INVESTING IN CONDOMINIUMS

INVESTING IN CONDOMINIUMS

STRATEGIES, TIPS AND EXPERT ADVICE
FOR THE CANADIAN REAL ESTATE INVESTOR

Brian Persaud
and
Randy Ramadhin

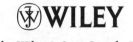

John Wiley & Sons Canada, Ltd.

Library and Archives Canada Cataloguing in Publication Data

Persaud, Brian, 1980-
      Investing in condominiums : strategies, tips and expert advice
for the Canadian real estate investor / Brian Persaud, Randy Ramadhin.
Includes index.
Issued also in electronic formats.
ISBN 978-1-11-804385-1

      1. Real estate investment—Canada.   2. Condominiums—Canada.
I. Ramadhin, Randy, 1975-   II. Title.
HD316.P47 2012   332.63'240971   C2012-905214-8
ePDF: 978-1-118-04412-4; Mobi: 978-1-118-04411-7; ePub: 978-1-118-04413-1

Production Credits
Cover design: Mike Chan
Typesetting: Thomson Digital
Cover image: Ian Koo
Printer: Solisco-Tri-Graphic Printing Ltd.

Editorial Credits
Executive Editor: Don Loney
Managing Editor: Alison Maclean
Production Editor: Jeremy Hanson-Finger

John Wiley & Sons Canada, Ltd.
6045 Freemont Blvd.
Mississauga, Ontario
L5R 4J3

Printed in Canada

1 2 3 4 5 LBF TRI 16 15 14 13 12

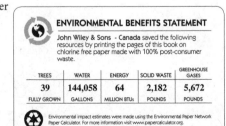

ENVIRONMENTAL BENEFITS STATEMENT

John Wiley & Sons - Canada saved the following resources by printing the pages of this book on chlorine free paper made with 100% post-consumer waste.

TREES	WATER	ENERGY	SOLID WASTE	GREENHOUSE GASES
39	144,058	64	2,182	5,672
FULLY GROWN	GALLONS	MILLION BTUs	POUNDS	POUNDS

Environmental impact estimates were made using the Environmental Paper Network Paper Calculator. For more information visit www.papercalculator.org.

Contents

The Pre-Construction Condo: Leap of Faith or Wise Investment?

What buying a pre-construction condo involves. The pluses and minuses of a condo investment. The REal Experts Property Analyzer helps you make educated investment decisions.

Imagine pulling up to a red carpet in a chauffeured limousine, with elegant greeters ready to usher you, arm-in-arm, to a party being held in a sales centre that cost over $1 million to construct, a sales centre that will soon be demolished to make way for a hip, urban living space for the crowd of party-goers who have come to celebrate their good fortune on this night. Alcohol flows, canapés are consumed, and you mix and mingle with people who are eager to buy, just like you. To the condo developer, you are "VIPs"— Very Important Purchasers.

Inside, hundreds of VIPs and real estate agents crowd around the architect's renderings of the lavish new condominium. Eye-catching images of the building's architecture are displayed, alongside illustrations of bikini-clad women enjoying the pool, and stunning, life-like depictions of the fantastic amenities (amenities that will seldom actually be used). The nattily dressed developer walks out to applause, and his attitude is like that of a preacher giving a sermon to his fold: "The market is strong across the city, prices are still going up and the population keeps growing. Our building is at the best location in the most up-and-coming neighbourhood."

"Luxury finishes," and "A view like no other" are the homilies of the day to grab the attention of purchasers and indoctrinate the crowd of enthusiastic real estate agents. These hovering and attentive agents are only too eager to spread the marketing maven's gospel to their clients. Their incentive, of course, is the commissions they will earn.

All builders have a formula: an array of pretty renderings used to evoke an emotional response, presented at sales launches hosted within slickly designed sales centres. The formula is used to shift your focus from price to the "this could be yours" fantasy of how nice it would be to live in the builder's version of urban paradise.

But to be a smart investor you cannot be swayed by the builder's dog-and-pony show. Doing your homework on both the macro and micro level of investing in a pre-construction condo is paramount. From understanding market conditions to itemizing the smaller details such as finishes, being an educated investor is the best way to equip yourself with the tools to make a sound, strategic decision.

There is a reason why builders invest heavily in the pretty pictures, stories and emotions: When you buy pre-construction condos you're not really buying real estate—something with bricks, mortar and wood, all the tangible things you can see and touch. Instead, you are buying a promise, and accepting a promise requires faith. Our experience has shown us that when people get caught up in the hype of buying a pre-construction condo, they are more susceptible to making irrational investment decisions. And when things go wrong, investors tend to point fingers at the developer, their agent or the government rather than take personal responsibility. The question, then, is: How can you ensure you make a wise investment decision when buying a pre-construction condo? That is the most important question we aim to answer in this book.

What Exactly Is a Condo?

Before determining if investing in a pre-construction condo is right for you, let's start with a basic question: what is a condo?

Almost any piece of real estate—any building, or even open land— can be a condominium, since the word "condominium" refers to a legal structure of ownership rather than to a particular type of building. Condominium ownership is made up of two parts:

1. the unit (the part of the property that is owned by the purchaser); and

2. the common elements (the part of the property that is shared among individual unit owners).

(Just to make the terminology clear, in British Columbia a condominium is a Strata Corporation; in Quebec, a Syndicate or Syndicate of owners; and in all other provinces, a Condominium Corporation.)

While fancy brochures focus on lifestyle and amenities, you must always bear in mind that when you purchase a condominium, you are also entering a world of regulations, obligations and restrictions that may impact the very lifestyle being advertised. Condominium governance is comprised of: (1) by-laws, which govern the use of units and common elements, as well as the administration and regulation of the corporation, and (2) rules, which the condo board may make to govern the corporation's common elements and assets. Rules cover, among other things, the use of visitor parking, the scheduling of use of common elements and even fines for breaking any rules.

The following are some considerations to keep in mind when thinking about how condo living is different from owning a detached single-family home. These are important to keep in mind, whether you decide to buy a condo as an investment, or as your own home for the short or long term.

- Whether you are living in a townhouse or high-rise condominium, *noise levels* can become annoying. You will be living in close proximity to neighbours, and, if your unit is near any mechanical system, noise levels can be amplified.

- You will not have complete *independence* or the final say over alteration to your own space, how your building is maintained or how the common elements are used.

 TIP

Know the rules

In 2008, a condo owner in Ontario was sued by his condominium corporation after he installed hardwood flooring in his unit. The installation was deemed "annoying, disruptive and constituted a nuisance to other occupants in the building."[1]

 TIP

Breaking the rules will cost you!

If a condo owner breaks a rule, the board could decide to levy a fine on that owner, and a provincial court action can be taken to back up its fine. There are few avenues for appeal. If the owner refuses to pay, the fine is added to his/her condo fees. If the amount remains unpaid, a caveat can be filed against the owner's property title, preventing sale until the debt is cleared.

- In a single-family home, your *lifestyle* is entirely up to you. Having a pet or firing up the barbeque is done without a second thought.

But you might not be able to enjoy these activities in a condo. You need to be mindful of your neighbours and abide by the condo by-laws.

- Having increased *security* in a condo building means that your guests won't be able to come and go as they please. Many buildings require guests to sign in.

- Some buildings restrict the *number of tenants* that can occupy an individual unit, while others may not have such restrictions.

Risks Associated with Buying Pre-Construction

Buying pre-construction real estate is really a leap of faith. As much as five years could pass from the time you sign the offer until you get the keys to your unit. Many "moving parts" could affect how long it takes, and how profitable your investment will be. Here are some examples:

- the state of the economy today and in the future
- legal changes
- strikes and work stoppages
- the availability (or not) of skilled labour
- builder reputation and construction quality
- changes to the neighbourhood
- legal risks
- taxes and fees
- zoning risks.

The State of the Economy Today and in the Future

If you buy a pre-construction condo today as an investment with the hope that the future value will be much higher, you're banking on the assumption that the economy will be healthy and keep growing. How can you forecast economic fundamentals in the future? While it might seem like an arduous task, using the REal Experts Property Analyzer will guide you and empower you to make the right decision.

TALES FROM THE TRENCHES

by Wade Graham, investor, Calgary

In 2006 we bought a condo in Calgary for $170,000 and got a great tenant who rented it for $1,400 a month. By 2008 that condo was worth $280,000. From that success we bought another for $400,000, thinking we could tap into the lucrative furnished rental market and rent the unit out for $4,000 a month. After the recession started, the market was flooded with units at the same time. The condo's value went down substantially, and I could barely get a tenant to rent it at $1,650. It just goes to show that the market takes care of us in the best of times and kicks the crap out of us at the worst. From this experience, we learned to study the economic fundamentals to have a long-term outlook.

Legal Changes

Above and beyond condo regulations and by-laws, changes to the law—from local by-laws right up to federal laws—can have a considerable impact on the future value of your condo, especially if these occur during the construction phase. Federally, laws on foreign ownership of real estate can change. Regionally, land-use policies can change (Ontario's Places to Grow Act, for instance, can make the surrounding area more valuable). Locally, property taxes can change, which may have a severe impact on the desirability of your property, if and when the time comes for you to sell.

TIP

Watch your taxes

In some locations, condominium hotels are a popular choice as an investment because they offer flexibility: If you don't plan on living in the unit, you can add it to the hotel pool to earn cash-flow. Be aware that city regulations may re-classify your property taxes from the cheaper residential rates to the more expensive commercial rates, which can harm your cash-flow and make future financing of the building more difficult, since lenders will demand a higher down payment.

Strikes and Work Stoppages

Prolonged strikes for trades or government can significantly delay the time it takes for your project to be completed. For example, the City of

Toronto union strike in 2009 caused permit delays and occupancy certificate delays.

The Availability (or Not) of Skilled Labour

The general quality of the local construction workforce can have an impact on your condo building, but even more important is availability. If there is a shortage of skilled trades, rising costs and delays are more likely.

Builder Reputation and Construction Quality

Look for a builder with a reputation for completing projects on time and with high-quality standards. That good reputation should be consistent across many projects. Keep in mind that builders that don't have their own construction team could have different trades with different construction managers, meaning that it can be difficult to judge quality from previous projects.

Construction quality is impossible to guarantee when buying pre-construction, which is why it presents a huge risk when buying. Since there is no way to see into the future, steps can be taken to mitigate risks—that means doing your due diligence, which we outline in this book.

Changes to the Neighbourhood

Neighbourhoods that are going through "gentrification" or renewal are in a process of great change. Perhaps the neighbourhood has had a high crime rate, or many of the amenities that draw people to a neighbourhood have been missing (parks, schools, shopping, mature trees), or there was a lot of noise from traffic or construction. These can all be turnoffs to end-users if the area hasn't fully transitioned by the time the building is complete.

Other things to consider in rapidly developing neighbourhoods is your potential view. It's possible that a new building will pop up and block your fantastic view. Zoning by-laws could change suddenly, with the effect of eliminating desirable neighbourhood features (such as restaurants and bars) or encourage undesirable characteristics (such as a new landfill site).

⊚ YOU SHOULD KNOW

Choosing the wrong building will affect your resale ability

When selecting a neighbourhood and condo building, it is extremely important to know your neighbours—not just the lovely young couple in the unit down the hall, but also the various "neighbours" down the street. Are there industrial activities being carried out on nearby properties? Or perhaps there is a large structure nearby or planned for the future that could block an otherwise lovely view.

Years ago, before construction was completed near Woodbine Beach in Toronto's east end, potential buyers were told that the above-ground Olympic-sized D.D. Summerville pool complex that sat between new townhouses and the lake would be torn down within the not-too-distant future. Fast-forward almost 10 years and the pool still opens its doors each summer to thousands of laughing children—great for the kids, not so great for the property owners whose "lake view" is on permanent hold. This example shows that simply taking the word of your real estate agent or condo developer about things that are "likely" to happen can be dangerous. Although plans for things such as demolitions and new constructions may be well intentioned, until they are officially approved and/or underway, there is a question mark associated with them. It is vital that prospective buyers ask themselves what they can and cannot live with if nothing about their condo building or condo neighbourhood were to change in the short to medium term.

Legal Risks

Builders' contracts are thick and complex documents, certainly more daunting than an agreement for the purchase and sale of a typical single-family home. It is imperative you hire an experienced lawyer to review your contracts, a lawyer who has represented clients who have purchased condos. It's even better if the lawyer has represented investor-clients. (We'll go into more depth about legal contracts in Chapter 5.)

Taxes and Fees

New-home buyers in provinces such as Ontario and B.C. got a bit of a shock when the Harmonized Sales Tax (HST) was introduced in 2010. New homes had previously been subject to the 5% Goods and Services Tax (GST), but with the introduction of the combined federal and provincial sales tax, new-home buyers were suddenly left to deal with a substantial increase (12% in B.C., and 13% in Ontario) in the cost of buying a property, without anything in return. Since changes in taxes can be made at the whim of a local or provincial government, they must be taken into account.

Taxes can come in many forms. One form, charged by local governments, is development charges. Development charges can range from education levies and regional development levies to municipal levies, and can add a substantial amount to the cost of the property.

Along with taxes and development charges, closing fees are also higher with new condos than resale condos. Closing fees are normal with any real estate transaction, but newly built properties are subject to many more fees, including new-home warranty fees, paperwork fees, legal fees, utility hookup fees, and more. Some charges, such as those for guest suites or superintendant suites, are buried in the condo maintenance clause.

What's worse, fees and taxes are constantly changing, hidden in the builder's contract, and very hard to calculate beforehand, and many cannot be financed by banks (meaning you have to be prepared to pay for them on top of your down payment).

Zoning Risks

Today, many developers start pre-selling their condos before zoning changes and approvals are given by the city. When a developer pre-sells a substantial number of the units in a building, they are able to get financing to complete their project fairly cheaply, which allows them to sell the units at an affordable price. This carries an inherent risk, though, since in some cases the city will reject a developer's plan. If this happens, any buyers will have their deposits returned (if the deposits have been held—as they should be—in trust by a lawyer and protected by a solid trust agreement).

In addition, zoning changes after a project is completed can significantly increase the operating costs of your condo. Different uses have different property tax rates—residential property tax rates are usually lower than hotel or business tax rates—so if the city assesses your property as a different class, it can change your residential rate to the higher hotel and business tax rate.

ⓧ TALES FROM THE TRENCHES

A Flexible Strategy Is Best
by Mark Savel, realtor, Toronto

It's good to have a clear strategy and purpose for buying, but I also think one should be prepared to be flexible. A lot changes in the three- to five-year period it takes for most condos to be built. As a golden rule for my investors, I always suggest purchasing a layout you'd be comfortable living in if need be. If you're an end-user, it's advisable to pick a location that can be easily rented out should your family grow and the unit no longer fit your needs. I've worked with all sorts of purchasers—flippers, end-users and investors. Typically, the best profit is seen from those who hold onto their units the longest!

Why Buying a Condo Has Its Rewards

Over the past 10 years, the popularity of buying pre-construction real estate has been well documented. Sometimes even an element of hysteria comes with the launch of a new development. While lining up to buy a condo in a wave of hysteria is not recommended (homework and due diligence are still required), there are some definite pluses to investing in a pre-construction condominium:

- profit potential
- staggered deposits
- ease of management and low maintenance costs
- proven demand for tenants
- an affordable "cottage" (urban getaway or low-stress vacation property)
- affordability and liquidity
- modern architecture
- modern amenities
- opportunity to decorate to your unique tastes
- new technologies and modern construction
- modern layouts

Profit Potential

When you buy your unit in today's dollars and prices, or at a discounted price, with a small investment you may stand to earn lots of profits tomorrow. If we look at the price growth in Toronto and Vancouver by examining the general price index of pre-sale condos, we see returns of as much as

400% for a unit purchased between 2001 and 2007. (See more on how you can profit from a condo investment in the next section.)

Staggered Deposits

As an investor, you are leveraging a small amount of capital initially and the rest of the capital to be invested is spread over time, so you're not putting down a substantial amount of money all at once.

 TIP

Get familiar with the warranty

Ask whether your deposit is covered by a warranty program and know the exact amount that is covered (in some provinces, the warranty provider will not cover the entire amount or provide any coverage at all). In addition, you may be able to negotiate the deposit, depending on what stage the developer is at in sales.

Ensuring your property is covered by a warranty program will also give you, and the other owners, peace of mind that if issues crop up you and they are protected from any costs in the first few years. (We look at new-home warranties in some depth in Chapter 5.)

Ease of Management and Low Maintenance Costs

Condo buyers are more than willing to forego grass-cutting and snow-shovelling. With exterior maintenance taken care of by the property management company, condo owners get the benefits of convenience and fewer demands on their time.

Most of the costly items of maintaining a property are shared by multiple owners. The condo board should have an accurate and frequently reviewed plan for spending on maintenance and repairs. Most owners are not involved in the day-to-day grind of maintaining landscaping or dealing with major repairs directly. Other than minor suite issues, most condo owners have a turnkey property.

Proven Demand for Tenants

Renters will pay a premium to live in high-quality units with terrific amenities over living in purpose-built rental buildings that may be older and poorly maintained. All things being equal (location, amenities, etc.), tenants would prefer being in newer buildings rather than resale.

An Affordable "Cottage" (Urban Getaway or Low-stress Vacation Property)

Downtown cores of many cities across North America are being revitalized, offering many terrific attractions for families living in the suburbs. Restaurants, theatres, concerts, sporting events, museums and shopping are to be found within walking distance of many condo developments, and the added population density that condos bring has the effect of increasing the attractions available. Owning a condo makes perfect sense to families who have a more urban lifestyle and want to be "closer to the action"—there is also strong resale potential for well-located condos.

Affordability and Liquidity

Condos are usually built in urban centres where people çan be close to transit, shopping, entertainment and work. We instinctively know that neighbourhoods that provide many opportunities for people to live, work, play and move around will always be in high demand by buyers. This is why people get excited about buying a condo; they know they can easily resell it if their circumstances change.

In addition, because of the smaller size of most condos compared to single-family homes, and the economies of scale, builders can offer many different pricing options to attract a large pool of buyers seeking an affordable place to live.

Modern Architecture

The visual, psychological and physical effects of living in a neighbourhood of architecturally stunning buildings are profound. Beautiful buildings, properly integrated into a neighbourhood, are anchors in a community. The look of buildings creates a sense of place and an identity for residents. Buildings with poor architecture can make a neighbourhood desolate, attracting crime and decay.

Modern Amenities

Condo developers have the benefit of using foresight when designing a great building. With amenities in particular, developers can look at previous buildings to see what works (pet facilities, basketball courts, video-game rooms) and what doesn't work (rock-climbing walls).

Amenities are one of the great benefits of owning a condo. How else can someone afford to have a squash court for their own? It would be better to share the costs with many owners who can also share the use.

Popular modern amenities include:

- theatre rooms
- multimedia rooms
- quiet study rooms
- shared TV and internet use rooms
- high-end coffee lounges
- swimming pools
- saunas
- health clubs

- exercise rooms
- pet-grooming facilities
- barbecues
- sun decks
- dance, yoga studios
- massage tables
- pedicure facilities
- enhanced security and concierges.

Opportunity to Decorate to Your Unique Tastes

Buying from floor plans gives you the unique opportunity to make changes that would be impossible or costly if performed after construction. Converting a three-bedroom suite into two larger bedrooms, or eliminating small balconies to give you more indoor space, are examples of what can be done to customize your living space.

In addition, buyers like to choose their own finishes and colours. Knowing that something is designed the way they want it on the first day they walk in will appeal to many buyers, who might otherwise spend $15,000 or more on cosmetic renovations.

New Technologies and Modern Construction

Building codes and energy efficiency standards change over time, so when you purchase a new home, you are also buying a property that should be the most up-to-date in terms of plumbing, electrical, materials, energy efficiency and building practices.

Modern Layouts

Have that old crusty dining room in your home that no one uses? Well, you may if you bought a home built prior to the 1980s. Today's floor plans feature more usable and fluid spaces that are more enjoyable and tuned to the modern family's lifestyle.

Open-concept floor plans, with spaces naturally separated according to use rather than with walls, allow for a condo to be smaller without feeling smaller.

Running the Numbers on a Condo

To analyze the investment potential in a fast-paced environment of condo sales, two different formulas for quick comparison should be used for the rentals, and a separate analysis must be done for the appreciation in prices during the pre-construction period to completion.

The first ratio is the Gross Rental Multiplier: GRM = Sales Price divided by Gross Monthly Rent.

Sales Price is the price you are buying the condo for plus your estimate for all closing adjustments (see also Chapter 5).

Gross Monthly Rent is the current gross monthly rent for the particular submarket. Use your local real estate board as your source for rental market information.

 TIP

"Brand new" doesn't necessarily bring in more rent
Research provided by Toronto's leading researcher of the high rise condo market, Urbanation, found zero difference in index rents between projects registered in 2007, 2009 and 2010 in Toronto. The research suggests that as long as a condo has been built within a four-year window, tenants will not pay a premium for a newer building, all things being equal.

The next ratio is the Net Income Multiplier: NIM = Sales Price + Closing Cost Estimate/Net Income

Net income = Effective Gross Income – Operating Expenses

Effective Gross Income = Potential Gross income – Vacancy Allowance[2]

Operating Expenses = Maintenance/Condo fees + Property Taxes + Utilities + Repairs and Maintenance + Advertising costs for rentals

A gross number is a quick comparison with different condos and a net number includes differences in maintenance/condo-fee costs.

Appreciation Factor

Most of your investment return will come from the appreciation factor. Appreciation is a difficult number to get comfortable with and analysis of the supply and demand factors, the layout and floor plan must be done by you or your agent. The key for the appreciation factor is to focus on choosing a unit that will be highly demanded once the building is complete for the best price possible using the tools we've already outlined in the REal Experts Analyzer.

$$\frac{\text{Opening Index Price}}{((\text{New sold index price} + \text{Resale index price})/2)}$$

In Chapter 2, we'll learn more about "price aggressiveness." For now, it's enough to know that the more aggressive the price, the lower the potential for appreciation, unless the demand factors show the building to be exceptional. Naturally, based on the criteria given, buying a pre-construction condo cheaper than the current resale prices would be the best bet, but given the inflationary pressure on labour, materials and land costs, this may not be possible.

The biggest determining factor to any end-user is the monthly carrying cost of their home. A quick way to get an idea of what demand will be in the future is to do a comparison in carrying costs between your condo and its competition for potential end-users.

Carrying costs = Mortgage costs + Insurance + Property Taxes + Maintenance/Condo Fees

Mortgage costs = Mortgage at 80% (size of a standard deposit is 20%) Loan To Value and 25-year amortization with an estimated interest rate for when the building will be complete.

For example:

$300,000 condo with a 20% deposit will require $240,000 mortgage

$240,000 mortgage with a 6% interest rate = $1,546.32/month

Property tax estimate = $300

Maintenance fee estimate = $300

Insurance = $100

Total monthly carrying costs = $2,200

CONDO A	CONDO B	HOUSE C
Carrying costs = $2,200	Carrying costs = $1,800	Carrying costs = $3,000
Location: Avenue Infill in the battery district. Walk to the subway, dining, shops and entertainment	Location: Urban Renewal in the film district, easy access to streetcar and highway	Location: Quiet cul-de-sac subdivision in the inner suburbs. 5-minute walk to bus, close to highways and shopping mall
Size: 9' ceilings and 1 bedroom, 525 square feet	Size: 10' ceilings and 1 bedroom, 601 square feet	Size: 3 bedrooms, 1,600 square feet.
Amenities: 24-hour concierge, rooftop pool with cabana bar, private dining room	Amenities: Bicycle storage, party room, sauna and barbecue area	
Finishes:	Finishes:	Finishes:
Kitchen/laundry	Kitchen/Laundry	Kitchen/Laundry
5 matching appliances, granite counter tops, high-end custom cabinets	6 appliances (4 stainless steel and white washer/dryer), quartz counter top, basic European-style cabinetry	Original kitchen cabinets, 4 appliances of various ages
Flooring	Flooring	Flooring
Wide-plank engineered hardwood floors in living areas and carpet in bedroom	Laminate in living areas and carpet in bedroom	carpet in basement, hall and bedrooms; hardwood in living areas, vinyl in kitchen
Bathroom	Bathroom	Bathroom
Large porcelain tiles in bathrooms, stainless steel sinks, chrome faucets, oversized shower	Basic tiles and ceramic sink, 5-foot soaker tub	Recessed lighting, vanity, ceramic sink and tub
Special features: Individually controlled HVAC		Updates required: $6,000

As prices, interest rates and condo fees increase, fewer and fewer people are able to afford a condo. When this occurs, price appreciation will occur more slowly, or not at all, as fewer buyers are available in the market-place. The graph below, created by Barry Lyon and Associates, shows the income required for a family to qualify for a condo apartment mortgage. As indicated, if rates, prices and operating costs increase further, it will take close to $100,000 in household income to afford the average Greater Toronto pre-construction condo in 2012. The average household income was $80,343 as of the 2006 Census, meaning a large percentage of people within the city are already priced out of living in a new condo.

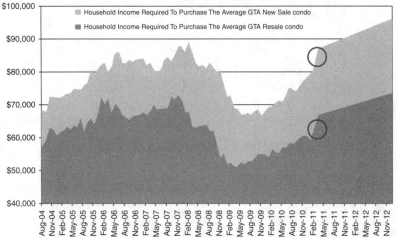

Income Required to Purchase a New or Resale condo
Greater Toronto Area: 2004–2012

Notice the spike when mortgage rules changed the maximum amortization from 35 to 30 years.

The study was based on the following assumptions:

- 35% of gross income was used for qualifying.

- Covers average insurance, property taxes and utilities.

- Unlike the Royal Bank of Canada's affordability index, maintenance fees are included.

- Mortgage payments were calculated based on Royal Bank of Canada's interest forecasts.

- Mortgage payments were calculated using the maximum amortization rate insured by CMHC (note the spike after August 2010 when CMHC shortened the maximum amortization from 35 to 30 years).

- Forecasted 2.5% annual appreciation rate for pricing with data collected from RealNet for new sale and Toronto Real Estate Board for resale.

- Historical data are adjusted for inflation.

 TALES FROM THE TRENCHES

by Caitlin, condo purchaser, Toronto

I am 26 years old, straight out of my mom and dad's suburban house. As an up-and-coming single female, I purchased my first home at the DNA 2 development in downtown Toronto. It was a huge milestone and accomplishment in my life to start living on my own in downtown Toronto. Little did I know that my cute condo was also a gold-mine investment. I've been living here since 2006 and the resale value of my suite has gone up beyond my wildest expectations. If I sold today I could easily make a sweet $170,000. Not many people my age can say that! I'm a happy homeowner and a smart real estate investor, as it turns out.

 TALES FROM THE TRENCHES

The Importance of Buyer Confidence

by Andrew la Fleur, realtor, Toronto

I had a buyer for a two-bedroom, southwest corner unit at X2 (which has a view of the CN Tower). My buyer signed for the unit, then backed out during the 10 days because he just thought the price was too high and it could never go up from that point; he thought he'd never make his money back as no one would ever pay more. Prices for that unit went up about $60K to $70K in less than a year.

Spotting Problems Before You Buy

Those who have lived in an apartment or a condo know all too well that problems can be broken down into "the 5 Ps": Pets, Parking, People, Personalities and Parties. Here's a guide to asking the questions that will help you spot problems with the 5 Ps before you buy. Using this checklist, together with the REal Experts Property Analyzer that follows, will help you gather all the information you need to determine if condo investing— or a particular condo—is for you.

Pets

- ☐ Do the condo by-laws created by the developer allow for pets? Is there a size/weight limit?
- ☐ Will you be able to bring your pet into the common outdoor space?
- ☐ Are there pet-friendly amenities?
- ☐ How well insulated are the walls? Will you hear a dog barking?
- ☐ How far will you have to travel to access services for your pet?
- ☐ Are there off-leash parks in the neighbourhood?
- ☐ Is there space for your pet to eat, sleep and get cleaned?

Parking

- ☐ Are there going to be any future developments that would eliminate parking spots (either street parking or parking lots) in the future?
- ☐ Can you secure a convenient spot in a good location?
- ☐ Are there safe-access parking facilities?
- ☐ How much extra are the maintenance fees for a parking spot?
- ☐ Does your chosen floor plan let you purchase a parking spot?
- ☐ Will adding a parking spot net you a good return?
- ☐ Are there enough spaces available for visitor parking?

People and Personalities

- ☐ Is the street noise loud at the floor height you're considering?
- ☐ Is the unit you're considering too close to elevators, garages, mechanical units and garbage chutes that can get noisy?
- ☐ Are the walls insulated enough that you won't hear your neighbours?
- ☐ Are there any restrictions on renting the unit out?
- ☐ What kind of security will the building have?
- ☐ Is there a 24-hour concierge?
- ☐ Is there space to entertain your guests? How much will it cost to use it?

- ☐ What type of public space is nearby? Who tends to use it?
- ☐ Where can you store your bike? Will they allow it in your unit?
- ☐ Are there good daycare facilities nearby? Do they have a waiting list?
- ☐ Is the condo close to good schools? A hospital?
- ☐ What will be at the ground floor? Will there be retail that you would use (e.g., bank, grocery stores, restaurants)? Is it confirmed?
- ☐ How will the condo share the facilities with the retail at grade? Do they have adequate delivery loading and unloading space? Will their operations cause a disturbance?
- ☐ Are you comfortable with the condo regulations?
- ☐ Is the heating individually controlled?
- ☐ Are there enough elevators?

Parties

- ☐ Is the unit too close to common elements? Is the hall near the unit you're considering used as a thoroughfare?
- ☐ Is the unit's outdoor space or window(s) too close to common space?
- ☐ How close is the unit to nearby buildings? Can your living room be easily seen?
- ☐ Is there a guest suite for visitors? How much will it cost to use on a per-use basis? What are the common monthly fees to be paid for it?
- ☐ Is the unit too close to bars, restaurants or nightclubs with loud music?
- ☐ Is the unit too close to sports stadiums and arenas? Will you be able to handle the traffic and the noise?
- ☐ What is the intended demographic of end-users (e.g., retired persons, young singles, families) for the building?
- ☐ Are there designated smoking spaces?
- ☐ Are the stairwells secure?

The REal Experts Property Analyzer

Hindsight is always 20/20. It's easy to see how pieces fit together after the fact. Since it's impossible to see into the future, having an effective model of investing that enables you to do all the necessary due diligence is the next best thing. With a model for analyzing information you will put yourself in a position to earn high returns while investing in pre-construction condos and ensure that the decision you make will be free of any emotional bias.

To build a model for investing in pre-construction real estate, it's important that you be able to apply it in any city and in any neighbour-hood, on any street. This is why our REal Experts Property Analyzer is a model built on strong, tried-and-true fundamentals. The more fundamentals a project has in its favour, the higher the probability for a substantial profit—and you do want to earn a high profit, right?

Furthermore, investing in pre-construction real estate requires a large financial investment. This large investment necessitates that you follow the REal Experts Property Analyzer to the letter—before you write the first cheque.

The REal Experts Property Analyzer is a checklist of questions you need to answer for any project you are looking at as an investment. Consider it your due-diligence checklist. It is exhaustive, but not exhausting: over time, you will be able to do this research quickly and you will become familiar with how other members of your team (for example, your realtor, mortgage broker, accountant and lawyer) can help you gather the information you need.

Market

- ☐ Is there anything limiting land supply for new housing (e.g., legislative barriers or natural barriers)?

- ☐ Are the costs of labour and/or materials increasing?

- ☐ Is credit for both buyers and developers easy to access?

- ☐ Are interest rates low or expected to go down?

- ☐ What kind of demand for condos is being seen in the resale market?

- ☐ Is the area creating jobs?

- ☐ Is the employment diverse? Is the diversity deep (e.g., lots of trade associations, head-office jobs, centres for excellence)?

- ☐ Is the area's population growing?

- ☐ Is population growth being concentrated by the municipality to encourage high-density development?

- ☐ Is the growth more than the construction capacity for the area?

☐ If condos are new to the market, are the monthly costs to own the condo lower than or comparable to the average cost to own a single-family home in the area?

☐ Does the area score high for quality of life?

☐ Is there a lot of international investment into the area?

☐ Is buyer confidence high? (Look at retail sales, MLS® transactions and new sale transactions as indicators.)

Neighbourhood

☐ Is the neighbourhood within 450 metres of a rail transit?

☐ Does the area score high on the "Walk Score"? (Check out www.walkscore.com)

☐ Is the area comfortable for pedestrians to walk? (Look for crosswalks, large sidewalks, good street lighting, lots of sunlight, low wind, bike lanes, slow traffic.)

☐ Does the area have more than one primary use (commercial, office and residential)?

☐ Does the neighbourhood have short blocks?

☐ Is the area an urban area with buildings of a variety of ages?

☐ Does the area have a sufficient population density?

☐ What are the demographics of the neighbourhood?

☐ Is this an area going through significant renewal or gentrification? Will it be unsafe for a time period? If so, how long could the renewal or gentrification process reasonably be expected to take?

☐ Are there any barriers (e.g., large wooded areas, rail lands, dead-end roads, large highways) preventing the area from gentrifying or becoming vibrant?

Site

☐ Is the site clear from any active uses (e.g., highways, railways, industrial buildings, manufacturing plants, landfills, sewage treatment plants)?

☐ Is the site close to any area that could be developed or that could hamper your view or your enjoyment?

☐ Are you buying in an early phase in a master-planned community or an urban renewal community?

☐ Is the proposed building actually part of the neighbourhood you want to live in or does the marketing material make it appear closer than it actually is?

Builder/Design Team

☐ Does the builder have the requisite experience?

☐ Is the builder active in trade associations (such as the Building Industry and Land Development Association) for the betterment of the industry for consumers, or active in its communities to build its brand? Does the builder care how its development impacts the neighbourhood?

☐ Does the builder have a reputation for providing high-quality finishes as its standard?

☐ Is the builder using up-to-date technologies? Will it build beyond minimum building code? Is it committed to building sustainable communities?

☐ Does the builder have a reputation for building quality homes? Are they responsible for the construction where you can more accurately gauge quality?

☐ Does the builder value customer service and after-sales service? Is it known for its communication and access? Are they proactive with their customer service?

☐ Is the builder "upfront"? Does it market its product transparently? Is it focused on building a brand rather than developing through shell companies? Is it known for not assessing extra fees after owners take possession?

☐ Does the builder keep its word and promises as measured by third parties (e.g., past customers, real estate agents, lawyers, property managers, new-home warranty sites, the Better Business Bureau, etc.)?

☐ Is the builder known to treat its customers with respect?

☐ Does the builder's finished product rent for a higher amount than the competition's?

☐ Is the design team experienced in projects of this type? What awards have they won?

☐ Are they part of any associations?

☐ Are they active in bettering their industry by giving lectures, sitting on design review panels, judging awards?

☐ Are they using up-to-date technologies (as seen in the features and finishes)?

☐ Does the design team have a reputation of not compromising on quality? Do they keep their word on quality?

Realtor

☐ Do they have real front-line access to a preferred project by a developer?

☐ Do they understand the contract? Can they advise you on clauses that are normal in the marketplace? Do they understand which closing adjustments are legit?

☐ Will they provide you with service after you sign the contract? Are they willing and able to help you sell your unit before construction is complete? Are they willing and able to be there for you during the pre-closing inspections? Will they give you updates as price changes and construction milestones are met?

☐ Have they actually experienced closing a transaction with a client with a particular developer? Each developer has a unique operating procedure; can your agent help you navigate this for you?

☐ Does the agent have experience in the rental market? Is the agent experienced in renting out units to high-quality tenants? Do they know the market rents in other buildings and do they know which buildings cater to a certain demographic?

☐ Is the agent capable of reading a floor plan and a floor plate (a plan that shows the unit's location on the floor of the building)? Are they capable of advising you on how saleable the unit will be in the future by understanding the nuances of the floor plan and location of the unit on the floor?

☐ Is the agent knowledgeable in their local market? Do they under-stand what unit types are valuable in your marketplace, have knowl-edge on the finishes, amenities and condo fees in other buildings, know what other sites will be built upon that will compete with your unit or impact the end-user's enjoyment?

☐ Is the realtor involved in trade associations or networking groups where they could gain insider knowledge about a builder's track record or understand new issues as they arise in the local marketplace?

☐ Do you trust that the agent has your best interests at heart? Can they give you references of past happy clients? Are they willing to negoti-ate on your behalf?

Building

☐ Are the maintenance fees comparable to other buildings?

☐ Have you considered "the 5 Ps" (Pets, Parking, Personalities, People and Parties)?

☐ Are the amenities in the building better than the amenities in other buildings?

☐ Is the architecture of the building pleasing?

☐ Does the building have quality outdoor space built in?

☐ Does the building fit well with the neighbourhood?

☐ Did the builder use durable, quality materials?

☐ If there is to be a retailer at the base, has the retailer been confirmed?

Unit

☐ Are the standard finishes in the building better than the finishes in other buildings?

☐ Are the finishes on display in the sales centre the standard finishes rather than the upgraded finishes?

☐ Does the suite allow for a lot of natural light?

☐ Is there an adequate number of ceiling light fixtures?

- ☐ Is there an adequate number of electrical outlets?
- ☐ Are the fan coil unit and breaker box placed in good locations?
- ☐ Is there an adequate amount of storage?
- ☐ Does the floor plan have lots of usable space?
- ☐ Does the floor plan allow for a lot of flexibility? (e.g., a den that could double as a bedroom, or two full baths)
- ☐ Will the view be breathtaking? Is there anything that could block the view in the future?
- ☐ Are there measures to ensure the unit will be comfortable to live in? (i.e., adequate ventilation, heating and cooling, humidity controls, insulation to protect from noise)
- ☐ Does the floor plan allow for maximum privacy? (e.g., two bathrooms; bedrooms placed at a maximal distance apart)
- ☐ Does the unit have 9-foot ceilings (or higher)?
- ☐ Have you ensured that no mechanical systems or ductwork will lower the ceilings in high-use areas (i.e., bedrooms, living room)?
- ☐ Is the unit located away from party rooms, mechanical systems, elevators, or anything else that would impact the end-user's enjoyment or privacy?

Contract and Disclosure Documents

- ☐ Have you chosen an experienced, knowledgeable and battle-tested lawyer?
- ☐ Has the lawyer completed the key information chart?
- ☐ How long do you have for the rescission ("cooling-off") period?
- ☐ Is the deposit held in trust?
- ☐ Does the warranty program protect the deposit money?
- ☐ If so, what is the maximum?
- ☐ What is the interest rate to be paid?
- ☐ Are deposits for upgrades protected?
- ☐ What are your financial obligations?

- [ ] Are sales taxes included in the price?
- [ ] Are you eligible for any rebates?
- [ ] Did you cap your closing costs?
- [ ] What do the maintenance fees include?
- [ ] What's included in the fees (e.g., utilities)?
- [ ] What leases does the condo board have to take on?
- [ ] What purchase agreements or loans is the condo board obligated to take on?
- [ ] What is being leased in the unit and common areas?
- [ ] When do the lease agreements start (one year after closing)?
- [ ] What are the terms and financial obligations of the loans and leases?
- [ ] Has the reserve fund been funded? (applicable provinces)
- [ ] What are the builder's obligations toward the reserve fund?
- [ ] What is the likelihood that common expenses are too high or too low as compared to similar buildings in the area?
- [ ] Does your contract include room-size measurements and total square footage?
- [ ] Is a measured floor plan attached?
- [ ] Does the builder have the right to change size or layout?
- [ ] What provisions are in place to ensure what you are sold is what you get?
- [ ] What substitutions are possible (e.g., materials or colours)?
- [ ] Are all important items mentioned in the marketing material (including fixtures and appliances) also included in the contract?
- [ ] Is anything missing from the feature sheet? (The sheet is a list of maximum features, not minimum.)
- [ ] What are the ways the contract can be cancelled by the builder?
- [ ] Is the contract conditional on your ability to get financing?
- [ ] What conditions need to be satisfied before the condo registers?
- [ ] Under what conditions can you cancel your contract?

☐ When does the developer expect the condo be completed?

☐ How long can they extend the completion date?

☐ What conditions does the developer have to satisfy before they can start to build?

☐ How much are the occupancy costs expected to be and will the amenities be included?

☐ Do you have the right to pay more money on occupancy to reduce the interim occupancy fees (unpaid interest portion)?

☐ Can you assign the contract? If so, are there any conditions (such as 90% builder sales)?

☐ Is there an assignment fee?

☐ On assignment, do you remain responsible for performance of the original contract if the assignee defaults?

☐ Is there a prohibition on advertising/listing/marketing or Internet promotion even if you have permission to resell or lease?

☐ Do you need permission to lease your unit?

☐ Is your unit covered by a new-home warranty program by the builder? If not, is there one available?

☐ How long is the warranty? (e.g., 1, 2, 7 years)

☐ What is covered by the warranty program?

☐ What is not covered?

☐ Are there manufacturers' warranties for the different components?

☐ Are there any warnings about the location?

☐ Can the developer make changes to the community plan?

☐ What is the developer obligated to complete? (e.g., shared amenities or recreational areas)

☐ Are there any zoning issues you cannot object to?

☐ Can you object to any noise, dust, hydro lines, vibration and smell issues from nearby buildings now and in the future?

☐ Are there restrictions on the use of the condo (e.g., business)?

☐ Is there enough parking for residents and visitors?

☐ Are pets allowed?

☐ What kind of modifications are you allowed to make (e.g., hot tubs, satellite dishes, etc.)?

☐ What type of commercial uses are allowed for units at the base?

Investment Analysis

☐ Can you buy early in the sales process? If not, does the price (or other incentives) make it attractive as an investment?

☐ What are average rents for comparable units in the area?

☐ Have you investigated the cost of view premiums and floor premiums?

☐ Will the unit generate cash-flow?

☐ How do the Gross Rental Multiplier and Net Income Multiplier compare to competing units?

☐ Is the unit priced non-aggressively by the builder?

☐ How does the price compare to similar resale units in the neighbourhood?

☐ Is the unit in the affordability "hot zone," to open it to a large pool of end-users?

☐ Have you done a break-even analysis to ensure the condo can create cash-flow if you have to rent it out and hold it for a period of time?

☐ Is the building backed by a powerful brand that would attract international investors?

There may be items in the checklist that you don't understand right now. Rest assured that each point will be discussed in greater detail and depth throughout this book, and you will come to see how each point is necessary for you to get the whole picture of the investment decision before you. The REal Experts Property Analyzer is a checklist that you will return to again and again as you make real-estate investment decisions.

Depending on your circumstances, the answers to some of these questions will have more weight in your decision-making process than others. To some, the number of questions will seem daunting. But asking the right questions causes the mind to focus and search for answers, which will help you become an expert in buying pre-construction condos. The search for answers will ensure you make a wise and successful investment.

The Economics of Real Estate and Condo Investing

The economics of real estate, leading market indicators and how condominiums fit into the real estate market. How you can use all of these indicators to predict successful real estate investing.

Please bear with us as we revisit a subject we were all taught at school: economics. One of the most fundamental aspects of economics is an understanding of the law of supply and demand. The intricate relationship between the two is the backbone of a market economy.

"Demand" refers to how much (quantity) of a product or service is desired by consumers or buyers. The quantity in demand is the amount of a product people are willing to buy at a certain price. The relationship between price and quantity demanded is known as the "demand relationship."

"Supply" represents how much a market can offer. The quantity supplied refers to the amount of a certain good producers are willing and able to supply when receiving a certain price. The correlation between price and how much of a good is supplied to the market is known as the "supply relationship."

The ultimate price of a certain good—and, specifically for our book, a condo unit—is a reflection of the supply and demand relationship. Where

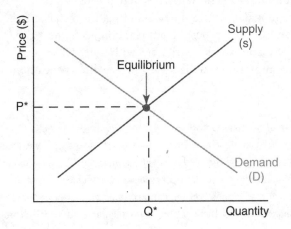

the two lines on the above graph intersect is theoretically where we will find our market price for a condo unit. This is called the point of equilibrium.

The basis of an economy is a supply of goods and services that are demanded by consumers, which in turn determines market price. With respect to condos, there are five major factors that contribute to the condo supply relationship:

1. land supply

2. materials supply

3. skilled labour pool

4. access to capital

5. condominium inventory.

1. Land Supply

The owners of land in urban city centres seek its most profitable use, which can be referred to as its "highest and best use." According to the Appraisal Institute of Canada, the term is defined as follows: "That use which, at the time of appraisal, is most likely to produce the greatest net return, in money or amenities, over a given period of time."

"Highest and best use" takes into consideration both the legal use of the land and the practical uses of the land. Legal considerations are related to property rights created by federal, provincial, municipal and private contract laws in the form of zoning restrictions, easements, environmental protection legislation and historical property rights, to name just a few. Practical considerations fall under the current and future uses of a building. The building's current tenancies may prevent a property from being demolished to make way for a new building, for instance; other practical realities preventing a property from realizing its highest and best use are grading of the land, depth restrictions with water tables or rivers running beneath the property, or public transit subway lines beneath the building.

 TIP

Be aware of political factors

The political climate created by local property taxpayers, the local ward councillor elected by the taxpayers and the municipality, has a major say in the zoning and therefore the market value of any piece of land. Depending on political motivations and regulations, some cities will be more open to re-zoning than others. There can be environmental factors, such as protecting parkland or environmentally sensitive areas. There can be historical factors, such as having certain neighbourhoods or specific buildings declared as historic sites and therefore rendered immune from significant changes or the wrecking ball. Sometimes, fierce opposition by existing taxpayers and residents can influence a government's decision.

Although as an investor you will not be directly involved in having land re-zoned or seeking out possible condo-development sites, you should be aware of what changes might be coming in the near future that will affect the supply of condos available in your chosen city. If the government in your city is fairly restrictive on allowing re-zoning, and desirable neighbourhoods are becoming more and more scarce, this can be a very positive consequence for the value of your unit. If there is nowhere left to build a condo, more people will be interested in your unit, which will likely drive up the price.

On the other side of the coin, if you own a unit in a good area and suddenly developers are allowed to build new units in an even better area, or even one of equivalent reputation, there will very soon be a greater supply or inventory of available units, and potential buyers now have more options. Your unit, although it has not changed in quality from our last scenario, is now less appealing to buyers because they have more choice. It is for this reason that an understanding of the available supply is important to you as in investor.

Condominium developers are constantly seeking land that is currently zoned for high density (allowing a large number of living units rather than a low number) to allow high-rise condominium development. The higher the density, the more valuable the land; where only low density is allowed, developers may seek a zoning amendment to increase the allowable density on a given plot of land. The zoning and use of adjacent pieces of land can create additional density. So the supply of condominiums is not only restricted by the amount of available land, but also to the areas where the city will allow density.

CASE STUDY

Greater Toronto

Land supply can be used to support high-rise growth over low-rise growth, resulting in significant appreciation in prices. In Vancouver, a city landlocked by mountains, an ocean and an agriculture land reserve, condo towers were built out of necessity as the population grew. Other cities, such as Calgary and Edmonton, and to a lesser extent the Greater Toronto Area (GTA), could afford to build homes out to the suburbs. This all changed in 2005 for the GTA when the province of Ontario introduced legislation legally requiring land developers and builders to build high-density communities to handle the region's growth. This had the following profound effects on the market:

- High-rise land investment increased, driving up the value of land and the cost of labour and materials.

- High-rise units started to outsell low-rise units as supply of low-rise dwindled.

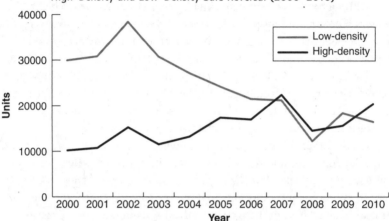

High–Density and Low–Density Sale Reversal (2000–2010)[1]

As fewer options became available for low-rise products, buyers were forced to buy condos. High-rise sales started to go up and prices of new condos started to increase substantially.

2. Materials Supply

Materials supply refers to the supply of basic building materials, such as wood, concrete and steel, and higher-end materials, such as hardwood floors, plasticized concrete, polymers, glass and steel rebar. The players here are steel suppliers, forestry companies, glass manufacturers and the like.

The international markets for wood and metal resources affect supply costs. When you look at the Producer Price Indices for construction materials from 2002 to 2010 (graph below), you can see a definite escalating trend in resource costs. With the low-interest rate environment in North America over this time period, the cost to borrow and build infrastructure, including condominium development, has had a definite impact on the demand for steel and concrete.

With greater demand, prices escalate, which then has a direct impact on condominium investors and developers: the condominium they sell today will be priced in today's dollars, but the condo building could be built in three to five years, at which point materials prices may be far higher. This reality has put tremendous pressures on the developers. Their cost analyses, as well as those of the lending institutions that provide capital for these projects, have very complex hedging strategies to take into account the cost of materials. Developers are careful not to underprice condominiums to be delivered in three years.

A smart condo investor is aware of these materials price trends and understands that a condo to be built in five years' time will be more expensive, just factoring in the higher cost of materials. One can conclude that materials supply trends are directly correlated to new condominium prices in the future, thus affecting in a positive way the resale values of condominiums in the market.

 YOU SHOULD KNOW

CMHC has guidelines for developers, too
Canadian Mortgage and Housing Corporation (CMHC) lending guidelines for condominium development require the borrower (developer) to obtain a fixed-price contract, and at least two-thirds of hard construction costs, including major contracts (structural, mechanical, electrical, forms and concrete), must be signed prior to the first insured advance of funds. Developers then are required to negotiate with suppliers to commit to pricing upfront.

ⓘ TIP

Watch for "price aggressiveness"
Savvy investors who have a keen eye on a particular submarket (a smaller segment of a neighbourhood containing condos) look at the "price aggressiveness" at which developers open up their units. Aggressiveness is calculated by taking the opening price of a condo and comparing it to the sale price of resale condos and the sale price of existing-inventory new condos. If developers are particularly aggressive in their pricing, they may be confident in the market or padding the price to account for future cost increases. If you have already bought a pre-construction unit, watching the aggressiveness of opening prices is a good leading indicator of where prices are heading when your condo is complete.

If you are looking to buy a unit, and a developer is particularly aggressive with its prices, careful analysis is required to ensure you are not overpaying for what the market will bear in the future.

Opening Index Price

((New sold index price + Resale index price)/2)

Price aggressiveness in Toronto is monitored by Urbanation

World Carbon Steel Product Prices (October 2002 – August 2010) $US/Tonne

Hot Rolled Coil (Aug 09-Aug10) 28.7%
Hot Rolled Plate (Aug 09-Aug10) 29.6%
Cold Rolled Coil (Aug 09-Aug10) 26.7%
HD Galv. Coil (Aug 09-Aug10) 22.4%
Electro Zinc Coil (Aug 09-Aug10) 32.8%
Wire Rod (mesh) (Aug 09-Aug10) 21.7%
Structural Sections and Beams (Aug 09-Aug10) 13.9%
Rebar (Aug 09-Aug10) 17.2%
Merchant Bar (Aug 09-Aug10) 14.6%

September 2008: Beginning of Global Financial Crisis

August 8, 2008: Beginning of Summer Olympics in China

Post-Recession Recovery

Emerging markets - Growth far exceeding that of developed economies

2004: Construction starts for 2008 Olympics in China

Mergers, acquisitions, import surges, bankruptcies and market weakness have been rolling the North American steel industry

$US/Tonne

Altus Group

Source: AGCC Based on MEPS Data

Besides understanding the impact the rising cost of materials has on price appreciation, buyers should understand costs, because it's important to know the builder's ability to manage such costs. An experienced builder can manage the cost of the big-ticket items, such as concrete and mechanical, a lot better than an inexperienced one. The increased savings due to expertise and a preferred relationship with suppliers of big-ticket items means that a developer can afford to spend more on finishes, which has a direct impact on the bottom line of investors.

Builders that manage their own construction may have an advantage over developers that contract out their construction. Ask if your developer does the construction themselves.

To build a condo tower, costs are divided into hard costs (those associated with materials, labour and construction) and soft costs (those to do with legal, accounting, financing, design and taxes).

A typical cost breakdown for a builder for hard costs is as follows.

SPEND CATEGORY	% OF TOTAL HARD COSTS ON A HIGH RISE	BIG TICKET ITEMS
1. General Conditions & Fees	9–13%	
2. Site Work & Earthworks	3–6%	
3. Concrete	22–26%	24%
4. Masonary	1–2%	
5. Metals	1–2%	
6. Carpentry	5–6%	5%
7. Thermal & Moisture Protection	5–6%	
8. Doors & Windows	6–9%	8%
9. Finishes	8–10%	9%
10. Specialties	0–1%	
11. Equipment (Appliances)	3–4%	3%
12. Furnishings	0%	
13. Special Construction	0%	
14. Conveying Systems (Elevators)	2–3%	3%
15. Mechanical	13–17%	15%
16. Electrical	7–9%	8%
	100%	**75%**[2]

YOU SHOULD KNOW

Hard construction costs are by no means uniform across Canada[3]

Condo Tower Construction Costs by Geography

Building Type	Vancouver ($/sq ft)	Calgary ($/sq ft)	Edmonton ($/sq ft)	GTA ($/sq ft)
Basic Condo	170–210	145–205	140–195	155–175
Basic Medium Quality	190–240	205–245	195–235	175–220
Basic High Quality	240–290	240–325	230–310	225–400
Medium Quality Tower (50–80 storey)	260–350	n/a	n/a	225–295
High Quality Tower (50–80 storey)	330–400	n/a	n/a	275–450

Notes:

a. This is a general guide and includes no contingency costs.

b. Assumes a level, stable and open site with no restrictions from adjoining properties.

c. Costs may change because of the following factors:

   o quality of building

   o location

   o building shape, size and height

   o topography and soil conditions

   o schedule and timeline

   o site restrictions

   o market conditions

   o type of contract

   o extent of site works (environmental remediation or demolishing buildings)

   o design method

        ◦ user requirements

        ◦ purchasing power of developer/contractor.

d.   Soft costs are not included.

e.   Cost varies between regions due to supply of existing labour pool.

f.   Cost increases for taller buildings due to the extra mechanical systems for ventilation and elevators and extra depth.

Soft costs can range from 30% to as much as 60% of the total hard costs for a project. Soft costs include the following:

- architectural and engineering fees
- government registered programs
- insurance and bond costs
- legal fees
- special design consultants
- special equipment and furnishings
- management costs
- site services outside the property
- interest charges and lender's fees
- marketing and advertising
- levies and development charges
- tenant incentives
- permits
- purchaser upgrades
- appraisals
- soil and environmental tests
- land surveys
- realty taxes
- broker commissions.

Development charges are used by municipal and regional governments to offset costs directly resulting from new growth and are used as a revenue-generating source for the governments. Over the past few years, the speed of increase in these charges has alarmed many, who feel that new home buyers are unfairly burdened with higher costs.

DEVELOPMENT CHARGE INCREASES, 2001–2008[4]	
Toronto	338%
King Township	313%
Brock Township	185%
Town of Newmarket	148%
City of Brampton	128%

Development charges are definitely passed down to the end-user, and should be looked at as a hidden tax on your condo unit. Government-induced charges include the following items:

- infrastructure charges (municipal/regional government)
- land dedications (municipal/regional government)
- development application and processing fees (municipal/regional government)
- building permit fees (municipal/regional government)
- property taxes (municipal/regional government)
- home warranty fees (provincial)
- registry and land-transfer fees (provincial)
- provincial sales taxes (provincial)
- provincial levies and applications (provincial)
- GST (federal).

These items can be substantial, and in some cities can add up to $40,000 or more in total costs on a single unit. The following graph shows development charges for condo apartments in cities across Canada.

Development Charges for Condo Apartments (CMHC 2006)[5]

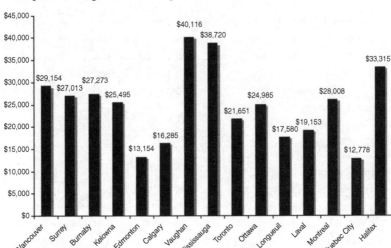

3. Skilled Labour Pool

The supply of skilled labour is contingent upon our colleges and universities and training programs offered by technical schools and trade schools. Universities and colleges provide skilled engineers, architects, project managers and professionals; trade schools train electricians, carpenters, HVAC tradespeople and pipefitters. Trades and professionals are required at different phases of development. Labour shortages lead to rising wages and result in costly construction overruns which are borne by the developer in the short term, but by the purchaser in the long term.

CASE STUDY

The Effect of Labour Shortages

From 2001 to 2007, the lack of available labour and the skyrocketing costs that were created as a result caused substantial instability for Calgary condo developers. Construction costs were increasing so rapidly that some developers were forced to redesign and retender contracts for construction at higher costs when they got ready to build. For some builders, the prices rose so dramatically that they were forced to cancel the contracts they had with purchasers and return their deposits, as the project was no longer viable. To rub salt in the wound of would-be purchasers, they were then offered units to buy—at a $40,000 increase.[6]

Access to Capital

Next to demand, access to capital is a hugely important factor for a developer's success. Beyond the revenue generated by condo sales, developers must be able to secure financing in order to begin—and complete—the project.

Savvy investors understand this, because if a developer is unable to qualify for financing, construction will never begin, and their investment could be put at risk.

CASE STUDY

Loan Defaults in Florida, 2006
In Florida, at the height of the condo boom in 2006, many pre-construction condos were being sold for as much as $1,000 per square foot. When the boom ended and prices plummeted, construction finance lenders moved in to foreclose on projects as builders began to default on their loans. The result: construction of the towers stopped midway. Since the state of Florida allowed builders to put buyer deposits toward construction, many investors lost hundreds of thousands of dollars in buildings that may not be completed. Even if they are completed, the units will definitely not be worth as much as the buyers paid for them.[7]

CASE STUDY

Birchwood Village Greens, Alberta, 1999[8]
In Alberta, under the Condominium Property Act, a developer's lawyer must withhold in trust 50% of the unit sale proceeds for residential purchases until there is substantial completion of the common property. In the Birchwood Village Greens case, purchasers bought into a bare land condominium, where they could park their mobile homes or build a permanent property on their plot. The common elements for these condos included roads, perimeter fences and the utility infrastructure.

During the construction, the developer experienced cash-flow problems and failed to complete the project. A huge problem occurred because the lawyer representing the developer released all funds, leaving no holdback, and because of the cash-flow problems, the developer was unable to refund the purchasers' investment. Since there was no warranty program protecting the purchasers, they had to sue the developer for breach of trust.

The developer and their lawyer argued that the property was a recreational resort and not residential, therefore the holdback rules didn't apply. The purchasers argued that they intended to use the property as residential, either for their mobile homes or for permanent homes.

The Alberta Court of Queen's Bench ruled in favour of the purchasers and found the developer, the developer's lawyer and the realtor in breach of trust; as a result, they were all liable for the condo's completion cost.

Construction lenders evaluate developers based on the 5 Cs of credit: Character, Capacity, Capital, Collateral and Conditions.

Character: What is the developer's reputation? This is a subjective category, but a lender must try to evaluate the developer's trustworthiness to repay the loan. The lender will look at the developer's past history, education, experience, references, past litigation or bankruptcies, and their reputation in the field.

Capacity: Can the developer repay the loan? The lender will want to see a detailed plan showing cash-flow projections and timing of repayment to determine the probability of success of a loan repayment. Naturally, the ability to repay a loan depends on how profitable the project becomes, but as costs go up, a lender will want to know that a developer has the skills to handle themselves with business savvy, because their revenues are based on purchase and sale agreements that have locked-in prices. Lenders will look for: past credit history with other lenders, experience, a high degree of attention to detail, what kind of team they have assembled, and past projects they have been involved in.

 TALES FROM THE TRENCHES

Why Pre-sales Are a Must
by Harry Stinson, developer, Hamilton

Builders would much rather finance and build a condominium, and then sell the suites on completion at current market value. Builders certainly do not like to lock in and cap their revenue years in advance, while enduring subsequent years of ever-increasing costs. The concept of pre-sales at the very beginning of a project is essentially a banker requirement, not a builder's trick to inconvenience consumers.

Capital: How much cash or equity does the developer bring to the project? The higher the percentage of capital to cost, the more likely the lender will finance the project. The higher the equity that a developer has, the better their ability to cope with financial setbacks. (As a buyer, you can ask the salesperson if the developer owns the land outright.)

◎ YOU SHOULD KNOW)

Joint ventures minimize risks
Many developers do joint ventures with land owners, in which the developer will supply the money and expertise to get necessary zoning approvals in place and pre-sell a project, and the land owner will supply the land equity to ensure favourable financing terms. In doing so, the developer doesn't have to risk a huge amount of capital to buy land that may not get re-zoned or get the required number of sales, and the land owner will get a premium price for the site.

Collateral: What assets are backing up the loan? This is where the lender will look at the size of the deposits collected from buyers; the end-user/investor mix; how much buyers are qualifying for from lenders; the assets the developer is putting against the loan; and the value of the land it is building on (taking into account that land becomes more valuable when an approval for high density is in place). In some cases, where developers have shown they are unable to complete a project, lenders want to know if they can bring in another developer that can easily take a site to completion. The lender will look for: the number and value of pre-sales in current and past projects, how marketable the project is, and location of the site.

◎ YOU SHOULD KNOW)

Design has monetary value—in more ways than one
Some lenders who provide construction financing to developers have begun to look at design as a form of collateral. Lenders know that well-designed projects, from both an urban planning and architectural perspective, will be more profitable.

Conditions: What conditions have to be satisfied before the developer will receive construction financing to break ground? This has an impact on what will be included in your purchase and sale agreement. Items such as how many units you could buy, deposit amount, payment structure, your qualification criteria, your ability to flip or rent units, and the ability of the developer to cancel the contract if certain other conditions are not met, will be added to your contract, depending on the developer's financing terms. Lenders will consider the local political climate and economic fundamentals of the time, trying to determine the likelihood that the development will receive its approvals from the city and if the unit mix will sell quickly in the current economic climate. Ask the developer how many units have to be sold before construction financing is released, and how long they have to sell those units.

During robust economic times, lenders tend to be more lax with their lending policies, as they have confidence that the potential profit outweighs the potential risks of the project. This means that developers have greater and more flexible access to money and therefore are able to go forward with proposed projects, thereby giving buyers favourable buying terms (e.g., lower deposits that are more spread out than usual).

The other side of the coin is that the money supply can contract during tougher economic times. Lenders do have provisions to cancel construction financing, even after a developer has met their pre-sale and deposit requirements. If the economic fundamentals change, causing labour and/or material costs to inflate and prices to fall, a development can stop midstream during construction, leaving an empty hole like we've seen dotting the landscape in downtown Calgary.

CASE STUDY

1 Bloor East, Toronto[9]

In November 2007 hundreds of people lined up for days to buy into 1 Bloor East in Toronto. By May 2008 more than 80% of the condo units were sold, with more than 20% deposits. Construction financing was to come from a consortium of European banks led by the French bank Société Générale. After the credit crisis in the fall of 2008, the European banks cancelled their commitment. Unable to secure construction financing, the developer was forced to cancel the project and return all deposits to buyers.

How often are projects halted? While it doesn't occur frequently, it is common enough that there are stories of it happening across Canada. In Vancouver, in the fall of 2007, a proposed 119-unit condo project was halted due to financing concerns. The Eden Group, which had pre-sold 55 of these units (and was also working on another $30-million townhouse project in the city), made the decision to stop work on the project and ultimately return the deposits. The purchasers were fortunate, as this does not always happen so readily and easily for the buyers. Fortunately, Bill Eden had the foresight and integrity to halt the project while he still could, saying, "It's a financing issue. It's a scheduling issue. And it's a labour issue. I refuse to put my investors in harm's way. We're selling the site."[10] A year later, in Calgary, construction was put on hold on the Skytower.[11] This was likely partially due to excess of supply within the Calgary condo market, but might also have been attributable to financing obstacles. In the past, financing through lenders was often triggered once 50% of units had been sold, but lenders had become more pessimistic and were beginning to require 75% pre-sales, making financing an even greater hurdle than before.

As an investor, it's important to understand the general outlook for access to money, both in your market and for your developer.

OPPOSITION TO DEVELOPMENT

Not in My Back Yard (NIMBY)

According to research done by the Saint Consulting group, 74% of Americans believe their neighbourhood is overbuilt and don't want any new development in their community. Resident opposition represents a significant risk to developers when deciding they are going to buy a site to develop a condo tower, and it's something that needs to be carefully considered.

Residents oppose developers for a number of reasons:

Strongest Reason for Opposition	Percent Surveyed (adds to 100%)	Specific Explanations
Protecting Community Character	23%	Building is too high
		Too much sunlight will be blocked
		Construction will be too disruptive
		Building design doesn't fit with neighbourhood
		Too much light at night
		Noise and dust will be a nuisance (especially with a building's loading and mechanical systems)
Protecting the Environment	22%	Will destroy natural habitat
		Area is contaminated and must be cleaned up
		Will destroy old trees
Protecting Value of Home	16%	Debris, noise and traffic will make home less valuable
		Destruction of greenspace will make neighbourhood less desirable
		Development will increase property taxes

Too Close to Home	13%	Privacy will be endangered
		Bring too much crime, drugs, alcohol
		Dust, noise and smells will make living difficult
Too Much Traffic	13%	Long commutes
		Difficult left turns
		Bad air quality
		Use residential streets as shortcuts
		Children/elderly endangered
Other	13%	

 TALES FROM THE TRENCHES

Challenges for the Developer

by David Nakelsky, lawyer, Toronto

Even if there is no opposition from the neighbourhood, working within the bureaucracy of a city's planning process can be difficult and time-consuming for a developer.

In a city with an active condo market, developers are actively searching out sites to develop, competition is fierce, and you have to move fast. Once a site becomes available, a developer typically puts a conditional offer on the property. During this period, the developer's team studies the market to understand the market risk.

The developer works to determine the optimal price, suite mix and how many units they have to sell. If the developer determines that the project is feasible from a market point of view, they give this information to their architect. The architect develops a plan for how a building can be created on the site to contain the necessary suite mix, and determines how much it will cost. The architect and the developer also work with the local planner to determine if the density of suites they need from the project in order to be financially feasible is possible.

Before the end of the conditional period with the land owner, the developer will have a good idea of what kind of suites will be built, how fast they will sell, how many units they need to sell in order to obtain financing, what the cost will be, and how difficult it will be to obtain an approval from the community.

If the developer works out they will profit if 200 units are built, and they know it's likely they will get approval for that amount of density or more, they will move forward. If, after doing their due diligence, they find the only way to make the project profitable is to increase the density beyond what will be easily approved, the developer must decide whether to take a risk and fight the city to get the project approved.

After the developer's due diligence is complete, they can decide to start pre-selling units, even if they have not received the required approvals from the municipality. Those who buy into these projects need to understand the risks of not obtaining the full approvals: if approvals aren't obtained and the project stalls or is cancelled, their deposits can be tied up for years without earning much of a return.

CASE STUDY

Stage East Lofts, Toronto

Stage East Lofts in the Leslieville neighbourhood of Toronto started marketing in April 2008, with the expectation that purchasers would move in as of October 2009. Due to administrative delays between the developer and planners, as of June 2011 approvals had still not been granted. Purchasers who made their deposits in 2008 are still waiting for the building to be completed. The purchasers have earned very little on their capital and all were given the option to back out. Many are supporting the developer, hoping the project can still be built. Others in the industry feel the developer will end up cancelling the project, because costs have gone up substantially since most of the sales occurred.

---

5. Inventory of New Condominiums

This refers to the number of new unsold condominiums on the market. An important distinction must be drawn between finished units that remain unsold versus available pre-sales. A prudent condo buyer should be aware of these numbers throughout the purchase and completion phases of a condominium, in order to determine the potential market value of the condo or the ability to charge a reasonable rent if they decide to keep it as an investment.

New inventory can be broken down into many parts: number of units sold, number of units unsold, number of units pre-construction, number of units under construction and number of units set to be delivered.

A high number of units sold in a short period suggests that investor activity into a submarket is large and could be inflating prices. In these areas it's better to get in early and ride the wave of investor demand, as it will cause a spike in prices. Low numbers of units sold can mean longer pre-construction periods and lower appreciation once the project is built.

Low unsold inventory in an area means the area is currently underserved with respect to demand, and prices could be poised to rise. If you are one of the first people to buy into a submarket, watch other sites being developed to see what impact they will have on your appreciation or ability to rent in the future.

Developers and lenders typically look at absorption rates when determining demand. Absorption rate is calculated by taking the number of units sold and dividing it by the number of units available. In submarkets with large investor activity, absorption rates could be over 80% in one year.

The number of units in the pre-construction category can include units in projects that are in various stages of the process. Projects can be pre-selling and waiting to hit pre-sale requirements for their lenders or waiting to get approvals from the city to build. These projects have yet to move forward and could be cancelled. For units under construction, it's very hard to forecast when units will be delivered, however, it's usually a good sign that your condo won't be cancelled.

The number of units set to be delivered indicates the number of units for which buyers are receiving their keys to move in. In some jurisdictions, this could mean the occupancy phase begins prior to the condo registering and where buyers are able to get a mortgage.

The number of resale units available, the sales-to-listings ratio, days-on-market stats, and sale prices (not listing prices) for comparable units are all good indicators of what end-users are paying to buy in your submarket. Lease-to-listing ratios and vacancy rates are good indicators of rental demand.

Areas with sales-to-listing and lease-to-listing ratios are calculated on total sold or leased, divided by the total listed. This data can usually be found from your local real estate board.

- Under 0.40 is a buyer's market. It means that less than 40% of all properties in a market have been sold in a given time frame. Buyer's markets are a leading indicator that prices have a good chance of falling.

- Between 0.41 and 0.50 is a balanced market for buyers and sellers. This is a good indicator that prices will hold steady.

- 0.51 and above is a seller's market. Seller's markets can mean that prices have a good chance of increasing.

What happens when this ratio is above 1? It means the market is so hot, and demand is so high that buyers and their agents are door-knocking to find properties, undoubtedly pushing prices of everything else higher.

Total days on market indicates how long it takes to sell or lease in the given market conditions. In some areas, these numbers can change significantly over a seasonal basis.

Vacancy rates indicate the amount of supply available for rent. Areas with higher vacancies will have a lower lease-to-list ratio and a higher number of days on the market. This can push down yields (which we will discuss later).

Markets that are showing signs of too much investor activity will show more appreciation on a price per square foot basis for new unsold inventory over resale price per square foot and lease price per square foot. In these times, as more and more investors enter the market, yields will begin to erode. This is the time to be extra careful in your due diligence, as other investors are banking on appreciation for the bulk of their returns. If new supply keeps entering the resale market, the extra supply can create problems when you decide to flip your condo or decide to rent it. For those looking to flip, if there is a large supply of condos less than four years old, buyers are more likely to purchase those units than take the extra risk of assuming your contract from a developer. For those looking to rent, renters won't pay an extra premium for your condo if there is an adequate supply of condos less than four years old in your submarket, so as the price appreciates, the yield you receive from rents will diminish.

Demand Factors

Buying pre-construction condos has been thought of as buying a real estate future in a particular submarket, because the development of condos goes hand-in-hand with neighbourhood gentrification and revitalization. It's easy to see how buying a unit in the right area can be profitable.

Buying pre-construction condos can be tricky: buying too early in the real estate cycle in your neighbourhood can make your condo obsolete by the time appreciation is set to occur; buying too late will leave very little room for growth and result in low rental yields.

Since real estate is cyclical in nature, buyers will need to understand how demand for their condo will look 5, 10 or 15 years in the future.

Those seeking high yields need to see both price and rent appreciation in the areas they buy into. This involves studying the economic and demographic fundamentals and political climate of the area where you plan on buying.

These are the factors that need to be considered when determining demand:

1. employment, incomes, economic diversity and job density

2. immigration, in-migration and population growth

3. ease of financing, affordability and cost of living

4. quality of life

5. expectation of rising prices.

1. Employment, Incomes, Economic Diversity and Job Density

When contemplating purchasing a condo, especially one you plan to rent and hold as an investment, it is important to research the health of the economy within the area where you intend to invest. A growing and diverse economy provides employment and income to residents; without stable employment and its resulting income stream, the pool of condo buyers and renters will be stagnant. In areas that have growing businesses and thriving industries, we tend to see an increase in population and also an increase in consumption. People who have jobs in which they feel secure tend to feel more comfortable settling down, either buying properties or renting places on a semi-permanent basis. A healthy economy therefore works to create or increase demand for housing.

To scope out areas that are poised for growth, look at the region's employment numbers. Unemployment measures the amount of people who are actively looking for work, but doesn't take into account those who have given up; unemployment numbers may also be skewed by rapid population growth, which brings in more people looking for work. The number of people employed is a better number to look at. If the number of jobs is growing, this forces wages up. When incomes go up, people can afford more for rents or for mortgages, and this will drive price appreciation and rent.

The employment numbers give us an indication of how many jobs have been created, but how do you determine employment numbers in future?

This requires forecasting, and there are various fundamentals that housing economists look at. They include:

- GDP (gross domestic product): As the region's GDP increases, the number of jobs being created increases.[12]
- Retail sales: Retail sales reflect confidence in the market. As sales increase, companies will hire more employees.[13]

Investors should also consider the diversity and density of employment in a region. Diversity reflects the range of industry that can be found in a particular city, while density reflects the number of jobs in those industries. If a region is diverse, it could buffer recessions a lot better; if a region is particularly dense, talent will always be attracted there, ensuring employers will follow. If the region has a diverse employment base, but it's not sufficiently dense, large job losses in one industry can cripple the confidence of the local population, which can be disastrous for the real estate market.[14]

Employment density can be tracked by looking at the number of head-office jobs, colleges and universities, industry associations and centres of excellence.

2. Immigration, In-Migration and Population Growth

As people are attracted to a city or town, the demand for housing rises. Immigration refers to people moving into an area from foreign countries; in-migration refers to people moving into an area from other parts of the country. In areas with strong immigration or in-migration, we tend to see a corresponding decrease in rental vacancies, as people often will choose to rent rather than buy upon first arriving in a city. As there are fewer and fewer available rental units, property owners can begin increasing their rents. This increase in rental income soon translates into an increased demand for investment property, as prospective investors identify an opportunity to increase their monthly cash-flow and overall rates of return on investment. Eventually this effect begins to trickle into the resale market as well. Research has shown that immigrants tend to buy housing three to four years after arrival. People who are renting begin to look at the monthly cost of being a tenant, and when they are able to afford it, they decide to become buyers instead. Either way, increasing populations positively impact the demand for condominiums.

Population change and growth is best tracked through census and research data, which is generally readily available online or through government bodies. Although there are many resources on population and demographics, the Sauder School of Business is a great source of up-to-date information on population and demographic trends across Canada. The Canadian Mortgage and Housing Corporation also regularly updates its website with current information on population and demographic information for would-be buyers.

Buyers must consider both the rate of change and the actual number of new immigrants. In large cities, such as Toronto, Montreal and Vancouver, population appears to grow very slowly if one only looks at percentages, but the actual numbers are in fact consistently high. In these cities, this means that population growth typically exceeds the total building capacity that can be delivered, thus causing prices to appreciate significantly as demand far outpaces supply.

CASE STUDY

Yaletown, Vancouver

Population growth rarely spreads itself uniformly around a city. Certain sub-markets in certain neighbourhoods will have enclaves of gentrification and renewal that will be attractive to end-users once complete. For example, Vancouver had one of the fastest growing residential downtowns in North America for some time, but Yaletown, a neighbourhood within the city, grew faster than others, spurring real estate prices in that submarket to rise. Statistics Canada reported that the population of Yaletown grew 15% from 2001 to 2005, compared to 3% for Vancouver. During this time, prices of resale condos in Yaletown increased a median of $267.78 per square foot in 2001 to $501.81 in 2005 (an 87% increase), while the rest of Vancouver, excluding Yaletown, experienced a 71% increase in property values.[15]

3. Ease of Financing, Affordability and Cost of Living

In discussing supply factors, we looked at the importance of the developer being able to access money easily and affordably. This is also true on the demand side of the formula. Just as developers require funds to build condos, purchasers require funds to buy the individual units. The two largest factors in determining whether access to credit is "easy" or "difficult" are the criteria for credit approvals and the cost of borrowing.

Credit criteria generally focus on a buyer's debt-servicing ratios and their credit worthiness. Debt-servicing ratios are simply a way to quantify a buyer's financial ability to repay a mortgage. The formula used by most lenders involves the percentage of the borrower's gross annual income that is required to service all their debts, including a mortgage, credit cards, leases and other loans. Most lenders have a set maximum that this percentage can be, usually 40%.

The credit worthiness of a buyer refers to their past history of repaying debts. Have they honoured past agreements and been responsible in their credit usage? This history gets quantified and is expressed in a numerical value, called a Beacon Score, which is reported by a credit bureau such as Equifax or TransUnion, and is then evaluated by the lender. (We'll discuss access to credit in greater depth in Chapter 6.)

The Canadian government plays a huge role in determining how easy or difficult it is for someone to obtain a mortgage. The Canada Mortgage and Housing Corporation (CMHC) underwrites (insures) some mortgages for the banks. In 2011, CMHC changed its down-payment requirements and put limits on the length of the mortgage's amortization period, both of which will impact the number of people able to access credit to buy a house or condominium.

Interest rates also have an impact on the consumer's access to money. As interest rates climb, the theoretical amount that a lender will lend to a buyer decreases as the buyer's monthly carrying cost of a mortgage increases. As rates decrease, the loan amount will increase accordingly, as the cost to service (or repay) that mortgage decreases on a monthly basis. In late 2011 and heading into 2012, we still find ourselves in a historically low-interest rate period, as illustrated by the following chart:

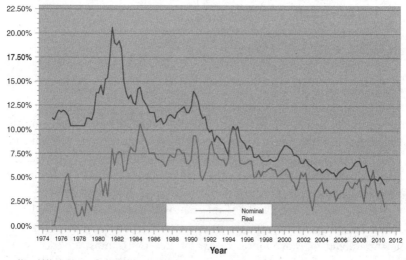

Average Residential Mortgage Lending Rate: 5 year

Notes: (1) Nominal Average Residential 5 year Mortgage Rate: Cansim Series Number v122497

If interest rates are low, or expected to get lower, the pool of buyers who are able to purchase your condo when it is completed will be higher. If the overall availability of credit is loose, and an asset, such as a property, is seen as scarce, demand will tend to increase and the price of condos will also tend to rise accordingly.

Finally, investors who plan to resell their condo in the near future should look at the cost of living in their area. Cost of living includes an end-user's mortgage payment, property taxes, utilities, insurance, transportation and food. When the price of real estate goes up, the affordability of home ownership (whether single-family homes, semi-detached or townhouses) erodes; as a result, the demand for condos tends to increase substantially, as long as condos remain affordable.

On a quarterly basis, the Royal Bank of Canada (RBC) calculates the affordability of condo units in cities across the country. RBC bases affordability on the following criteria:

- average condo prices taken from Royal LePage's quarterly House Price Survey

- principal and interest payments, calculated with a 25% down payment and a 25-year amortization at the five-year fixed interest rate

- average property taxes and utilities

- an estimate of the gross median income, based on numbers from Statistics Canada

- (maintenance fees are not included in condo calculations).

As long as the affordability index is in the "hot zone"—meaning that the cost of condo ownership is less than 40% of the median income—the property will be open to the widest range of buyers within the city.

Cost of living is something employers look at when they are considering expanding as well. Companies look at property taxes and commercial lease rates before deciding to move into an area to bring jobs.[16]

4. Quality of Life

Cities with high quality of life will attract and keep people looking to buy real estate. Quality of life measures many factors, such as political, economic, environmental, health, education, climate, culture and recreation. Cities with a high quality of life will be attractive for Baby Boomers looking to downsize or buy a second property; quality of life will bring in immigrants and ensure they stay there; and it will bring in international investors looking to buy into a city for lifestyle and security.

On a local level, certain submarkets will increase their quality of life faster than others, resulting in significant price appreciation. Urban planning plays a substantial role in this. The ideal area is one that combines condo development with great urban planning, including making the area more walkable, the addition of trains and light rail, and access to retail, restaurants and entertainment.[17] We'll discuss this more in the location fundamentals section later in this chapter.

5. Expectation of Rising Prices

A demand factor that is a little bit less quantifiable is consumer confidence in rising prices. If a potential buyer believes that a property is going to increase in value, he is more likely to be excited about buying and feel more confident in his decision. He is also more likely to be willing to pay a bit more for a property, simply because he believes he will recover his investment—and more—in the future. This consumer confidence or exuberance is created and affected by several factors, including media (such as headlines, which often lean to hysterical pronouncements), past personal experiences, advice of friends or acquaintances, and how risk-averse the buyer is. Of these factors, the media has arguably one of the greatest effects. The following graphs show historical housing price changes in Vancouver, Calgary and Toronto.

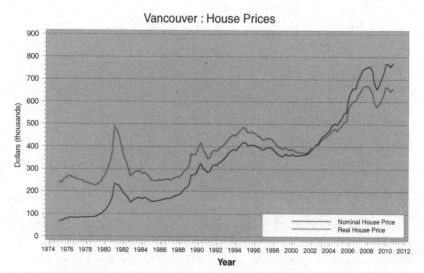

Notes: (1) UBC Centre for Urban Economics and Real Estate calculation of Royal LePage Survey of Canadian House Prices data for standardized house type: avg. of bungalow and two-storey executive
(2) Real prices in 2002 Q2 Dollars

Calgary
Nominal House Price—Percentage Growth (Over Previous Year)

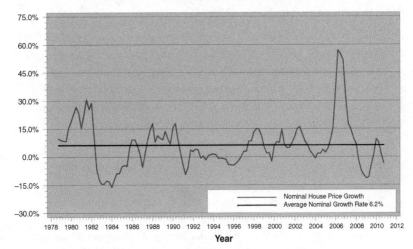

Notes: (1) UBC Centre for Urban Economics and Real Estate calculation of Royal LePage Survey of Canadian
House Prices data for standardized house type: avg. of bungalow and two-storey executive
(2) Real prices in 2002 Q2 Dollars

Toronto : House Prices

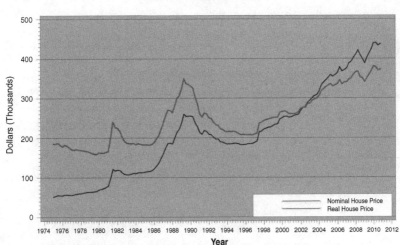

Notes: (1) UBC Centre for Urban Economics and Real Estate calculation of Royal LePage Survey of Canadian
House Prices data for standardized house type: avg. of bungalow and two-storey executive
(2) Real prices in 2002 Q2 Dollars

TALES FROM THE TRENCHES

Expecting Rising Prices Can Backfire

by Manny Riebeling, realtor, Vancouver

A client of mine got caught up in the hot condo market of 2008. He thought that prices would never stop increasing and that it was a safe idea to buy a condo and then sell it. So he decided to buy a pre-construction condo in a not-so-good area. At the time he was qualified to get a mortgage. Two years later, the market had gone south and getting approved for a mortgage was harder (he had also overstretched his credit by buying more properties).

When the condo was finished, he tried to get the mortgage, but was unable to because the value of the condo was now less than what he agreed to buy it for. Then he tried to sell his contract to purchase the unit (known as an assignment), but first he needed to get the approval of the developer to market the unit—and he didn't get it. Long story short, the developer sued my client, and the developer took over the unit and sold at a loss. My client had to pay for the difference plus lawyer's fees.

Overview of Supply and Demand

We have examined key elements that contribute to both the supply and demand of condominiums. Having a general idea of these factors will help you make a sound real-estate investment decision. This is not only important when purchasing a property, but also when deciding how long to continue to hold it once it has been purchased.

 TIP

As supply increases, the investing landscape changes

As city plans for certain neighbourhoods change, entire condo submarkets can be created within a neighbourhood as a new supply of land becomes available for re-zoning. These submarkets within a neighbourhood can be vastly different in terms of price and the demographic of end-users; therefore, looking at the neighbourhood zones created by local real estate boards may be ineffective for comparison purposes. When making a decision, carefully look at what areas are included in the submarket you are buying in, to determine the local supply and demand fundamentals. This may mean just looking at units in a few buildings within a real-estate board zone. To find which are the best buildings for comparison, take a walk in the neighbourhood or consult with a local realtor who is experienced in condo sales.

Location Fundamentals

Analyzing the location for a condo can be difficult, because you may be investing in an area that is going through revitalization or gentrification and may have an existing negative reputation. In order to make the best decision, you must have a clear understanding of the urban planning of the site and the submarket.

Let's look at how a developer assesses a site for development potential.

When a developer is determining whether a property can be considered adequate to build upon, they consider the zoning potential of the site and the physical makeup of the site.

Zoning Potential

- number of units they can build upon a site
- cost and time to gain necessary approvals
- cost and logistics around preservation of historical buildings
- development charges and levies for developing the site
- city parking rules and costs to build parking spots

Site Issues

- site layout and design challenges associated with it
- shared municipal services (gas, sewage, electricity, storm water) with other land owners and easements
- cost to upgrade or build new infrastructure
- demolition and environmental clean-up costs
- access for heavy equipment and ease for construction
- existing tenants and leases if site is occupied
- air rights over site and neighbouring properties

 TIP

Beware the awkward site

Some sites are very difficult and costly to build on and this translates into an expensive project—even if it's in a desirable submarket. An awkward site may be too long, too shallow, irregularly shaped, neighbouring an established building or highway, or just in an area where the city planning rules cause the developer to take unusual steps to satisfy them.

The resulting building may be clumsily curved, have too-large setbacks, or a higher-than-usual ratio of exterior to interior space. Not only will building costs be higher for this tower (which will result in high prices), but the cost to maintain it will be higher (especially if it's next to a highway, body of water, or an active part of a building such as a chimney), substantially limiting your ability to make a profit when compared to other buildings.

Photo by Chris Ho.

The above tower at the far right is an example of a building that, once completed, experienced a dumping of units because of its poor location and high investor activity. During the third quarter of 2010 the building had 128 units (of 401 units in total) for sale and just 6 sales (a sales-to-listing ratio of 5%). Thankfully, the developer charged a fair price originally and the building was completed during a seller's market (at the time that many owners decided to sell). On paper, based on the price of six sales, most owners made a profit when their units sold; however, if conditions had been different, the outcome would have not have been as positive for the owners.

We will discuss more about how you can look for a well-designed building to maximize your profits in Chapters 3 and 4.

Now that we understand the importance of understanding the site of the building, how do we determine which submarkets created in certain neighbourhoods will appreciate the most or create a living space we want? In order to understand this, we need to break down submarkets into different types and explain what will result from them.

Types of Submarkets

1. Urban Renewal: These projects are in established areas that are going through massive changes from a city planning perspective. The area is going to be open to a massive amount of development within an existing city streetscape. The city planners are basically banking on using the existing city infrastructure to absorb the new residents. These areas will be revitalized quickly, as there are many large sites (parking lots or older buildings ready for demolition) for a developer to buy into. Within Urban Renewal areas, the price of the condos will be higher, since the developer has to account for higher land values, and you might have to pay a premium price, above market value. These areas will be for those looking for a more vibrant lifestyle, those who don't mind living in areas with crowds. Prices usually go up very quickly after the first few towers are completed. Since these areas are already established, the walkability and Walk Score may be limited, due to the existing urban planning and street network.

2. Avenue In-fill: These projects may be in heavily urbanized streets or a suburban street or an old plaza parking lot. The differences between Avenue In-fill and Urban Renewal is that the critical mass required for the area to change in a resounding way may take time to occur or may never occur at all. When buying into these projects, the buyer is basically looking to live in an established neighbourhood, but may not be able to afford to buy a detached home there, or prefers the condo lifestyle. These projects may include conversion of existing churches or schools and may be found on residential streets.

3. Brownfield Redevelopment: These projects are in urban areas and may be on former manufacturing and industrial sites that have been remediated for development. The sites are often so large that a developer is able to create a master-planned condo community of many towers with a new street network. The whole lifestyle of these projects is created with collaboration between city planners and developers, so careful study is required. Prices change dramatically depending on what phase of the development you buy in.

4. Suburban Greenfield Development: These projects are typically found in suburban areas around major malls or transportation hubs. These areas will typically offer a more suburban lifestyle and may be master-planned. Suburban Greenfield developments are more reliant on cars and offer a predictable lifestyle. It may take some time for a critical mass of services and amenities to be developed that are within walking distance, unless the urban planning for the entire area will be redesigned.

CASE STUDY

The Benefits of Master-planned Communities: Concord City Place, Toronto

Usually when developers first launch a master-planned community, prices are very low, since the developer knows that in the beginning, the community will have little in the way of vibrancy, and it's very difficult for buyers to envision how the community will look. To offset buyers' hesitation, the developer will kick-start the process by offering low prices: with one building up, the developer hopes that people can get a clearer picture of how the community will look as residents and businesses move in and amenities are built. A good example of this is Concord City Place in Toronto. The first building, Matrix, completed in 2002, sold for $230 per square foot at the original launch, and prices went up 103% in eight years. As prices went up during the later phases, price appreciation from the pre-construction launch to first quarter of 2011 ranged from 101% in the earliest buildings to 35% in the newer buildings. From the chart below we can see that buildings completed from 2005 to 2009 all have similar resale numbers and opening prices were significantly lower, depending on how early the building was bought.

Development	Year of Registration	Total Units	Original PSF	Q1 Resale Index $	Maint. Fee	Appreciation Since Launch
Cityplace Matrix A 361 Front St W	2002	308	$230	$466	0.65	102.6%
Cityplace Matrix B 373 Front St W	2002	344	$235	$472	0.65	100.9%
Apex at Cityplace (C) 381 Front St W	2003	264	$245	$482	0.65	96.7%
Apex at Cityplace (D) 397 Front St W	2003	366	$245	$488	0.64	99.2%
Optima at Cityplace 81 Navy Wharf Crt	2003	397	$260	$475	0.69	82.7%

The Gallery (Cityplace) 15 Brunel Crt	2008	139	$265	$490	0.51	84.9%
Harbour View Estates I – Tower 10 Navy Wharf Crt	2005	416	$260	$517	0.75	98.8%
Harbour View Estates I – Lofts 9 Spadina Ave	2005	102	n/a	$509	0.67	—
Harbour View Estates II 35 Mariner Terrace	2005	517	$273	$502	0.54	83.9%
Harbour View Estates III – "C" 3 Navy Wharf Crt N	2006	253	$295	$463	0.63	56.9%
Harbour View Estates III – "D" 5 Mariner Terrace	2006	349	$298	$504	0.67	69.1%
Luna at Cityplace— Podium, LTD & Villas 8 Telegram Mews	2010	334	$343	$479	0.52	39.7%
Luna Vista 25 Capreol Crt	2010	378	$397	$539	0.57	35.8%
Montage (Cityplace) 25 Telegram Mews	2009	529	$315	$507	0.51	61.0%
N Tower (Cityplace) 15 Fort York Blvd	2008	429	$365	$493	0.49	35.1%
Neo (Cityplace) 4K Spadina Ave	2009	353	$305	$489	0.5	60.3%
Panorama (Cityplace) 38 Dan Leckie Way	2010	401	$438	$493	0.53	12.6%
West One (Cityplace) 11 Brunel Crt	2008	613	$285	$501	0.59	75.8%

Urban Planning Issues

In this section we talk about how the urban planning of the area your building is in will impact both profitability and liability. In her book *The Death and Life of Great American Cities*, author Jane Jacobs outlined the making of a vibrant area as follows:

1. create mixed-used areas

2. have short blocks

3. have a mixture of buildings of different ages

4. have a sufficient population density.

Create Mixed-use Areas

"A district and many of the internal parts must serve more than one primary function: preferably more than two. These must ensure the presence of people who go outdoors on different schedules and are in the place for different purposes, but who are able to use many facilities in common."

—Jane Jacobs

In the past, residential areas were separated from other uses because urban planners thought that it was the best way to protect property values. History has shown us that this is not the case. Mixed-use areas create a sum greater than all the parts. Think of the most vibrant areas in your city, or a city you have visited. Office workers, residents, shoppers, visitors, tourists and curious people are intermingling throughout the day on the streets. New moms can stop at the local café to grab a tea and their favourite *pain au chocolat* and run into a friend who is on her lunch break. After work everyone from the office can get together at the city square and watch a free concert. The outdoor patio becomes the dinner table and the beach becomes the kids' play room. Starting to get the picture?

Primary uses include:

- employment space (manufacturing buildings, court houses or office buildings)
- residential (condo towers, mid-rise buildings or a nearby street with houses)
- entertainment (theatres, comedy bars, sports arenas, opera houses)
- education (colleges, universities, schools, libraries)
- recreation (community centres, parks, basketball courts, gyms, museums, galleries)
- tourism (hotels, aquariums, monuments, beaches).

The different uses must not separate people from each other; therefore, the people visiting a neighbourhood must use the same street or facilities, and the uses must fit in with the existing neighbourhood character. For example, putting a low-income community centre near an opera house would naturally alienate people from each other, but putting a community centre next to a library would create a synergy.

Synergies are further created by the proportion of the different uses. So putting a single condo tower of 100 units in a downtown financial district where 40,000 people work through the day would not create a vibrant community. The area's heavy uses during the work week and light uses during evenings and weekends will not create a vibrant neighbourhood around your buildings.

There are pros and cons of financial districts

Financial districts are good examples of why packing in many primary uses at the same time is ineffectual. On weekdays, people are jammed into the area; as a result, uses such as shopping and dining are crowded between 11 a.m. and 2 p.m. and seemingly abandoned the rest of the time. Since office workers make up a large portion of people using the area, other uses that might drive visitors there during other times of the day can never flourish, making the area less vibrant.

Cities do see the value in financial districts, which is why they allow for different zoning rules within them. In cities such as Toronto, New York and Chicago, office towers and hotels don't have the same zoning restrictions on height and density. Where land is increasingly in demand on the residential end, creative developers may build an extra-tall tower with residential components in financial districts, and also include a hotel or office component.

In Avenue In-fill projects, seeing the character of the neighbourhood is very easy, because it's already there. In the other types, the future character of the neighbourhood will be more difficult to determine. This is why it's a good idea to understand the urban planning for the area. In Brownfield Redevelopment and Suburban Greenfield projects, developers usually create a block plan (a map of the area showing how the development will look after it's complete); for Urban Renewal projects you may need to contact the city planner for the area. Cities are notorious for getting urban planning wrong. A good plan augments what is already there to create the vibrant urban space that is so sought-after.

When looking at the block plan, the key is to imagine the different times that people will be visiting the streets and why they will be there. If there is a constant flow of people in a neighbourhood throughout the day, using the same streets, you have yourself a vibrant area. When mixed-use areas are created with these ingredients, the neighbourhood becomes fertile ground for secondary uses, such as restaurants, shopping and retail. Over time, because of the constant people traffic, the neighbourhood character starts to develop and specialized shops start to sprout up. It can be really exciting to see the neighbourhood change as cool shops, such as an organic artisan bakery, start bringing more and more people into your neighbourhood, wishing they lived there.

Maple Leaf Square, Toronto

A great example of an area that has experienced great appreciation as a result of the mixing of primary uses is Maple Leaf Square. The two towers of Maple Leaf Square sit on a 9-storey podium that includes a grocery store, a sports bar, retail, office space and the Hotel le Germain. The tower includes 872 residential units and across the block is the Telus Tower (an office building), the Air Canada Centre (recreation) and Union Station.

In 2006, Maple Leaf Square launched at $450 per square foot. Today, units are going for north of $700 psf. Other buildings at the time were selling between $350 and $440 psf and are now just above $500 psf.

Source: Lanterra Developments Limited.

Have Short Blocks

"Most blocks must be short; that is, streets and opportunities to turn corners must be frequent."

—Jane Jacobs

Simply put, if blocks are too long, people won't walk on the sidewalks. When people don't walk on the sidewalks, no shops will open on the streets. When there are no shops and no people, the streets become isolated. Long blocks keep people far apart and prevent mingling, which causes isolation. Isolated streets are boring and predictable, and because there are few eyes on the street, they could be unsafe and promote crime.

From a traffic perspective, when certain roads, transit lines, shopping centres or office complexes become large areas of single use, traffic is consolidated and those areas or roads become overcrowded. Like many streams pooling together in a large river, the water pushes through, not giving a drop where it's needed. High traffic increases commute times, makes it difficult to find a seat on public transit and tough to find a parking spot while shopping.

If the blocks were shortened, paths would be mixed and mingled, which would create spots that are feasible for retail, and give you opportunities to run into friends. For those who love following Starbucks as signals that a neighbourhood has become cool, you will note that most, if not all, Starbucks cafes are found on corners.

For Avenue In-fill and Urban Renewal developments, unless the city is planning on connecting roads that were once blocked off or is actively working to change the streetscape, you are stuck with what you have. Check out the urban plan to get a sense of what's going on in the neighbourhood.

Brownfield Redevelopment and Greenfield Development projects offer an exciting opportunity to be part of a development as it grows. Carefully study the block plan.

 TALES FROM THE TRENCHES

The Entertainment District
by Roy Bhandari, realtor, Toronto

One of the neighbourhoods that exemplifies the success of an Urban Renewal development is Toronto's Entertainment District. Short blocks dominate the neighbourhood and it has become the natural choice for developers to start projects, especially with the addition of some new amenities. Since it was announced that the area around King and John streets would become the new home for the Toronto International Film Festival, the area has added two high-end hotels (the Ritz Carlton and the Hotel le Germain), exclusive restaurants and a number of new condominium, developments which has turned this district into one of the hottest in Toronto.

Festival Tower units initially sold at approximately $500 to $550 per square foot in 2006, and today those units are on MLS® for as much as $800 psf. Similarly, buildings such as M5V and Charlie sold for around $500 psf in 2007 and as of May 2011 are selling remaining inventory for approximately $700 psf.

 TALES FROM THE TRENCHES

Yaletown, Vancouver
by Don Ho, developer, Vancouver

In the early 1990s, Vancouver city planner Larry Beasley and I worked to redevelop Yaletown. Overlooking False Creek and within walking distance to downtown, Yaletown was primed for redevelopment. Larry and I put together a proposal for a thin tower and a podium holding townhouses, office and commercial units. The thin, tall tower gave a nice density of residences while allowing for views of the waterfront. This worked out really well to make the area diverse. Yaletown was originally zoned as commercial, but adding residences was key to its renewal. As the development proceeded, the waterfront brought in many visitors seeking leisure and recreation. Additionally, the lack of space for cafes, spas and hair salons in the downtown core drove many businesses into the area, which made it even more vibrant. Today Yaletown is a diverse mix of people and is a demand area because of the work we did many years ago. Prices have gone up from $200 per square foot to almost $800 psf today, and the businesses that bought units that were strata titled increased their business value much more than their cash-flows ever could.

Have a Mixture of Buildings of Different Ages

"The district must mingle buildings that vary in age and condition, including a good proportion of old ones."

—Jane Jacobs

As we read earlier, cost of construction is constantly growing; as a result, only a few businesses can support the new costs of construction in terms of mortgages or leases. High operating costs result in high turnover of business tenants, and diversity becomes limited to those businesses (such as large chain stores) that can afford the higher rents.

For new businesses and ideas to flourish within a neighbourhood, Jacobs notes that "there must be leeway for trial and error and experimentation," and this could only be fostered if there are old buildings within a neighbourhood that can offer cheaper operating costs. These new businesses are needed to incubate new primary diversity elements within a neighbourhood.

Only in a city, with its mix of high people traffic walking in a street in an established neighbourhood, could yoga studios, board-game cafes and vegan bakeries survive. This is the single most important reason why Avenue In-fill projects are so popular: it gives folks the opportunity to live in one of these established neighbourhoods, and development is slow enough to keep lease rates from going up too quickly. In Urban Renewal, finding aged buildings with low lease rates may be problematic, because land gets priced based on its development potential, which will increase property taxes so much that "experimental" businesses cannot afford to set up shop there.

This is how an area becomes a victim of its own success: the cool shops and businesses make an area popular, thus driving demand for people to live there too fast. This causes those businesses and shops to be priced out, forcing them to go to another neighbourhood. This is where the theory of "following the artists" to find a hip neighbourhood came from.

For Suburban Greenfield and Brownfield Redevelopment, having aged buildings nearby is problematic. These developments begin by starting fresh. The area can still become diverse and vibrant if the other three conditions are met.

Have a Sufficient Population Density

"The district must have a sufficiently dense concentration of people, for whatever purpose they may have there."

—Jane Jacobs

If the population in the submarket around your condo is too thin, the area will be handicapped from ever being diverse and popular. Cities such as Detroit have very low density, and it is one of the contributing factors that have made the city difficult to live in. High population density has been associated with low crime rates, diversity and liveliness, all of which Detroit sorely lacks.

Jane Jacobs notes that population density is not the same thing as overcrowding, which she defines as 1.5 people per room in a dwelling. Overcrowding is a problem and leads to social problems of its own, while population density is a positive thing for cities.

All major cities across the world share one thing in common: they are substantially dense.

Some of The Largest Cities in the World by Population Density (City Mayors Statistics)

Major City	Density (People / Sq km)
Mumbai (1)	29,650
Beijing (12)	11,500
London (43)	5,100
Moscow (47)	4,900
Tokyo (50)	4,750
Paris (69)	3,550
Toronto (97)	2,650
San Francisco (104)	2,350
New York (114)	2,050
Montreal (118)	1,850
Ottawa (122)	1,700
Vancouver (123)	1,650

Many people talk about wanting to slow down and live in the country. On a mass scale, this has not happened. From Boomers to first-time home buyers, the majority of people want to live in a dense core because of the vitality it creates, the availability of transit, and the variety of amenities it supports. What's more, employers are starting to see the benefits of density. Cities with high population density create industry sectors with high density. Research has shown that density of industry clusters creates economic strength and diversity, thereby creating more jobs.[18]

For those looking to buy pre-construction condos, it's important to note that some neighbourhoods are going to be denser than others. It's important to see how many units are allowed for in the city plan for the specific area.

Considering Jane Jacobs' factors is very important. Though we could find exceptions to the rule, lively areas are the most universally enjoyed and sought-after. The neighbourhoods that incorporate all of Jacobs' ingredients will always be in demand, which will lead to greater quality of life if you choose to live in a condo in such a neighbourhood, and will significantly help your resale potential.

Walk Scores and Price Appreciation

Extensive research has been done on the impacts of "Walk Scores" (http://www.walkscore.com) and price appreciation. Research from the University of Arizona analyzed 4,200 office, apartment and industrial properties from 2001 to 2008 in the United States. The research found that, "all things being equal, the benefits of greater walkability on the market value and investment returns were capitalized into higher office, retail and apartment values."[19] The paper found that a 10-point increase in walkability increased values from 1% to 9%, depending on the property.

Another study by Transport for London found that making a street more walkable adds significant price appreciation to surrounding apartments.[20] Other research done by Impresa, a consulting firm specializing in economic analysis, shows that neighbourhoods that were walkable held their values better than other neighbourhoods after the U.S. housing market crashed in late 2008. This is simply due to the increase in demand by people who see walkable neighbourhoods as valuable.

Why are walkable neighbourhoods so highly valued?

- Studies have shown that the average suburban American family spends 25% of their income on its cars, and dropping one car can increase a family's mortgage capacity by $100,000.[21] Furthermore, according to the Urban Land Institute, 80% of car trips are lifestyle based (over work based). If you can walk to buy groceries, for entertainment or to take the kids to school, the savings from not being in the car for those trips start to add up.[22]

- Studies have shown a person's least favourite activity is commuting. Economists who measure the costs and benefits of long commutes found that the erosion of well-being for long commutes can only be balanced by a 40% increase in salary. Other economists found that every 10 minutes spent commuting results in 10% fewer social connections, leading to isolation and unhappiness.[23] Essentially, if you spend less time in the car and more time walking to a friend's house, you will be happier.

- The leading cause of death for children up to 19 years of age in the United States is auto accidents.[24] Getting out of the car and walking more is much safer for families.

- People living in walkable neighbourhoods have more access to high quality, reasonably priced, fresh food. The USDA research on American cities that are dependent on cars show that many people live more than a mile away from a grocery store, but are an easy commute to a fast-food outlet like McDonald's. The higher availability of junk food makes it more likely for you to make poorer choices. Over time, less walkable areas in Canada are following trends that are similar to those in some U.S. cities, as more and wealthier residents leave the neighbourhood, deflating property values.[25]

- People who walk more are healthier. Research done by the World Health Organization has shown that every dollar a government spends to encourage walking reaps $3.50 in savings from decreased hospital admissions, premature deaths, pollution and traffic congestion problems.[26]

- Walkable neighbourhoods are safer. Crime rates are much lower on busy city streets because there are more eyes preventing crime. Additionally, research done by the Center for Neighborhood Technology in Chicago shows emergency vehicles take longer to travel to neighbourhoods with suburban cul-de-sacs than to those streets in a traditional urban grid. If you are suffering a heart attack, you are more likely to survive in a walkable neighbourhood.[27] Research also shows that if health-care facilities are within walking distances of people's homes, they are more likely to be used for preventive care.

- Walkable communities also benefit the local economy. Despite increasing property values and retail spending, walkable cities bring in more high-paying technology-based jobs.[28]

We will see in later chapters how developers can make your condo more pedestrian friendly, and therefore more valuable once it's ready to enter the resale market.

IT'S ABOUT THE NEIGHBOURHOOD

by Ken Greenberg, landscape architect and author of *Walking Home*

Selecting a place to live used to be about the size of the unit and the ameni-ties in the apartment or townhouse, plus the private yard or long view on the horizon. Today it is about neighbourhood, celebrating life outside the front door. This dramatic change in priorities is increasingly being driven by the rise in the cost of energy, as the need for mobility options other than the private automobile kicks in, but it is also about a whole range of trade-offs that make walkable neighbourhoods the most desirable places. People are swapping their larger living spaces for walkability, convenience and less time spent in the car.

A key new measure of success is being able to walk to more destinations. By doing many things in close proximity, we play chords rather than single notes—a trip to buy food, or to go to school or daycare or work, becomes a chance to do several errands and enjoy more sociable encounters as part of daily life. A critical mass is needed to make close-in walking, cycling and transit viable or to allow neighbourhood street retail to function. But it is not just density in the abstract that matters, it is how we make neighbourhoods dense and compact that is critically important—the way buildings shape pub-lic spaces and what happens along the sidewalks. An enhanced experience makes us more likely to take the walk.

This shift is gathering momentum as we move to more sustainable ways of living, with significant collateral benefits. Daily exercise from walking is a key contributor to heath. Lively neighbourhoods offer greater opportunities for neighbourliness and stimulation for those who desire it, and clearly an increasing number of people do. It often begins with young singles and couples and empty nesters, who are the pioneers in newly forming neighbourhoods—the "poplars" in a natural succession—but soon to follow are young families, as the first arrivals have kids and the large cohort of Baby Boomers arrives to extend their independence until that inevitable moment when the car keys will be taken away.

This raises a whole new set of criteria that come to the fore when choosing a place to live. It often starts with the most basic of needs—food. Where is the grocery store? What shopping is available within easy walking distance? Is there a market? Is health care available? Where is the nearest hardware store? Where can you go to the movies or hear live music or see a play? Or get your hair cut? Are there convenient and appealing neighbourhood restaurants and cafes? And for families with kids, where are the daycares, schools, community centres and playgrounds? Are the streets safe and comfortable and are there enough people around during the day to provide casual surveillance? What nearby places can you walk, take transit or cycle to? Where is the transit? How frequent is the service and where does it take you? Can you get to the train station or the airport? Is there car share and bike share (often an excellent sign) available?

Does the neighbourhood have a story, or contain a unique piece of local history? What makes it special? Green spaces and parks are a key attractor. Paradoxically, in urban neighbourhoods, residents often have greater access to nature than their suburban counterparts. It is not just the "yard," but the whole area, with a combination of natural features such as waterfronts, ravines and larger, more generous parks, linked by trails and lively sidewalks.

Is this a neighbourhood where people can "age in place" as they move from one stage of their lives to another, should they choose to put down roots and stay? Are there affordable options for a diverse population? And do the residential buildings themselves provide the things needed to serve this diverse population beyond the individual units—things such as bicycle storage, a courtyard, play space, gardens, green roofs and terraces? Does the neighbourhood allow for a real mix? Are there places of business, providing a daytime population? And are there places to open a business or a home office successfully?

Neighbourhoods are not static and few neighbourhoods will provide all these things. Our neighbourhood choices are usually based on a combination of what is already there and what is likely to come. The art lies in selecting a place that has the capacity to evolve in positive ways. The older pre-war neighbourhoods have a distinct advantage. With smaller streets and shorter blocks that encourage shared use, such as local shopping, they are inherently more walkable; they also typically have better access to transit. But because there is only so much pre-war neighbourhood fabric to go around, the challenge has now become how to make new, affordable places that have these desirable characteristics.

This is putting pressure on city planners and transportation departments to rethink their accumulated rules and standards, in order to "legalize" in new areas the characteristics and intricacy that these older neighbourhoods possess, but which had been rendered illegal by prescriptive zoning that separated land uses, and by road designs that created streets devoted to the free movement of automobiles but were inhospitable to pedestrians. It also poses new tests for a development industry that had become expert in producing one isolated real estate "product" at a time—either residential (in homogeneous groupings), retail (in malls or power centres) and office buildings (in office parks or clusters). The industry is now being challenged to break the mould and begin re-combining all these uses in new walkable, mixed-use neighbourhoods. Those developers that rise to the opportunity and embrace this new paradigm will surely be the most successful.

What Am I Going to Get for My Money?

An introduction to sales techniques, location and amenities. How condos are priced and sold. Choosing the right building and the right suite: layout, views and finishes.

When you find yourself looking for a pre-construction condo, the experience can take on a magical quality. Clever headlines, fantastical videos, stunning computer-generated images and photos of gorgeous models obviously enjoying an amazing lifestyle pull at your chequebook. Developers seem to spare no expense when it comes to promoting their new developments and hiring marketers, publicists and designers with a single goal: by showing their project in the best possible light, to sell as many condos as they can, as quickly as possible.

Developers have come a long way from selling their condos from a feature sheet, floor plans and a few renderings. Beware! You can get yourself into a lot of trouble when you make a decision solely based on "magic." A condo buyer must balance the seduction of powerful marketing with extreme caution and proper due diligence. It is very easy to make a costly financial mistake that can set you back for decades.

A BRIEF HISTORY OF MARKETING

by David Allison, partner with Braun/Allison, Vancouver[1]

We are living through a massive change. Change is being driven by the consumer, who is waking up to the incredible power they now have to talk to builders (and all other kinds of companies). Thanks in part to technology, but also to a new sense of empowerment brought on by the recession that started in 2008, consumers now feel entitled to ask questions and demand answers in a more aggressive and far-reaching manner than they have ever done before. They are forming groups online to protest things they don't like. They are sharing videos and photos of things that delight or annoy them. They are fiercely loyal when a company gets things right (look at Apple as one example) and fiercely vocal when they feel a company is trying to pull a fast one. We are entering a participatory age of consumerism, a time of great energy, a time that I believe will change the real-estate development industry for the better, and for good.

Any discussion of the real estate development marketing process has to keep this notion of change top-of-mind.

The old ways are still in use, side-by-side with developer activity that is focused on a response to this new consumer. As with any change, there are early adopters and there are slow-moving laggards. Someone who wants to can find plenty of examples of companies that are using the old ways exclusively and doing just fine. My over-arching point is that this might continue to work for some time to come. But the new consumer won't put up with the old ways forever. There were companies that resisted building websites, and companies that were slow to adopt fax machines, and companies that refused to consider cell phones. Eventually, everyone catches up. Or they close their doors and walk away, mumbling about the good old days when things were easier.

Let's look at the old method. Using billboards, signs and print advertising, along with simple and uninspired websites, the old method was based on something referred to in the industry as "fear of loss." It was predicated on the notion that the real estate on offer was a hot commodity, and for many years that predicated notion was bang on. The market was rife with stories about people buying a pre-sale condo and selling the contract for a huge profit before the building was ever built. It was not uncommon for one contract on one condo to be sold many times over before the building was built.

In that kind of market, where equity gains were almost guaranteed, people were scared of missing the boat. And that meant all the power was in the hands of the developer. Marketing was simply a matter of teasing people with little bits of information. A kooky headline on a billboard and a few print ads were enough to get a flood of prospects to visit your website and register for a chance to win the lottery—the chance to buy a piece of paper that would allow them to make a profit.

In that kind of environment, you didn't need to work very hard to market and sell real estate. Even mediocre product in a "B" location could generate a line-up of people waiting for their chance to buy. I stood inside on opening day at many sales centres and heard people say things like, "I don't care which one you sell me, I just want one," and "What do you mean, I can only buy two?"

For the most part, these people had no intention of actually living in the home they were buying. It was all about flipping the contract and making a fast buck.

Real estate agents played a role in this, too. If you were a real estate agent with a good relationship with a developer, you were treated like a rock star. You were invited to a champagne-and-caviar VIP event and could reserve a block of suites for your best clients. Developers wooed those agents who could deliver multiple buyers—it made everything easier. Agents were in the business of lining up buyers who they could count on to buy great batches of everything the agent pointed them to. Some of these agents built huge and profitable "marketing" companies by being the matchmaker between developers and hungry investors.

The Marketing Arrows in the Developer's Quiver

Developers have common tools they use to market condos. Marketing companies are usually hired to create a brand identity, which governs how a project will be marketed. When you understand what tools developers use, and how, you will be in a better position to understand how to determine what information is actually important to you.

Renderings

These are computer-generated models of a building's exterior and interior. Renderings are pure sales and marketing tools, designed to present the product offering in the best possible light.

Renderings are usually created at a stage where design and floor plans are barely finalized and the construction untendered, so naturally they are subject to change. Exterior materials, interior finishes and amenity space may be different, based on availability of finishes and equipment during the time of construction.

 TIP

Ask questions about renderings if you see something in particular that "sells" you. Find out if there have been any changes to the plan since it was completed.

Actual building. (Photo by Kent James.)

Rendering.

Lifestyle Photos

These are typically pictures of people enjoying a certain lifestyle, meant to create emotional responses in you to encourage you to buy.

Websites

Websites with cool graphics and flash animations, combined with glowing copy, are nothing more than online brochures and should not be relied on to get important information.

 TIP

Websites are a wealth of information
Recently, some developers have begun to use their websites as tools to offer more in-depth information that will help potential buyers determine what is important to them. If developers' websites are inadequate, sites built by realtors or message threads on online forums could be a good supplement.

Print Material

Print material includes brochures, copy-written text, and direct mail or flyers. Condo brochures are typically printed on high-quality, glossy paper and are filled with nice pictures. Their intent is to grab the attention of a potential buyer and sell the condo lifestyle. With respect to real estate, if you see words pushing you to visit a website, it is usually some form of copy material prepared by developers. Such copy can be found in direct mail flyers, free condo guides at newsstands and newspaper articles in your local paper. Copy doubling as a newspaper article can be a little deceptive; it will definitely be written with a bias.

 TIP

Keep marketing materials for your own use!
Keep any print material and use it to help sell the condo later on when you are ready to. The text and photos that grabbed you during the pre-construction process can be used again to grab buyers on the resale market.

TV and Radio

Not as prevalent today, but in some cities TV and radio ads can be used to promote a particular project or the developer in general. They are usually designed to drive traffic to a website.

Signage

Site signage can be an effective means to drive traffic to a website for people looking for a project in a particular neighbourhood. You will find signage on public transit, and less frequently, on billboards. With the advent and growth of social media, signage is becoming less effective as a means to generate traffic to developers' websites. Signage can also be found on the building as it is being constructed, for branding.

Sales Centres

Sales centres are often referred to as a presentation centre, a discovery centre or a multitude of different catchy names. Sales centres are designed to provide you with all the information you need to make a decision and are usually staffed with well-trained people to answer all your questions.

 TIP

You need a lot of information to make a decision on buying real estate pre-construction

Begin your research on a project by tracking an application as it goes through approvals. Attend community meetings, listen to the developer's proposals, and research comments on online forums. If a developer is using stunning pictures and a robust website to sell its product, it shows passion, but if that's all the developer offers, be careful and ask the hard questions.

Sales Staff

Inside sales staff in condos could be directly employed by the developer or could be sales agents hired by the developer. Most sales staff are well informed about the development and are prepared to answer all questions. In the real estate business, there is a lot of turnover of sales people, so the individuals who sell you a condo will most likely not be there when you move into that condo. You must ensure that what they say about the condo is written in the contract, otherwise their promise may be unenforceable, even if you record your conversation. (See Chapter 5 on contracts.)

 TALES FROM THE TRENCHES

Keep Emotions in Check
by Mark Savel, realtor, Toronto

Don't waste emotion on marketing brochures or sales centres. Look at these things with some degree of skepticism and dig deeper for the facts. Keep your emotions in check and expect changes on everything from the look of the lobby to the delivery dates.

Social Media Tools (Facebook, Twitter, Youtube, Blogs)

Developers have now begun to use social media to market their condos. Marketing companies such as Braun/Allison encourage developers to use Facebook and Twitter to actively engage with the public and post stories about their materials, architecture style and stories of the buyers who have already bought. However, many developers are still underutilizing social media tools.

 TIP

Find out what others are saying about a developer through Twitter and Facebook
Following Twitter lists of people in the industry are especially powerful tools to get information, as it's updated almost in real time. To get access to Twitter lists of experts in your region of Canada, visit www.twitter.com/BrianPersaud.

 TALES FROM THE TRENCHES

Social Media Marketing at The Hive: Lofts on the Queensway
by Sayf Hassan, builder, Toronto

While on-site signage was successful in bringing awareness of the project to commuters, the real marketing effort was on utilizing social media, Twitter in particular, to promote the project among industry insiders and potential purchasers alike. I handled the tweets personally, providing inside information about the project, responding to questions and comments on real estate forums such as Urban Toronto and BuzzBuzzHome. There was no third-party promotions company distilling the information into pre-packaged PR hand-outs; it was genuine insight into the project. The Hive was a hot topic on Twitter, trending on numerous sites as one of the hottest projects of spring in the GTA. There had never been a truly modern project in Etobicoke. Forum commentators wondered if the building design was too far ahead of the existing developments in the area, and if conservative, multi-phased development, mere blocks from the site, would absorb all the area demand. We welcomed any and all discussion, explaining the emphasis on end-user comforts and the boutique, intimate nature of the building. The idea was to be utterly transparent. Yes, we were more expensive than the competing developments in the area, but the value was justified. This wasn't an anonymous structure with copy-pasted features and finishes. The Hive had personality.

Response was outstanding. Peter Milczyn, the area councillor and an architect himself, was quoted as saying, "If successful, The Hive will demonstrate to a lot of property owners and developers that these smaller-scale, mid-rise buildings can be viable." And successful it was. By the end of the first month, we were 50% sold; by the end of the second, we were at 75%. Purchasers admired the building design, marvelled at the proposed stacker system for parking, and were excited by the intimate scale of the building. The marketing and presentation, focusing primarily on the standard materials and finishes within the units, educated and informed. It was transparent and honest in a way most development outside the core was not. This imbued the project with a quiet confidence that comforted and assured potential buyers. Our strategies worked not simply because they were unconventional, but because the thinking behind them was manifest.

At the time of writing, The Hive is set to begin construction in a few months, and we have future mid-rise projects in the works, with different locations and lot sizes, each meriting a unique, divergent approach. The possibilities are exciting.

Sales Techniques Developers Use

Land is money. To maximize their profits, builders want to begin selling condos as soon as possible. As a result, a developer rolls out sales at different stages and for different prices. As a rule of thumb, the earlier you buy, the better the deal. Some developers will start selling as early as they have the property under control from the landowner, but before the developer actually closes on the site. The builder may not even have the necessary contracts for you to legally buy into a project, but they can take reservations from the clients of a few select agents who have been given the opportunity to sell a number of suites for the best possible price to their investor clients.

Platinum Brokers, V VIP Agents, Friends and Family

Buyers at this level are usually investors and don't take much time to perform due diligence. Some investors, either because they are familiar with the process or because they trust their advisor's ability, make a decision to buy based solely on the VVIP (Very Very Important Person) agent's or the developer's recommendation. Their reward for acting quickly is usually a substantial discount over what would be offered to the public later on.

To get access to these prices, you usually have to work with a top broker, be employed by, or have a close relationship with, the developer, or have bought a number of units from the developer in the past. Brokers can have an entire floor reserved, and in some cases they will sub-broker units to other agents and take a cut of these agents' commissions. For VIP brokers, having access to sell is key, and they are more than willing to pay part of their commission to keep their clients loyal.

In a seller's market, there is a lot of demand for units at a VIP sale. These sales can almost resemble an after-Christmas rush at a major department store, where people are clamouring to buy anything and everything in sight. At a VIP event, the developer and good agents know which units are the most valuable. When the rush starts, all agents are fighting to get these units. Watching units getting snapped up in a competitive environment puts a lot of pressure on a buyer to buy—and quickly. The sales are happening so fast, sometimes going in you don't even get your first, second or third choice. An investor could end up with a less desirable unit. The fast pace can make the buying pressure unbearable.

VIP sales can occur in two ways:

1. at in-person events: agents or clients line up to get into a sales centre.

2. through remote events: agents submit worksheets to the developer via fax, outlining the top three choices of their clients.

In-person events are the traditional events that we are used to seeing in the media, where agents and their clients line up to reserve a unit.

Remote events are used when the developer may not have a sales centre large enough to handle the expected demand at a condo opening, so agents must fax a condo worksheet to the developer to reserve a unit for their clients.

In either case, a developer will invite agents and their clients to pre-view events, where they can see a scale model of the building and get the brochures and entire unit availability. After the preview event, agents must submit a worksheet to make the reservation. Worksheets have the client's personal information (name, phone number, address, SIN number and a photo ID number), along with the suite number they would like to buy.

 TALES FROM THE TRENCHES

by Linda Mitchell Young, developer sales representative, Toronto

From experience, developers have noticed that model suites outsell other suites by a considerable margin. If they know a particular suite may not sell, a developer may use that suite as the model to ensure that units will sell. For projects that don't have a model suite, a developer could invest in a virtual reality tour instead.

 TALES FROM THE TRENCHES

by an anonymous realtor

We had clients looking to buy a condo in a popular project in Toronto. The developer told us that worksheets could be faxed in Friday, and no units would be reserved until Sunday evening. We handed in three worksheets as soon as the lines opened on the Friday, and were told that since no units would be allocated until Sunday evening we stood, a very good chance of getting our first choice units. Knowing what I know, I decided to drive down on Saturday to: a) make sure that a human being had seen my worksheets, and b) see that the worksheets were actually at the top of the pile.

When I got there, the sales office was in a frenzy, with agents signing deals before the allocations had even begun. All three of my clients' first choice floor plans were sold, and we had to scramble to find alternative choices—36 hours before they began "allocating."

 TALES FROM THE TRENCHES

by Giovanni Marsico and Susan Toughlouian, realtors, Toronto

During the sales cycle, a developer can increase pricing several times, from the initial launch to agents, to the public grand opening, to start of construction, and prior to occupancy. Some of our most memorable moments in the industry are what we call our "price increase" phone calls. There's no better feeling than to call a client and say "Hi Tim, the developer just increased the price of your model again by $20,000!"

In the past few weeks, we've made 30 of these calls to investors who purchased at a hot new project in Toronto's Entertainment District, where the average price increase was roughly $25,000 within one month from the start of sales.

 TALES FROM THE TRENCHES

by an anonymous agent

It's sometimes mind-boggling to consider how developers increase prices so rapidly. One story that really stands out for us happened during a launch in downtown Toronto. It was a one-day sales event that was organized and it was a mad rush for units. Our client was interested in a specific unit that was no longer available, but he had decided on another suite that matched what he was looking for. After considering it, the client decided not to go ahead, because it wasn't the right unit for him. We told the client to reconsider, especially given that there was a ten-day rescission period if he wanted to change his mind, but there is a fine line between being a pushy agent and being an advisor.

The next day, the client called to tell us he had made a mistake and wanted to get the unit we talked about the previous day. We called the developer and the suite had increased in price by $30,000 *in one day*. Knowing that prices can change quickly adds another layer of pressure to make snap decisions when purchasing pre-construction condominiums, and it is very important to have someone by your side who understand how it works.

Limited Supply: Last Chance to Get Pre-construction Pricing

Why do sales and limited supply have such a strong hold on us? Frankly, it's human psychology to value things that have a limited supply. Take as evidence a study that was conducted at Florida State University. In the study, students were surveyed to rate the cafeteria food; most said it was unsatisfactory. The cafeteria was then closed for two weeks, because of a fire, the students were told. When students were again surveyed, they didn't complain about the quality of food, but did complain about not having access to the food they had previously rated as pretty much inedible.

In great locations, condos can be valued more because they are in short supply. Sometimes it is quite true that certain sought-after units are in short supply. But other times the developer could be holding back units to be sold later. Or sometimes the short supply is just a myth to create the illusion of scarcity. Either way, telling you that there is a limited supply or a limited time to buy is intended to increase your desire to buy. It's quite common for agents to play this tactic by asking if you will buy the unit before they actually check with the developer if certain units are available. Once you've committed to purchase, and the agent finds there is a unit available, the agent now has powerful leverage over you.

Here are two common ways developers increase the pressure on you to buy:

1. Limit information flow about pricing and availability. Since the developer has legal requirements for how they prepare information, to protect the buyer, it takes time for a developer to prepare the necessary documentation. The limited information flow is therefore most likely a result of practicality rather than a devious plot.

2. Create events to release only a select number of units to a crowd to create hysteria buying. Watching others sign contracts when you are unsure creates powerful buying pressure and is a great opportunity for developers to sell their more undesirable suites.

VIP Agents

In hotter markets or higher-demand neighbourhoods, after 20% of the units have been sold off to investor clients, friends and family, other sets of units are released to the next tier of brokers at a less discounted price. By this time, the contracts, condo disclosures and full marketing materials are finalized. In some cases, these brokers are only allowed to sell one or two units.

● TALES FROM THE TRENCHES

by James Kilpatrick, developer's sale representative, Toronto

A developer's acquisition costs for a client are expensive, which is why some areas sell upwards of 80% of their units with real estate agents with commissions ranging from 2.5% to 5%. This is a substantial investment, but developers know that real estate agents will do the legwork to pre-qualify clients, find who the decision makers are, and build trust over a long time period in order to get a signed contract.

TIP

Understand the fundamentals

Sales in the first few weeks after a condo is launched are usually a good indicator of the number of investors who have bought into a building. Heavy investor activity may not reflect actual end-user demand in the marketplace, though, which is why it's important to know the economics and demographic factors that will underlie end-user sales. Knowing who is buying and when they are buying is as important to your success as price, comparables and location.

TALES FROM THE TRENCHES

by Roy Bhandari, realtor, Toronto

The worksheet system was designed as a way to allow condominium buyers to put units on hold without the need to line up for weeks before a launch. Essentially, the developers ask clients to fill in worksheets with their top three choices for units, and then they are allocated on a first-come, first-served basis. The developers will tell us a time that the fax machines open, and after that it is a race to get the worksheets in.

There are both pros and cons to this method. The biggest pro is, of course, the ability to purchase without having to line up. Prior to the worksheet system, it was not uncommon to line up for longer than three weeks prior to a condo launch. It doesn't take a rocket scientist to figure out that this isn't an ideal situation, especially in our harsh winters.

However, there are cons involved too.

The Toronto market is hot and has been for a number of years. There have been a number of projects where the number of worksheets has far exceeded the number of units available. A couple of recent examples include Tableau (they received 1,200 worksheets for approximately 300 units) and PACE (they received 1,500 worksheets before they stopped counting, for approximately 250 units).

While agents are told that the worksheets are dealt with on a first-come, first-served basis, that isn't necessarily true. Let's say they opened the fax lines on a Friday morning, and worksheets are accepted until Sunday. If you are an agent that the developer has never heard of, it's likely they won't give you any units, even if you are the very first agent to fax in (especially when demand far outweighs supply). Developers will look at the agents who they recognize first, put them to the top of the list (whether they are first or last to get their worksheets in), and then deal with the rest on a first-come, first-served basis.

Of course, this isn't *always* the case, but we've seen it play out like this more often than not.

In addition, the worksheet system can put additional pressure on buyers. We have had calls that say, "we were able to get you your eighth choice unit, please let us know as soon as possible if your client would like to hold the unit, otherwise we have twenty other clients waiting." Clients now have to decide whether or not to buy their eighth choice (a unit they probably weren't interested in), or walk away. It's a fine line: if you put too few choices, you risk not getting called at all.

Given that the developers give preference to certain agents (agents who have a track record of selling pre-construction condominiums), it is not uncommon that clients call us and say, "we have been unable to get Unit X from our agent, can you help us?" and we are able to secure the unit. We have been on both sides of the coin, too: when we were starting out, after we had told our clients we were unable to secure the unit via the worksheet system, they were then able to get the exact unit they wanted from other agents, despite being told that the unit was "unavailable."

Another issue is that the worksheet system proves to be a logistical nightmare for the sales team. Imagine having 2,000 sheets for 250 units. How do you even begin sorting through them? While it is rare, there have been the odd instances where the same unit has been allocated twice. Imagine getting the call that you secured your number-one choice for your client, relaying that message to your extremely happy client, only to have to call them back to say there was an error and they no longer have the unit.

 TIP

VIP sales are not the only opportunity

During a VIP sale, agents usually compete to reserve a number of units. This process has been known to create huge line-ups with many inexperienced agents and their clients. In some cases, developers may inflate the number of true sales to spur demand even further (this is done by putting the famous red dots on the availability board). It's important to realize that if you don't get your first option, all is not lost; buyers do fall out within their cooling-off periods or developers may release other units at later "New Release" or "Ground Breaking" events. Waiting may work to your advantage. Hiring an experienced realtor, who has your best interests at heart, will be valuable in these situations.

General Public and General Agents

At this stage, the developer starts marketing to the general public, including purchasers attracted by the developer's marketing efforts, who have probably registered on the developer's website. At this time, the sales centre would be ready to receive buyers who need a slightly longer time to make a decision. Developers know that potential end-users tend to visit sales centres several times before they buy, as they are more risk averse and price sensitive than investors. As a result, the buyer who walks in off the street generally pays a substantially higher price, as the developer wants to recoup monies it gave up through its higher discounts to earlier buyers.

As the sales process continues, various short-term sales incentives may present themselves to encourage more sales. Incentives provide savings in lieu of the builder having to lower the price, which has terrible optics. Common incentives include:

- lower deposits
- free maintenance/strata/condo frees for a set time period
- reduced or capped closing adjustments
- right to assign the contract at any time
- free interim-occupancy fees for a set time period
- rental guarantees
- free property management
- cash back at closing
- free upgrade packages or furnishings
- free parking and locker combo at preferred locations.

In some cases, the incentives can be more valuable than the incentives received at the beginning of the sales process; on the downside, you won't get the best selection of units. No matter what incentives are offered, ensure you complete the REal Experts Property Analyzer so you've got the hard facts in front of you.

 TALES FROM THE TRENCHES

by Mark Savel, realtor, Toronto

A friend-turned-client of mine always had a difficult time saving. She thought it would be impossible for her to ever have enough put aside to purchase a condo.

She had the dream of owning but no plan or commitment. I was able to find a development that worked with her by creating an extended deposit structure. Having signed the contract, she was now committed to saving part of her pay cheques in order to honour the contract. Once complete, the suite appreciated $120,000, making her a very healthy return. Not only do pre-construction condos act as an investment, they act as a forced savings account too!

 TIP

How to hire a high-quality VIP agent

The Internet is full of inexperienced agents who are marketing their access to sell you a pre-construction condo. How do you know your agent is a high-quality representative rather than a glorified Internet-marketing order-taker?

Here are the key questions to ask when looking for a VIP agent.

1. Do they have real front-line access to a preferred project by a developer?

2. Do they understand the contract? Can they advise you on clauses that are normal in the marketplace? Do they understand which closing adjustments are legit?

3. Will they provide you with service after you sign the contract? Are they willing and able to help you sell your unit before construction is complete? Are they willing and able to be there for you during the pre-closing inspections? Will they give you updates as price changes and construction milestones are met?

4. Have they actually experienced closing a transaction with a client with a particular developer? Each developer has a unique operating procedure; can your agent help you navigate this for you?

5. Does the agent have experience in the rental market? Is the agent experienced in renting out units to high-quality tenants? Do they know the market rents in other buildings and do they know which buildings cater to a certain demographic?

6. Is the agent capable of reading a floor plan and a floor plate (a plan that shows the unit's location on the floor of the building)? Are they capable of advising you on how saleable the unit will be in the future by understanding the nuances of the floor plan and location of the unit on the floor?

7. Is the agent knowledgeable in their local market? Do they understand what unit types are valuable in your marketplace, have knowledge on

the finishes, amenities and condo fees in other buildings, know what other sites will be built upon that will compete with your unit or impact the end-user's enjoyment?

8. Are they involved in trade associations or networking groups where they could gain insider knowledge about a builder's track record or understand new issues as they arise in the local marketplace?

9. Do you trust that they have your best interests at heart? Can they give you references of past happy clients? Are they willing to negotiate on your behalf?

How Developers Price Their Units

The developer is keen to make a profit on a new development and carefully costs one out so that it can project its revenue targets. When calculating the individual price per unit, the development team considers the following:

- The cost to build a particular suite that has the design, finishes and amenities demanded by the target customer. For example, the builder may have to add an extra bathroom, or upgraded hardware and fixtures. If a building is to have many small suites rather than larger ones, there will be more plumbing, electrical and HVAC systems in the building, making the whole development more costly to build.

- The expected demand for a particular floor plan over another (all things being equal, higher floor suites and smaller suites are in demand in most areas). Suites with poor views, lower-floor suites and some floor plans could be priced more reasonably in relation to pricing for high-demand units. If a particular floor plan is in high demand, the developer may hold back units of that particular model to ensure the building sells uniformly.

- Units closer to mechanical devices (elevator, garbage chutes) or with awkward floor plans may be priced lower.

- Price of neighbouring competition. Developers generally try to keep their price per square foot similar to their competition. If condos are "new market," the developer will consider the monthly cost to live in neighbouring existing properties that are comparable.

- The gaps in price between different units. Developers try to keep pricing gaps small: they don't want to have someone miss out on a $250,000 unit and have the only other option a $350,000 unit.

- Maximizing the view for higher-priced units. If a building has an exceptional view in a particular direction, larger units will be given the superior view over smaller units. This will help the developer offset the high demand for smaller units.

- There will be a "floor premium" as you go higher in the building. This can range from $500 to $3,000 a floor.

- While not a hard-and-fast rule, builders generally say that the land should make up about 10% of the saleable square footage cost. For example, if a unit is priced around $500 per square foot, the land cost in that price would be about $50 psf.

Choosing a Developer

After making a decision regarding the potential of a neighbourhood (covered in Chapter 2), the next step is to choose a builder/developer. Buyers, and particularly investors, generally do not spend sufficient time looking into a builder's reputation. From experience, we can tell you that buying from the right builder will catalyze appreciation for your property much faster than buying from an average builder; indeed, buying from the wrong builder may result in slow or negligible appreciation, or may leave you with a time bomb of issues from poor construction. While we're on the subject of developers, it's a good time to differentiate these terms:

- **Developer:** The developer focuses on land development. Lawyers representing the developer apply for re-zoning by the city or municipality for high density. Some developers actually build the units as well; if not, they sell the land to a builder.

- **Builder:** The builder specializes in marketing and the after-sale service of condo units. Some builders may actually take on the construction themselves, while some do not. These companies hire general contractors or design-build contractors to manage it for them.

- **One-stop shop:** These companies are responsible for all facets of a project, from the development to the design and the construction of the project. One-stop shop developers usually have their

PRICE MATRIX CHART

SUITE	STUDIO	1 BEDROOM	1+DEN A	1+DEN B	1+DEN C	2 BEDROOM	2+DEN A	2+DEN B
SUITE NAME	KING	RIVER	MOUNTAIN	VALLEY	PLATEAU	OCEAN	FIELD	MEADOW
VIEW	NORTH	SOUTH	EAST	WEST	NORTH	SOUTH	EAST	WEST
12 PH	$244,900.00	$274,900.00	$304,900.00	$294,900.00	$304,900.00	$314,900.00	$354,900.00	$364,900.00
11 LPH	$239,900.00	$269,900.00	$299,900.00	$289,900.00	$299,900.00	$309,900.00	$349,900.00	$359,900.00
10	$237,900.00	$267,900.00	$297,900.00	$287,900.00	$297,900.00	$307,900.00	$347,900.00	$357,900.00
9	$236,900.00	$266,900.00	$296,900.00	$286,900.00	$296,900.00	$306,900.00	$346,900.00	$356,900.00
8	$235,900.00	$265,900.00	$295,900.00	$285,900.00	$295,900.00	$305,900.00	$345,900.00	$355,900.00
7	$234,900.00	$264,900.00	$294,900.00	$284,900.00	$294,900.00	$304,900.00	$344,900.00	$354,900.00
6	$233,900.00	$263,900.00	$293,900.00	$283,900.00	$293,900.00	$303,900.00	$343,900.00	$353,900.00
5	$232,900.00	$262,900.00	$292,900.00	$282,900.00	$292,900.00	$302,900.00	$342,900.00	$352,900.00
4	$231,900.00	$261,900.00	$291,900.00	$281,900.00	$291,900.00	$301,900.00	$341,900.00	$351,900.00
3	$230,900.00	$260,900.00	$290,900.00	$280,900.00	$290,900.00	$300,900.00	$340,900.00	$350,900.00
2	$229,900.00	$259,900.00	$289,900.00	$279,900.00	$289,900.00	$299,900.00	$339,900.00	$349,900.00

own construction team that manages the construction, the trades, materials and subcontractors. Experienced one-stop shop developers are usually more versatile and may take on more difficult projects or take more risks with design. These companies usually have a better track record for quality because they have more control over the construction. When buying into a project by these types of companies, a shop's experience and track record are easy to research.

- **General contractor:** The general contractor oversees all work related to the construction of the condo, from procuring materials and trades to managing the construction of the building. General contractors are usually hired by the builder/developer owner of the project, who is in charge of creating the development concept. Those buying into projects with general contractors may be exposed to an increased risk of change orders from the original concept, but developers, especially newer developers, can leverage the construction experience of a solid team.

- **Design-build contractor:** Design-build contractors are usually hired by a builder/developer owner to perform all the work regarding the conception of the project idea and its construction. The design-build performs the same duties as a general contractor, but is also responsible for hiring the architects and engineers to create the concept. These projects are usually simpler in design and form.

Understanding who is behind your project can give you insight into how your building will turn out. The development industry is a close-knit one, and just because you see a logo behind a project doesn't mean you can assume that you know who is behind the project you are buying into.

The Role of Architects

Most people think the architect's sole role is to design the look of the building, when in fact they do so much more. Architects are essentially creative problem solvers. They are the ones who look at the environmental and physical constraints of the site, the legal and planning rules, the type of construction and market demands, to create a building that works for the end-user and is profitable for the company the architect represents. Most developers bring in architects very early in the process, possibly even before the land is bought, to help the developer clarify goals and understand their options. During the construction process, an architect operates as the point of contact between the developer and construction team, ensuring the building is built properly.

Caveat emptor ("let the buyer beware") is still the motto of the day when choosing a developer. While there is legislation protecting buyers against buildings that take too long to construct, or fraud committed by the builder, or buildings that look and perform substantially differently from what you believed when you bought it, enforcing these laws falls on the shoulders of you, the buyer. This means huge costs in terms of time and money if you have to go to court. The best way to avoid these costs is to buy from a reputable builder.

How do we know if the builder we choose to buy from will actually build a home we can be proud of? The key is to understand what's important. Here are eight crucial points:

1. Does the builder have the requisite experience? Experienced builders have delivered (completed) a minimum of two projects with similar construction. The type of experience is important. Some single-family home builders may have many years of experience in their industry, but no experience with the challenges of a condo tower development.

2. Is the builder active in trade associations (such as the Building Industry and Land Development Association) for the betterment of the industry for consumers, or active in its communities to build its brand? Does the builder care how its development impacts the neighbourhood?

3. Is the builder using up-to-date technologies? Will it build beyond minimum building code? Is it committed to building sustainable communities?

4. Does the builder have a reputation for building quality homes?

5. Does the builder value customer service and after-sales service? Is it known for its communication and access?

6. Is the builder "upfront"? Does it market its product transparently? Is it focused on building a brand rather than developing through shell companies? Is it known for not assessing extra fees after owners take possession?

7. Does the builder keep its word and promises as measured by third parties?

8. Is the builder known to treat its customers with respect?

⊚ YOU SHOULD KNOW

Builders are the key to buyer satisfaction

Ask second-time condo buyers what their criteria are for a good deal and most of them will say "the builder"—and we tend to agree. The following press release from J.D. Power and Associates in September 2009, reporting on customer satisfaction among new-condominium buyers, showed that two of five condominium buyers (40%) in the Greater Toronto Area (GTA) would have purchased from another builder if given a second chance.

"Buyers who said they would opt for a different builder if given the choice cited a number of reasons, including poor communication from the builder; perceived misrepresentation; and delays in occupying the home. The overall satisfaction score among these buyers is 295 points lower on a 1,000-point scale than among buyers who were content with the builder they chose.

"An expectation that is frequently not met by condominium builders is the readiness of the home by the confirmed occupancy date. Nearly two-thirds of buyers (63%) indicate having experienced a delay, with an average wait of approximately seven months to take possession."

Poor customer service is just the tip of the iceberg and can be exacerbated by design flaws, construction flaws and sloppy workmanship. If you search online, you will find many disgruntled owners who are very vocal about their particular building or builder. Talk to owners in other buildings by the same builder. Do your homework on your builder before you commit to buying in the project. Have your realtor assist with this exercise.

DIVERGENT THINKING IN REAL ESTATE DEVELOPMENT

by Sayf Hassan, Symmetry Developments

I am standing on an unevenly paved parking pad at the rear of an abandoned rooming house at the corner of The Queensway and Lady Bank Road, in a traditionally suburban area of Toronto, Etobicoke. At 50 feet by 105 feet, it is roughly the size of my parents' home in a Brampton subdivision. This is my kind of lot.

My kind of lot is a development that calls for divergent thinking. Divergent thinking is the essential capacity for creativity, the thought process utilized in generating multiple solutions to a given scenario. It is the mode of thinking laterally, exploring possibilities in all directions instead of in a convergent, linear manner.

GTA developers are victims of "efficiency." That is, efficiently eradicating any ideas that do not fit preconceived, popularly accepted notions. There is a production-line mentality to development, masquerading as risk averseness, which consumes the industry. Build high, build often. It's about economies of scale and perfecting a formula for success, which is then mistaken for effectiveness. If a 30-storey high-rise, named after a European city, flaunting provocatively clad models in its marketing materials, sells well, then that is what consumers must want. If projects are located outside the core, it implies that the target market is a suburban one and the projects must be suitably suburban in intent. The sheer strength of the GTA market for such a prolonged period of time has meant that most developers see no need to deviate from their standard development formula.

Take the suburban Queensway lot as an example. City planners see the street as a perfect strip for mixed-use, mid-rise developments, but the site has been ignored by the vast majority of GTA condominium developers, simply because they feel that a 50 by 100 lot does not yield enough parking to build anything of worth.

But over the last few years, abetted by the short-lived market correction, a new strain of developers has emerged to satisfy demand by savvy purchasers. The old notion of imposing high-rises, brought to market with the assumption that the bulk of the inventory would be quickly bought by eager investors looking to cash in on a sure thing, felt the brunt of the correction as investors fled.

Developers and marketing companies scrambled to entice purchasers with true value. They realized the value of end-users, people who were purchasing condominiums as homes to reside in. Marketers replaced bikini-clad models, instead highlighting incentives and building features. Even after the GTA market made a stunning recovery, with sales quickly reaching pre-recession levels, the scars remained. There have been more creative, forward-thinking projects proposed since the recession, as smaller, nimbler developers took on challenging sites with gusto.

Utilizing "triple-stackers" at the Queensway site, we were able to provide 18 parking spaces for a six-storey, 20-unit building without having to go underground. This enabled us to achieve the much-needed retail space at grade that would provide the commercial continuity sought by the city along the Queensway. Most importantly, it made the project viable. We brought on Stephen Teeple, one of the premier modern architects in Toronto, to design the building, giving him the creative freedom to design a modern, cutting-edge downtown mid-rise. The result is The Hive: Lofts on the Queensway.

 TIP

Fees happen!

In 2009 an Ontario developer charged buyers between $7,680 and $11,280 for an "increase in fees" levied by the City of Markham. These fees had to be paid upfront by the buyers before they could get their keys, and in addition, the buyers could not finance these charges as part of their mortgage. While development charges from the city are normal, the problem was that the city never intended that the fees be passed along to the purchasers.

The lawyer for the developer argued that, according to the contract signed by the purchaser, the developer could charge purchasers for any new fees. Most buyers agreed to compromise and settled for a $3,000 increase in fees rather than fight the developer in court. Those who did sue eventually won their case and are expecting a refund.

Construction Quality

To avoid having to deal with lawsuits and paying expensive consultant reports for warranty providers, buyers should focus on finding a building that will be built solidly. A builder's construction quality is at times very difficult to determine, because the builder is at the mercy of local trades and deadlines. A construction manager who runs a tight ship with a clean construction site and ensures all the trades do quality work may be at one site, while the same developer may have another construction manager, who may not be as talented or motivated, at another site. Because of possible discrepancies such as this, buyers must focus on the builder's customer service record.

Here are some common ways to perform due diligence on a builder:

- Get the advice of a reputable realtor (see above on how to find one).

- Get a the advice of an experienced lawyer (see Chapter 5 on how to find one).

- Visit other construction sites, especially before the building is finished and is going through occupancy, to see if the builder maintains a clean site. What this will tell you: You'll get a sense of how much pride is being taken in the building of your property. With the number of trades being present at any given time, however, monitoring progress may be difficult.

◎ **YOU SHOULD KNOW**

Tarion sets standards for builders[2]

The new-home warranty program provider in Ontario, Tarion, publishes *Builder Bulletins,* a document that sets out requirements and standards that developers must adhere to in order to qualify for the warranty program. After analyzing the data from all warranty claims, Tarion has found that certain areas are prone to deficiencies and need to be inspected regularly during construction by field review consultants. Consultants are required to inspect and provide standardized reports every 60 days, or after specified stages within the construction period. Areas covered by the report include: design, sitework, structural, mechanical, electrical and acoustics. The aim of the review is to ensure that buildings perform properly and the quality of the finished project meets or exceeds expectations. (See more on new-home warranty programs across Canada in Chapter 7.)

- Visit newly completed buildings by the builder in question. Notice the little things as much as the big things. Do the doors close easily and are windows a tight fit? Pull out drawers, open cabinets, feel the walls and look at the windows. What this will tell you: you get to see how well the finishing touches are applied. You will also see a building that is still going through its growing pains with issues left to be fixed.

- Visit completed buildings, talk to existing residents, talk to property management companies managing the buildings, or review condo corporation documents. What this will tell you: you'll get a sense of the builder's customer service skills, after-sales care and the amount of pride it takes in its buildings. Condo board minutes may have some valuable information that documents the condo board's interaction with the developer. What you may not be able to determine, though, is whether the condo board is inept at managing the building—if this is the case, the issues are not the builder's fault. This is why it's valuable to get the advice of a good realtor or lawyer who is experienced in closing deals on the resale market for the developer. They will have a lot of knowledge, saving you from searching for a needle in a haystack.

- Go to third-party sources, such as Internet forums, social media, Youtube, and property managers. What this will tell you: you may be able to glean interesting first-hand observations and analysis. Beware of bias, however.

Because builders use many different trades, it may be hard to get an idea of construction quality. However, what can be measured is their willingness and capacity to deal with problems when they inevitably arise.

 TIP

Municipal building inspectors can't always save the day
Municipalities have a duty to protect their citizens from bad buildings. In major cities, the building department is required to inspect and approve condo plans to ensure that the building meets the city's building code standards before a building permit is issued. This doesn't necessarily mean a city is responsible if they approve building components that are faulty, once they are approved by an engineer or architect of the builder. In some situations where residents have tried to sue, courts have ruled in favour of the city as being not liable for approving bad plans.

Choosing the Right Building and the Right Suite

Today, choosing the right building is much easier than it was even five years ago. Why? So many more condominiums have been built that we can now tour condos on the resale market, use Google Earth to map our view, and use social media to see what other people are saying about the architecture, amenities and quality of construction.

To choose the right building and the right suite, the process starts with determining how "liveable" the building and the space will be when finished.

Imagine all the suites in a development as a horse race. At the start, all the horses are bunched together in a pack. Over time, the stronger horses pull away and hit the finish line first, and in doing so make their owners a lot of money. As a development is launched, suites are comparatively priced, and investors or buyers who aren't as well informed as others will focus only on price. This is a mistake. In choosing the right suite, a buyer must consider the following main points: layout or floor plan, views and finishes. We'll look at each of these areas in some detail.

Layout or Floor Plan

The first time people see a floor plan, they may not know what they are looking at and how to read it. Don't be intimidated. Here are the things you should focus on:

ABBREVIATION	MEANING
A/C	Air conditioner
B	Boiler, bathroom, bidet
BC	Broom closet
K, KIT	Kitchen
P	Pantry
D/W, DW	Dishwasher
F, REF	Refrigerator
W/D, W, D	Washer/dryer combo, washer, dryer
Sleep	Bedroom
WIC	Walk-in closet
Cook	Kitchen
Work/Play	Den
CL/CLO	Closet
BC	Bookcase
COL	Column
DR	Door
EF	Exhaust fan
ELEC, ELECT, EP	Electrical panel
SD	Smoke detector
W/O	Warming oven

Remember that everything is to scale. The smaller a suite gets, the more important scale becomes, to determine if your unit will suit your lifestyle or will be easy to sell in the future. You want to ensure every square foot is liveable space.

TALES FROM THE TRENCHES

by Elaine Cecconi and Anna Simone, interior designers, Toronto

Scale is so important when dealing with small floor plans because marketers can print the plan larger, which shows large white space and gives the
impression of a lot of space. To get a realistic idea of the floor plan's actual
size, ask the sales person for a drawing that shows the scale, then do the
calculations to determine the size of any item on the drawing. An interior
designer trick is to look at bathroom floors on the floor plan: when tiles
are shown, they are often on a scale of one tile=one foot. Door widths
can range from 30 inches to 36 inches, so if the scale isn't shown, ask for
specific measurements of doorways and cabinets (including depth). Once
you've got the scale figured out, you can draw your furniture into your plan
to see if it fits.

Determine if your furniture will fit. Get a tape measure and take exact
measurements of your furniture. Once you determine the scale of the
drawing, use the floor plan to draw in your furniture to see if it fits. Don't
assume that it will: some developers' drawings have been known to include
furniture pieces that may be smaller than normal to distort proportions.
There is a great tool online called Floorplanner (www.floorplanner.com).
It's free, and once you've recreated your floor plan online, you can add
your furniture to see if everything fits and if you will have enough clear-
ance to move.

 TIP

Contact the professionals
Get in touch with a design organization like ARIDO (Association of Registered
Interior Designers of Ontario) so they can put you in contact with a junior
designer—who you can hire at a minimal cost—to help assist you with furniture layout.

Use your fingers to walk through the plan. This process can lead to interesting discoveries. Ask questions such as: where do I put my shoes and
coats? How accessible is the washroom for my guests? Where will traffic
be heaviest? Is there sufficient closet space? Is there space for my art and
book cases? Where will I put my desk? Write on your floor plans to create a
"story" about how you will live in it (see the example below).

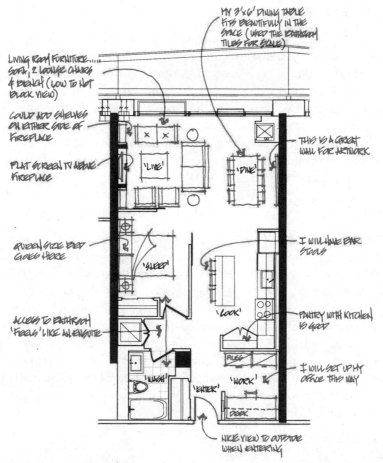

Source: Cecconi Simone.

TALES FROM THE TRENCHES

by David Allison, condo marketer, Vancouver

A good trick to help jog your imagination is to think back to all the places you have lived before, and try to remember the annoying little things that made those homes less than perfect. No home, unless you are custom building something to your exact specifications, will live up to every single one of your expectations. But it's important to know before you buy which issues will need to be addressed after you move in, and which ones you are buying along with the home. Some of these issues can be remedied yourself—you can build more closet space or reconfigure a closet door. Others will become part of your new life. Make sure you are okay with that!

Regional Preferences

Layout preferences vary from region to region, based on demand. In Canada, because of pre-sale requirements, most developers have to pre-sell 80% to 90% of their units in order to get construction financing. As a result, you will see buildings with many one-bedroom suites, or one-bedroom plus den, versus large two-bedroom or three-bedroom suites. In some cities, the residents demand closet space and storage space, while other cities demand more open space and less storage. In high-rises in New York, for example, its common to find suites that have no balconies, while in Toronto it's very rare to find a unit without a balcony.

Customization

The great benefit of buying a pre-construction condo is that it's somewhat customizable. Changes that don't involve moving plumbing, mechanical or electrical systems, structural walls or pillars are possible. How willing is a developer to move a wall if the electrical, HVAC or plumbing has to be completely re-designed? If ducts, pipes and conduits run in between the wall in question, they have to meet the building code. A developer may be more receptive to moving a wall for a higher-end condo priced at the top of the market, as opposed to a $150,000 junior one-bedroom, simply because of the costs associated with changes. Modifications can more easily be made to finishes such as counter tops, backsplashes, cabinetry, appliances, plumbing and light fixtures.

 TALES FROM THE TRENCHES

by Harry Stinson, developer, Hamilton

The administrative distance between the consumer who buys the unit and the trades who assemble the building is enormous.

Nobody in the "food chain" wants a project full of "one-of-a-kind" designs. The developer gets the best prices from his suppliers and contractors (and architects and engineers and lawyers) if the designs and finishes are standardized. Individuality is possible, but the developer will charge "retail plus." Frankly, I advise consumers to close on the property and do the customizing afterward. There are several reasons:

- They will save money doing it on their own.

- They really should move in and "test drive" the space before jumping to conclusions based on a floor plan and their own (probably incorrectly scaled) design ideas.

- Given that a few years will elapse between the original purchase and the move-in/closing, there is a very strong likelihood that something will change in their life and/or lifestyle and/or personal taste, and thus the money and effort spent on customizing is wasted.

- Given the option, a builder would rather deal with someone prepared to buy a suite "as is" than someone who is discussing changes, if the building and the unit are selling well. Trust me, the "change" person may find themselves without a signature from the developer.

Constraints to Modifications

Moving walls	Electrical outlets in wall have to be relocated.
Making changes to areas with dropped ceilings	The entire ceiling has to be re-configured. Duct work, plumbing and electrical may have to be moved. Could result in one area having a lower ceiling than another.
Adding showers to powder rooms	The need to add shower heads may result in the whole suite needing to be redesigned, impacting other suites above, below and adjacent to yours.

Assuming you are buying your condo as an investment, or you plan to live in it for a short time, it's important to ensure that there will be a large pool of buyers who will want to buy your condo when you are ready to sell it. So, making massive (and expensive) changes to the floor plan, or buying from a developer who has designed a floor plan that may not appeal to a subsequent buyer, is a huge mistake.

Suite Flow (Articulation)

In smaller units, every inch counts and designing small suites that create the illusion of open space is critical. Developers do this by maximizing three things: light, sightlines and height.

- They strategically place large windows in certain areas to maximize and extend sightlines and maximize natural light.

- They limit support structures by strategically placing columns in front of windows rather than building large supporting walls.

- They use continuous, uninterrupted flooring throughout to create the illusion of a larger space.

- They have mixed-use, open rooms that are not separated (kitchen, dining room, living room and laundry in an all-in-one space).

- They install compact appliances that don't obstruct views or take up space (such as the microwave/range hood combination).

- They reduce corridor space where sightlines can be obstructed.

- They limit dead space where no furniture can be placed. Buildings with impressive curved architecture, for example, can create large regions of dead space because furniture cannot be placed on the arching walls.

- They use bright lighting to brighten walls and corners.

Natural Light

People are always attracted to natural light. Almost all municipal building codes recognize the importance of natural light: they require that most rooms have natural light; interior spaces without any natural light cannot be called bedrooms, but must be referred to as dens.

It's hard to say which views will maximize natural light. Traditionally, south-facing views provide the longest exposure to sunlight, but in urban environments a south view may mean you're looking directly into another building or an industrial area. Keeping that in mind, the design of the unit to maximize light has to be considered. Wide suites have more natural light than narrower ones, so if you choose a narrower suite, ensure that you at least get some high ceilings with larger windows. Some condos may or may not have windows in all bedrooms; how much of an issue might this be when it comes time to sell your unit? To maximize natural light, look for suites where actual living space is concentrated around the windows. Ensure that you are protected from bulkheads being placed near the glazing. Good developers maximize sunlight in suites by adding finishes that allow light to permeate. Pieces such as glass panels (instead of walls) and glass sliding doors increase light. Floor-to-ceiling windows are nice, but your furniture will have to be placed in the middle of the room, which will limit the open feeling. Play with the furniture layout to balance this out.

CASE STUDY

Alternative Solutions to the Window Conundrum: 8 Gladstone, Toronto

At a new development by STREETCAR Developments, 8 Gladstone, the developer chose to make a one-bedroom unit—and the bedroom had no window. On the Internet forums, prospective buyers were concerned that they might not be able to re-list the unit as a one-bedroom when they were ready to sell. This would definitely not be the case, since the unit can in fact be considered a legitimate one bedroom. If the design of the suite doesn't permit a window to allow natural light, the National Building Code and the Ontario Building Code allow for "Alternative Solutions," as long as the room meets the minimum level of performance and safety by the code. In this case, the alternative solution took the form of frosted-glass doors that allow natural light to enter the room from large window openings to the balcony; they also provide an easy exit route in case of fire.

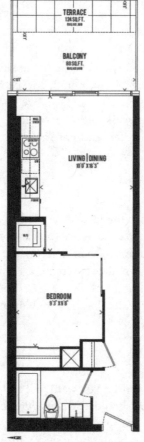

Source: STREETCAR Developments Inc.

Too much sunlight can overheat one side of the building over another, making cooling difficult if a building's cooling system is controlled centrally. Too much sunlight can also bleach art, pictures and the spines of books, which is less than ideal for people with valuable artwork or book collections.

Artificial Lighting

One of the common surprises that owners find after getting their keys is inadequate lighting in bedrooms or living areas. Some units will not have ceiling fixtures in bedrooms or in parts of the living room, so the owner must purchase floor lamps and table lamps. Since the walls are concrete and ceiling heights are so important, it might be difficult or impossible to install a fixture. Be sure to read your documents to see what lighting fixtures are designed for your unit.

Storage Space

Where will you put your vacuum, your entertainment system, your books . . . or your guitar? If your unit doesn't have adequate storage space, can you add a bookcase or armoire to a long hallway without interfering with the walkability? Consider the fact that you may want to buy a storage locker, and ensure it's of adequate size to hold your belongings.

Privacy

Investors have to consider the level of liveability for their tenants. Two-bedroom units or larger one-plus-ones (one bedroom plus den) are preferable, so that there is a master bath and a separate bath/shower in the other washroom to accommodate two renters. For increased privacy, most people don't want a common wall between bedrooms. If you are looking at resaleability, consider units that have two or more bedrooms that are adequately spaced.

Entertaining Guests

Again, the space and amenities you want will be based on your own personal preferences, but you should also consider the norm for your area. In urban areas, where you are surrounded by many amenities for meeting friends, such as restaurants, you can get away with a smaller unit with more open space and less bedroom and closet space. In more suburban areas, it would be very hard to resell a unit with a bedroom that cannot fit a flat-screen TV and decent-size furniture. At a bare minimum, in most regions, a bedroom must comfortably hold a queen-size bed, a night table and a decent-size closet. The key to understanding the future liveability of the space is to look at furniture layout. Play around with the floor plan by drawing in furniture; you might find that if you use "condo-size" furniture, the liveability of your unit increases immensely.

Ceiling Heights

In most cities the norm for ceiling heights is between eight and nine feet. Open-concept designs are best suited to higher ceilings, so if you choose a small unit it would be uncomfortable for most people to live in if the ceiling is lower than nine feet.

 TIP

Look overhead!
When your lawyer reviews the contract, ask him or her to look for (or include) a clause that will ensure no large bulkheads or modifications will affect ceiling heights in your unit.

Another solution is to buy a condo with in-slab ductwork. When ductwork is placed within the concrete slab of the tower, there is no need for a bulkhead outside the slab, and the end result is higher ceilings.

Bathrooms

Most condos can get away with one bathroom having a shower only as long as there is a bathtub in another bathroom (usually in the master suite). Bathroom fixtures and plumbing are quite expensive for a developer to build. To keep prices low, developers are staying away from adding a second bathtub and opting for a shower in extra bathrooms, or including only one bathroom altogether to keep prices affordable.

Is having one bathroom okay? All things being equal, most people would rather have a private bathroom and have another available for guests; however, as the trend continues to having people entertain less in their units by utilizing common areas, having fewer bathrooms may become the norm.

Views

In master-planned communities, developers plan every building to maximize great views, and you have greater certainty that your view won't be blocked by another development in the future. Stand-alone towers require more careful consideration as to how your views might be impacted down the road. Views of commanding features, such as a foothills or mountain vista, or water, are naturally in high demand and command a premium price. For some people, city views are preferred over natural views, because of the animation on the street or a great skyline, so it may be a good plan to pay less for a city view if your research shows that future development won't block it.

Privacy is another issue when it comes to views. Most cities demand that the distance between towers be equal to the width of the widest tower, or a minimum of 25 metres (whichever is less). Even at those distances, someone can still see clearly into another unit of the adjacent building, especially if one window is overlooking the other.

Sometimes developers build rounded towers to maximize views so they can increase demand for all suites in the building. Google Earth is a great tool to help ascertain what views will be like.

Developers usually charge more for units that are higher because the views are considered better. At some point there is a diminishing return the higher you go. Higher levels will definitely have better views, but the costs of the floor premium, the fear of heights some people may have, and the impact of wind if you have a balcony need to be balanced against the view.

 TIP

The optimal floor for views

Many people wonder: what is the optimal floor on which to buy your unit in buildings more than 40 storeys high? It's natural for people to assume the higher, the better. However, there is a cost to this when developers introduce floor premiums, and this leads to the question: if the building is built in such a way that all units in a stack are identical, what is the highest I should go to maximize my appreciation? (A stack is a set of units in the same location on the floor plate, e.g., the 01 stack may go from unit #201 to unit #2301.)

For this book, we analyzed thousands of units in Toronto and couldn't find a perfect rule for the best floor height you should buy. We found that the rigidly set floor premium that developers charge tends to disappear over time, being replaced by a more fluid pricing that changes constantly. The two main reasons for the change are that units will have different views the higher you go, and affordability.

Take for example, the Backstage project by Cityzen Development Group, Fernbrook Homes and Castlepoint Realty. The development team charged a $1,000 floor premium and they also used technology that sent a camera with a balloon so people could get an idea of the view from various directions.[3] The animation of the skyline and the CN tower make the western view a winner in our minds. As you can see below, the low floor west view is nice, but has less privacy and the noise from the street and railway might be troublesome. On the plus side, if you have a balcony, the space is more usable on a lower level for those who are afraid of heights and those who want to use the outdoor space as a place to entertain, because the wind impact will be low. From an investment perspective, these units will be by far the cheapest and most affordable, giving large appreciation potential.

5th floor. (Source: Ferncastle Esplanade Inc.)

The views from the 25th floor are spectacular and really capture the skyline, but start at $20,000 more. There is less street noise, but the balconies are less comfortable to use as entertaining space, with both wind and height being possible deterrents to use.

The view from the 36th floor is the most spectacular, as it captures much of the best parts of the western side of downtown Toronto. Seeing so much sky gives people a bright and open feeling, which can be awe-inspiring and make

25th floor. (Source: Ferncastle Esplanade Inc.)

small units feel larger. The balcony space may be too cold and uncomfortable from the constant wind, however, even on the hottest summer days. All outdoor furniture must either be heavy or stored indoors, since it could be blown away. (The worst-case scenario for balconies on such high levels is that they become little more than a place for smokers to have a quick break.) Higher floors, with their additional premiums, will attract more end-users than investors, because the units will not be as affordable as those on lower floors.

36th floor. (Source: Ferncastle Esplanade Inc.)

Looking at other buildings in the area of Backstage, we see that their units start to migrate away from the developers' initial rigid pricing to more market-driven pricing after about three to five years. Some units on higher floors will sell for less than the unit a few floors below; some units will sell for more. We see differences in price occur because of marketing, seller motivation, the quality of the individual unit, and the local market supply-and-demand relationship at the time the sales occur.

As a result, the best units to buy from an investment point of view are generally from the low to middle floors (i.e., 10th to 25th floor) of the building, and if all things are equal (i.e., view, floor plan, finishes and features), lower is better.

Finishes

Interior spaces include everything from the lobby, hallways and common areas (party room, fitness facility, games room, etc.), to your unit. The care put into their design and the choice of finishes are instrumental to how easily you can resell your condo, because finishes are the element of design that people most interact with. Here are the basic categories of "features and finishes" for the unit that buyers are usually able to select:

Kitchen

- cabinets
- counter tops
- backsplash
- island and breakfast bar
- appliances (stove, refrigerator, microwave, dishwasher, etc.)
- fixtures (faucets, sink, outlets, light switches, handles)

Bathroom

- vanity
- washbasin/sink
- cabinets
- tub and shower

- flooring
- fixtures (faucets, toilet, etc.)

General

- ceiling
- trim, doors, railings, baseboards and mouldings
- light fixtures
- paint
- fixtures (outlets, light switches, handles, telephone and high-speed Internet jacks)
- flooring (hardwood, carpeting, etc.)
- electrical box
- balcony and terrace (flooring, entryways, etc.)
- laundry (style of washer and dryer)

As with exterior architecture, how you respond to the aesthetics is personal. Good interior design employs the same principles that exterior design does to grab you emotionally and make you want to buy: light, sight and height are used to create the feelings of openness and awe, while material quality and texture can be introduced to create an experience.

The main difference between high-end and low-end condos, and those in between, is usually found in the quality of the interior space, features and finishes. But what determines what high-end is or what is standard in mid-priced and low-priced units? And how does this change by neighbourhood submarkets? These questions can only be understood by being very familiar with the market you are buying in, or by working with a qualified realtor. What would be considered an upgrade in one part of town will be considered standard in another. It takes some work to visit competing sales centres and look at resale data to see what works.

When choosing your colours, unless you're planning to occupy the unit yourself, you should consider what finishes would appeal to a tenant or subsequent buyer. If you plan to rent the unit, what type of finishes will be the most resilient? While a dark wood floor may look nice, a scratch is more noticeable than it would be on a light-coloured floor. The type of finishes may also determine the type of tenant you would attract. If you want a tenant to pay premium rent, it's generally more easily accomplished with the premium finishes.

Many buyers go for the hip and trendy finishes. Dark tones tend to be the preferred choice, as they can make a condo appear classy and sexy. But be careful: dark colours have a way of making a space look smaller.

Be careful of over-upgrading. It's easy to do this if you plan on occupying the unit. You may want the granite counter tops, stainless steel appliances, upgraded sinks, and the unit wired for surround sound, just to name a few upgrades. But if no one else in the building has done it and there isn't generally a demand for those upgrades, it would be more difficult to recover those costs when you decide to sell. When going with upgraded finishes, be sure to weigh the costs versus the benefits of doing so—every upgrade costs more money than the standard finish.

◎ YOU SHOULD KNOW

Finishes are subject to fine print too

Your purchase agreement will contain all the usual "fine print" when it comes to features and finishes, such as the following:

- "All features and finishes are subject to change without notice. (Errors and omissions excepted.)"

- "The Vendor shall have the right to substitute other products and materials for those listed in this Schedule or provided for in the plans and specifications, provided that the substituted products and materials are of a quality equal to, or better than, the products and materials so listed or so provided."

To some these are known as the "weasel clauses," because recent court cases give developers a huge amount of wiggle room for changes. And, since model numbers of finishes are not given, determining what is "equal or better quality" is very hard to do legally. (We'll discuss this more in the chapter on contracts.)

From a builder's perspective, it's difficult to build the exact interior look that you saw in the model suite and in renderings. It's not practical for the builder and developer to warehouse as many of the exact features and finishes they would need to outfit all units, especially taking into account that buyers will choose a variety of different finishes. And because two to five years can pass from when sales begin to when units are being completed, many suppliers can change their products or colours, leaving developers scrambling to find substitutions. When it comes to getting the quality you paid for, reputation is vitally important, and it's not just the developer's reputation that you need to look at, but also that of the architect and interior design team.

TALES FROM THE TRENCHES

by Elaine Cecconi and Anna Simone, interior designers, Toronto

Good developers that are serious about design will choose a design team that represents the design industry properly. These developers understand that good design is good branding, and they will do whatever it takes to give you what was promised in the marketing (though they may charge a higher price). Developers who care about design will work with designers from the beginning and won't let the construction side of the business devalue the work designers have done in the previous two to three years in order to position a project by making substitutions to keep construction costs low. Additionally, good designers will not be bullied into putting their names behind a builder that compromises their work.

Good developers work with a good design team and will value their recommendations, and a good design team will always take professional pride in the work they do. When you choose a developer and design team wisely, you are more likely to get the same—or equivalent, or even better—finishes and materials that sold you on the unit in the first place.

As the building is getting closer to completion, the builder will contact you to select your finishes. If the developer is design conscious, they will have trained interior designers who have created colour palettes for buyers, giving you a choice of colours for the various features that all match, making the process less overwhelming.

 TALES FROM THE TRENCHES

by Matthew Slutsky, condo marketer, Toronto

When I worked for a developer, we had people "dumpster diving" to determine which materials were being used during construction. Purchasers would actually go into the garbage to see the boxes being used for finishes to feel comfortable in protecting their quality.

Doing due diligence on the design team is very similar to doing due diligence on a builder. In fact, inexperienced builders can better their reputation by putting a solid team behind them.

1. Is the design team experienced in projects of this type? What awards have they won?

2. Are they part of any associations? Architects usually have designations after their name, such as OAA, FRAIC, MRAIC, AIA, LEED AP; landscape architects will have designations such as OALA, CSLA, MCIP; interior designers will have designations such as ARIDO or CIDA.

3. Are they active in bettering their industry by giving lectures, sitting on design review panels, judging awards?

4. Are they using up-to-date technologies (as seen in the features and finishes)?

5. Does the design team have a reputation of not compromising on quality? Do they keep their word on quality?

PRESTIGIOUS DESIGN AWARDS IN CANADA

Best Canada Design – Canadian Interiors
http://www.canadianinteriors.com/bestofcanada/

The Association of Registered Interior Designers of Ontario (ARIDO)
http://www.arido.ca/awards_of_excellence.php

The IDIBC (Interior Design Institute of British Columbia) Awards of Excellence
http://www.idibc.org/members/awards/

Pug Awards (Toronto)
http://pugawards.com/

Design Exchange Awards
http://www.designexchange.org/dxa/

Ontario Association of Architects (OAA) Award of Excellence
http://awards.oaa.on.ca/

Canadian Architect Award of Excellence
http://www.canadianarchitect.com/awards/

Royal Architectural Institute of Canada, Governor General's Medal in Architecture
http://www.raic.org/honours_and_awards/awards_raic_awards/2011recipients/index_e.htm

Urban Land Institute Global Award for Excellence
http://www.uli.org/AwardsAndCompetitions.aspx

Toronto Urban Design Awards
http://www.toronto.ca/tuda/index.htm

Pacific Coast Builders Conference
http://www.goldnuggetawards.com/

Mayors Urban Design Awards (Calgary)
http://bit.ly/CalgaryAwards

Ottawa Urban Design Awards
http://www.ottawa.ca/residents/planning/design_awards/index_en.html

City of Richmond LuLu Urban Design Awards
http://www.richmond.ca/services/planning/luluawards.htm

Lieutenant Governor of British Columbia Awards for Architecture
http://www.aibc.ca/pub_resources/aibc_outreach/awardslst.html

Canadian Society of Landscape Architects' Annual Awards of Excellence
http://www.csla.ca/en/awards-honours

The Ontario Association of Landscape Architects Awards
http://www.oala.ca/awards/

Awards for Excellence in Architecture, *L'Ordre des architectes du Québec (OAQ)*
http://www.oaq.com/larchitecture/prix_darchitecture/pea.html

Urban Development Institute
http://udi.bc.ca/

Home Builder associations (Visit individual branch offices for awards)
http://www.chba.ca/

Domus Awards, Provincial Association of Home Builders in Quebec (APCHQ)
http://www.apchq.com/

A Final Note on Choosing the Right Suite: Location on the Floor Plate

It's become the mantra for real estate agents giving advice on picking the right suite location: always pick the suite farthest from the elevator and garbage chute, and as distant from a garage door as possible. Your enjoyment of the suite may be impacted by its location on the floor plate, and in some cases, suite location can definitely impact your resale value.

- Choose a unit away from the elevator to limit the noise of the elevator motor that will enter your unit. The quietest unit will be a corner unit.

- Choose a unit away from the garage door to limit the noise you hear from the door-opener machinery and cars honking at one another. A unit over a garage may also be a little colder than a unit on higher floors.

- Choose a unit away from the garbage chute and loading bays to reduce noise and inconvenience.

Buying a locker and parking

As units get smaller and smaller, lockers will become more valuable. People always want extra storage to keep seasonal items such as Christmas decorations or sporting gear, yet the attention paid to lockers during the pre-construction phase is almost nil by most buyers and agents. From experience, we know this can lead to surprise and heartache. Locker size, location and types can vary tremendously. Some lockers are stand-alone, with solid walls, while others are no more than cages in a locker room shared by others, and as a result, they can be easily broken into. Although developers rarely allocate specific locker locations when people buy pre-construction, it's always a good idea to get in writing that your locker will be close to your parking spot.

With regard to parking spots, as cities work to become more dense, city parking lots will be eliminated, thereby increasing the value of parking spots over time, if your building is in a good location. The best tip for parking spots is to ensure your spot is as close to the elevator as possible, to make it valuable and convenient for the end-user (either you or the person you eventually sell to). Again, get this written into the contract.

In either case, parking and lockers do carry a maintenance fee and they are deeded, meaning they can be sold individually or rented if you decide you don't want to use them.

 TALES FROM THE TRENCHES

Buying Pre-Construction Units in College Park
by Hwi Young Kim and Myungjin Lee, Toronto

WHAT MADE YOU BUY A PRE-CONSTRUCTION CONDO?

We already knew pre-construction condominiums could appreciate well if we chose wisely. Usually condominiums in downtown Toronto are hard to cash-flow with limited down payment. We could afford to buy just one unit at that time, but we decided to buy three pre-con condominium units rather than one because it takes a 20% down payment before occupancy, and new condominium projects take several years to be done; we knew we could save more money for the down payment before closing, so that the units could cash-flow when it was time to rent them out. Since the expected completion dates vary, we decided to keep one of the units as our principal residence and we'll eventually move into the biggest one once it's completed.

WHAT KIND OF DUE DILIGENCE DID YOU DO?

We bought in the College Park development in Toronto, since we originally bought our principal residence from the same developer, Canderal Stoneridge, also in the pre-construction phase. We were comfortable buying from them again.

The location, as well as the amenities, is the first thing we considered after we decided we were ready to buy. We asked ourselves if we would live in the units over a neighbouring project. The answer was yes!

We chose suite types very carefully. It's easier to rent out a unit when the floor plans or/and the suite types can be easily split among tenants who want to share the space and the rent in downtown Toronto. We tried to buy units on higher floors with exposure to the south for the view of Lake Ontario.

WHAT MADE YOU DECIDE TO BUY IT?

Since the average house price in Toronto has been rising, a condominium is one of the affordable housing options for those wanting to live in downtown Toronto, so my wife and I started to look for a condominium.

We have been living in College Park (phase 1) since it was completed in 2006. This condominium is located at Bay Street and College Street. The location has everything nearby (the area's Walk Score is 98, according to walkscore.com). It is very close to shopping (Metro, Shopper's Drug Mart, Sears Centre, Canadian Tire, Best Buy), restaurants and even Service Ontario. It is also pretty close to the University Of Toronto, Ryerson University, MaRS entrepreneurship incubation facility, Sick Kids Hospital and the financial district. The Ontario Legislature and beautiful Queens's Park are also within walking distance.

One of the greatest things about my condominium is that you can take a subway without getting soaked by rain or snow. The building is connected to the College subway station and has very easy access to streetcars and buses. Highway 401, the Don Valley Parkway, the Gardiner Expressway and the QEW are extremely busy during the rush hour, which may be why so many people want to live in downtown Toronto, where they can go to work by walking or using public transit.

WHAT FEARS DID YOU HAVE ABOUT BUYING?

The cash-flow might be tough when the condo fee is very expensive. There's also the chance that it won't appreciate as much as we expect. The majority of condo buyers don't plan to live in the suite, which means the condo rental market can be very competitive.

HOW CONFIDENT WERE YOU IN THE OUTCOME?

There's no outcome for our purchase yet, as the building is not complete, but the unit I live in now has appreciated significantly. We are very positive about the appreciation for the purchase, but we are not sure how much it will appreciate.

ANY MEMORABLE STORIES OR PIECES OF ADVICE YOU WOULD LIKE TO SHARE ABOUT BUYING?

We bought the units at a VIP price and that helped a bit.

HOW MUCH DID YOU BUY THE CONDO FOR?

We bought three units:

1 Bedroom 1 Bathroom, 29th floor 584 sq ft ($545/sq ft)
2 Bedroom 2 Bathroom, 43rd floor 859 sq ft ($597/sq ft)
2 Bedroom 1 Den 2 Bathroom, 62nd floor 1,252 sq ft ($723.16/sq ft) [Executive Suite]

 TALES FROM THE TRENCHES

Making that First Investment Decision, by Nick Luca, Toronto

WHAT MADE YOU BUY A PRE-CONSTRUCTION CONDO?

When I bought my unit at Maple Leaf Square I didn't need another place, but I was considering different variables for the future. The first thing that attracted me to the building is that the sales person told me it would take four years, to build. I knew it would be slightly longer, more like four and a half years, and the building won't be registered for five years. I liked this because I didn't have to dish out the bulk of the investment for a long time because of the way my deposit was structured.

WHAT KIND OF DUE DILIGENCE DID YOU DO?

I really studied the brochure, reviewed the developer's websites and visited the model suite. I knew the developer had a great track record from visiting other buildings, and I ended up buying the model unit, so I knew my layout, finishes and view would be something I liked.

WHAT MADE YOU DECIDE TO BUY IT?

I was a season ticket holder for the Maple Leafs, and they gave us priority access before anyone else and we could save 2.5% of the purchase price. Additionally, I knew the property was in a great location (being close to the Air Canada Centre and Union Station), so if the property didn't appreciate, it would be pretty easy for me to hold on to it and rent it out to stretch out the timeline for me to make money.

WHAT FEARS DID YOU HAVE ABOUT BUYING?

I was always afraid of buying a pre-construction unit because you are never sure what your view will be, because you can never tell what building will come up to block it. This is a real unknown. This is probably why I bought the model suite; I knew what the view would be and I was confident that it wouldn't change.

HOW CONFIDENT WERE YOU IN THE OUTCOME?

I felt good about the purchase. When buying I considered a range of scenarios: Would the unit appreciate? If it didn't, could I hold on to it and rent it out? If I couldn't rent it out, my kids would probably want to live there while they were in university, and I could use it as a place to hang out after work and on the weekends.

ANY MEMORABLE STORIES OR PIECES OF ADVICE YOU WOULD LIKE TO SHARE?

I know its cliché, but when buying real estate the key is location, location, location. I lived in the Yonge and Bloor area for eight years, so I know how great it is to live in the heart of the city. The area is so vibrant that there was no way you could feel lonely. This has a huge psychological and unconscious impact on people.

TALES FROM THE TRENCHES

My First Pre-Construction Condo
by Neil Uttamsingh, Toronto

WHAT MADE YOU BUY A PRE-CONSTRUCTION CONDO?

My purchase, in the development known as The Village by High Park, was a successful pre-build purchase. It has convinced me that buying new construction is the best real-estate investment strategy.

As I look back, I remember hearing about this project in early 2008. One of my good friends had grown up, and was still living, in the Bloor West area of Toronto. At that time, I held one rental property in my real estate portfolio and was working as a realtor. My friend told me about a new condo project that was being developed a few blocks away from where she lived, in the heart of the "Junction" in Toronto. My interest was piqued, as I had recently heard many good things about the Junction from other real estate investors that I knew.

WHAT KIND OF DUE DILIGENCE DID YOU DO?

I Googled "Condo in the Junction" to see what I could find, and found the website of the not-for-profit company responsible for the development of this condo. The company is called Options for Homes (www.optionsforhomes.ca). The website was great, containing a lot of the information I needed. I signed up for an information session about the development and attended the session the following Saturday. There I was able to speak with some representatives of Options for Homes and find out everything I wanted to know.

I had heard a lot about the Junction and the tremendous revitalization it is undergoing. It was no secret that the City of Toronto was spending time and money in order to rejuvenate this area, which was once riddled by crime and prostitution, but was now seeing young families—many with above-average incomes—move in and call it home. Areas experiencing revitalization interest me very much, and I wanted to own a property in the middle of an area that was undergoing tremendous change.

Prior to purchasing the condo, I didn't really know anything about the builder. I simply had faith in the work that Options for Homes was doing, and I was convinced that the Junction was going to become the next hot spot of Toronto.

WHAT MADE YOU DECIDE TO BUY IT?

I was already sold on the neighbourhood; that was a given. I wanted to purchase a unit in this development, although I was slightly concerned as to what the deposit structure was going to be. Prior to finding this development, I had investigated many other developments, many of which were in Toronto, as well as in suburbs just outside of Toronto. Many of these deposit structures terrified me, as the developers were asking for very large deposits. Other developers were asking for deposits of 25% or more. In many cases, this worked out to more than $50,000. Being an astute investor, I was turned off by the idea of having to make such high deposits.

As I investigated the development by Options for Homes in the Junction, I was quite pleased by their proposed deposit structure. I was able to deposit $20,000 in order to purchase a unit. This allowed me to arrange my own financing for the mortgage of the condo. For a lesser deposit, $10,000 I believe it was, you had to arrange your mortgage financing through one of Options for Homes's recommended lenders. Due to the fact that I had a lot more real estate and financing knowledge than the average person, I opted to put down $20,000 as my deposit and have my own personal mortgage broker arrange financing for the property.

How much did you pay for the unit and how much is it worth now?

I purchased the condo unit in October 2008 for $222,245. The unit is a 665-square-foot, one-bedroom plus den condo, with a four-piece washroom. It is a north-facing unit with two large windows, one in the living room, and one in the bedroom. There is no balcony.

I estimate, by looking at comparable units in the building, that the value of the unit today is between $260,000 and $270,000, possibly even higher if upgraded nicely. I am very confident that the price of my units will continue to increase as the area continues to be rejuvenated.

What fears did you have about buying?

I had only a few fears regarding this purchase. At the time of buying the unit, I was not sure whether I was going to live in the unit or whether I was going to rent the unit out. Because this was a new condo building, there were absolutely no other comparable buildings in the area, which made it very difficult to know how much the units would resell for and how much I would be able to charge in rent. Due to these unknowns, I was afraid that I would potentially lose money on a monthly basis, as the rent might not cover all the monthly expenses.

I ended up moving into the unit and am currently living in it. If I do decide to rent the unit out down the road, the market is such that I will be sure to make a positive cash-flow.

ANY MEMORABLE STORIES OR PIECES OF ADVICE YOU WOULD LIKE TO SHARE?

The most memorable feeling I had during this entire process occurred after the building was constructed. I was impressed to see how amazing, new, fresh and modern the building looked from the outside. However, I was more impressed as I walked the streets about a week after I had taken possession of the condo. Being on the street level I could see first-hand how much this area was truly undergoing revitalization, and also how much more revitalization this area still needs to undergo. I see so many young people walking the streets. I see these same people in coffee shops and bars in the area. I sometimes overhear them say, "The Junction is an up-and-coming area." They have no idea . . . this is only the beginning! Property values are going to continue to go up. I am excited to see what this area looks like 20 years from today!

The ABCs of Condo Design

How condo design affects your lifestyle and the life of the neighbourhood. How to assess condo design from architects' renderings and layouts. Beyond the aesthetics of design: building performance and your comfort.

In the past, condos were designed from the inside out. Developers in Canada looked to architects and engineers to design a simple building that could be constructed with ease and have a nicely designed floor plan with the right finishes that would be attractive to the majority of buyers.

When a building is designed from the outside in, where spectacular exterior architecture is valued more than the design of the interior suites, the engineering may result in less useable living space and a building that is more costly to construct.

In Canada, the consumer values the quality of interior finishes and smaller suites to the point that every inch is valued, and most people compare buildings by the price per square foot. However, in cities such as Vancouver and Toronto, there is a growing movement of condo critics that demand a better looking building, and the use of social media is pushing this movement across the country. Many major Canadian cities have design review panels—made up of architects, engineers, landscape architects and other members of the community—whose sole purpose is to give professional and impartial advice to the planner on the design of buildings within the city.

Developers now understand that achieving a richer and broader mix of architectural aesthetics is valued by the consumer and, as such, premium pricing can be charged for an aesthetically pleasing building.

Tall buildings are defined by the City of Toronto as a building whose height is greater than the width of the street it's located on. Tall building design can be broken into three parts. The base is the lower portion of the building, the part that is most visible from the street. The middle portion of the building is sometimes also called the shaft. The top part (or roof) of the building may make the building distinguishable on the city skyline.

The Base of the Building

The base of the building is the part that interacts with the street. How the base is designed will determine the character of the building. The base of a condo can either be situated on a podium, where the main tower is set back from the street, or a tower erected off the foundation. The focus of the base design will differ according to the class of a building and the type of condo submarket it belongs to (Urban Renewal, Avenue In-fill, Brownfield, or Suburban Greenfield, as we discussed in Chapter 2), and each style will inherently appeal to a certain lifestyle. When analyzing the design of the base, you should focus on what is right for you, rather than argue design principles. Design can be used to encourage public interaction to create a vibrant and walkable street; however, not all people want this: some buyers prefer predictability and quiet. In either case, design should make people feel comfortable in a given location. Comfort for those walking the street is created from consistency, and through encouraging light, sight and height.

Keys to a Good Condo Tower Base Design

1. The base should be scaled against adjacent property.

If you would like a vibrant, walkable condo, buying a condo with a base that is "out of scale" is not for you. Deep setbacks will separate a building from the street life, and when separation occurs, the life at the base loses its vibrancy and becomes more predictable and quiet. On the other hand, if the setback is too short or nonexistent, the building could lose its identity. Either way, curb appeal and vibrancy for the street is facilitated when a consistent sense of scale is created for the entire street.

In certain projects, such as Urban Renewal, Urban In-fill or Avenue In-fill projects, a historic building could be retained and integrated into a new development, thereby keeping the character and integrity of the neighbourhood intact. To achieve integration in urban neighbourhoods where no such historic building exists, most cities require that the main tower sit on a podium that extends the length of the site, where the building walls are aligned with the street and have regulated distances to the sidewalk.

If you prefer a quieter environment, then having the base set back far from the street would be for you. Having a setback creates a buffer between the public and private realms. Large setbacks are typically found in neighbourhoods that don't have an active street life. From the diagram below, you can see that having a large setback from the street could allow the condo to be gated, thus ensuring enhanced security, or to have a garden or a plaza with benches and landscaping.

PLAZA
- ADDS ANIMATION

Scale is vitally important with buildings with large setbacks. In the past, cities such as Toronto built tower communities with no podium at the base and a large landscaped area; this type of development is known as "Towers in the Park." Towers in the Park are notoriously hard to maintain and secure, and are breeding grounds for crime. To avoid Towers in the Park scenarios, some cities have regulations in place to prevent it.

2. The design should fit in with neighbouring properties.

In order for people to feel at ease at the street level, consistency is very important. Consistency creates a sense of comfort and safety for people at street level. Consistency doesn't mean that the building be of cookie-cutter design; it just means that the use for a particular area is easily recognizable and seamless for residents and non-residents, both in cars and on foot.

The diagram below illustrates what the base of a condo should be optimally. A developer designs ground-floor uses to encourage public use by non-residents. The developer will ensure the sidewalks are paved to handle commercial activities and pedestrian traffic. The main entrance is clearly visible. The delivery and passenger drop-off areas, garbage storage, air vents, mechanical elements, building utility services and garage entrances are at the side of the building, off the main street and away from public view.

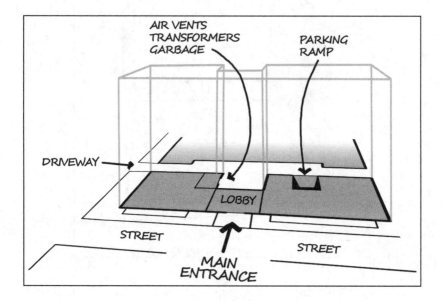

There may be commercial components at the base, with space to accommodate sidewalk cafes, for example, or storefronts. No matter what components are present, the design should fit the character of the existing street.

Even though your city may have guidelines for developers to follow, not every site will meet them exactly. A developer may undertake a tremendous amount of negotiation with the city, and sometimes a development represents the art of the deal rather than the art of urban planning. Do not take anything for granted; make sure you understand the condo block plan before buying. The photograph below illustrates an example of a base that is not well integrated with the street. The main garage is right beside the main entrance, which poses a risk to pedestrians as they exit the building. The facade, marked only with a small canopy, lacks any sort of curb appeal. The address is very easy to miss, which could prove frustrating if your visitors can't find you. It is also tricky to drop off passengers, and commercial deliveries are encumbered by pedestrian and vehicle traffic. Be sure to study your plan and ask the builder questions on how these things are handled.

Very little curb appeal and a parking garage right next to the main entrance lower the potential for this condo. (Photo by Chris Ho.)

Low height at the base of this condo lessens its potential to attract a quality retailer. (Photo by Chris Ho.)

If you are in hopes that a trendy restaurant, bar or grocery store will find a home at the base of your condo, it's best to consider the track record of the developer to build a space to attract these type of tenants, or wait until an agreement is already in place with a major retailer. Developers who are inexperienced can build a space that is not attractive to anyone looking to lease space at the base of the condo. The condo in the photograph above is an example of how an inexperienced builder applied residential construction techniques to a retail environment. The low ceilings prevent signage from being visible from the street, and those same low ceilings inside, coupled with awkward columns, would deter anyone from launching a cafe or high-end shop of any kind. With a base design such as this, it's very difficult for retailers to be successful. A poorly designed space results in high vacancies or small professional uses that kill the vibe at the street level.

Retailers are very cautious about the locations they choose; they want developers to design a space that is energy efficient, has adequate signage space, includes high ceilings, has few interior columns, can handle deliveries and has storage space for garbage. In Toronto, Chicago and New York, developers are required to build with a minimum ceiling height, so retail at the base is encouraged.

The design of the base reduces vibrancy at the street level. (Photo by Chris Ho.)

Regardless if you are in the suburbs or in an urban area, retail may not be able to be supported at the base of your building, for a number of reasons other than design. For one, the location may have too little traffic for retailers, and two, the use might not fit with the neighbouring properties (as in the case of in-fill projects located on predominantly residential streets, where commercial use is unlikely). The base of these condos could have townhouse or loft units around the building to ensure some street animation. Some cities allow for commercial uses, even in residential neighbourhoods, but generally the developer will opt for residential use because it's more financially advantageous for them to do so. This means the front entrances may have gardens, landscaping or some other space to transition or separate itself from the public streets.

If you are a hoping for a vibrant street life to be created later on as future development occurs, as we mentioned in Chapter 2, you must be mindful that the neighbourhood needs to establish the right proportion of residential and other uses. Offices, commercial, retail, entertainment and leisure usually arrive many years after the first residents, and their success depends on the initial character of the location, the demand of the particular class of developers, the skill of the city planners or other major renewal initiatives (such as adding mass transit systems or huge government brownfield remediation projects).

If the community plan has been thought out properly and the area already has plans in the works to develop primary uses other than residential (such as commercial or office space), the area will start to become vibrant. Once the primary uses are set, they will start to bring in a steady flow of people throughout the day; this is when secondary uses, such as retail, restaurants and cafes, will start to flourish.

CASE STUDY

Regent Park, Toronto[1]

Toronto's Regent Park had degenerated into a ghetto. Originally designed in the late 1940s as a low-income enclave with parks and recreation, the community became an enclave of dead ends, ambiguous space and criminal activity. As a result of the physical barriers in the community, residents were cut off from economic, education and health-care opportunities that would encourage upward social mobility. Clearly, just adding condo towers would not be enough to change the character of the neighbourhood; work had to be done to add primary uses that encouraged interaction among residents.

After doing extensive research on revitalization of neighbourhoods around the world, Toronto city planners embarked on an ambitious plan to completely change the character of the area. The plans, which began to be implemented in 2005, centred on creating a mixed-income community that would encourage interaction of people across entire city blocks. Interaction would be established in the following ways:

- Building facilities to foster a sense of community—such as shared courtyards, green space, a media arts centre and a cultural centre. These facilities will enable community programs and provide space for community festivals that will attract everyone in the neighbourhood. These initiatives will create a sense of community that all residents, regardless of income and culture, can be part of. When residents feel they are part of a community, they become attached and invest to make the community grow strong.

- Mixing low-, medium- and high-income residents: the city, in a joint venture with a private developer, tore down old low-density public housing buildings and redeveloped residences to house a mixed-income population. The public and private housing units were designed to a similar standard, and in close proximity, in an effort to increase social interactions among people from different income levels, thereby eliminating feelings of isolation.

- Physically changing the neighbourhood to increase accessibility. This involved physically changing the street to be more pedestrian friendly and involved creating space for retail that can cater to all residents of the community within its boundaries on the main streets.

- Creating opportunities for local governance. The city created groups, from tenant councils to community committees, that gave residents a voice to guide the direction of their neighbourhood. These groups provide a way for residents to become more attached to their communities.

Needless to say, a lot of resources, from a number of different stakeholders, are being invested to revitalize this neighbourhood.

The model that the Regent Park revitalization is following is going to be used in urban development across the country. Many cities are encouraging private partnerships on their social housing properties, to make the housing more desirable for residents with higher incomes and to eliminate the feeling of isolation by low-income residents.

3. The design should not limit skyviews.

In financial districts of major cities like Toronto, sky views could be limited because of many tall buildings close together. This makes for a claustrophobic feel and can block out the sun, which becomes uncomfortable for people looking to live there. Financial districts are meant to look strong and powerful, but in residential neighbourhoods "strong and powerful" can quickly become "dark and oppressive."

On sites with long street frontages, cities usually require the developer to design a building with a setback from the base (or to build the tower on a podium), to allow the tower to go taller without impacting skyviews.

4. The design of the base should be attractive and unique, and ensure privacy.

From street level, the human eye can see a maximum of five storeys. For this reason, the base of a condo is extremely important to the building's curb appeal. The base is the point of connection, in a sense where someone can touch and feel the building, where every detail can be seen up close. This creates an experience for people at ground level. Experienced builders who understand this put extra focus on the base, and as a result, they invest a little more time and effort to make it attractive. The base is where developers use high-quality materials and place unique aesthetic elements. This is great for visitors, because they can easily identify which building you are in when they pay you a visit.

Design also extends to the street. In Chapter 2 we mentioned that a high Walk Score is a good tool for determining appreciation potential, but what the Walk Score doesn't measure is how pleasurable the walk is. People are more likely to walk an area, and for longer distances, if the walk is interesting, comfortable and safe. This is why some cities require developers to provide landscaping and sidewalk trees, to resurface or widen sidewalks with quality materials, and to add public art displays and lighting to make the sidewalk look more inviting.

The design of the base also has to address privacy issues. For both the public and residents, lack of privacy can have a big impact. For the public, besides the obvious awkward feeling of seeing into someone's home, a building's curb appeal can be reduced if the owners' living spaces and possessions are visible from their windows and balconies. The building should be designed in such a way that this could never happen. A strong building is able to stand on its own design merits, rather than being dependent on the purchaser to keep it pretty.

Fort York, Toronto

Intersection is more centred around the car; as a result, not a comfortable pedestrian experience. This keeps people off the streets and lowers the vibrancy of the neighborhood. (Photo by Chris Ho.)

Fort York is an example of an area that has a great Walk Score, because it's close to many amenities, but is not a pleasurable walking experience; as a result, prices are much cheaper here than in other parts of the city with a similar Walk Score. As we can see in the photo above, the area was not designed with the pedestrian in mind, and massive change would be required to make the area vibrant. The sidewalks are narrow, there are infrequent pedestrian crossings and long blocks, and the street lanes are wide, which means cars can travel at high speeds. Crossing the street becomes a huge issue for pedestrians, with cars all around. Pedestrians and cyclists are completely out of scale as compared to the road, making for an uncomfortable street life experience.

 TIP

How to judge a sidewalk
The choice of sidewalk materials has a significant impact on a neighbourhood's atmosphere. In most Canadian cities, sidewalks are a mixture of concrete and cheap asphalt, used to repair holes. Concrete is cheap, durable and

able to reflect light (thereby reducing street lighting costs), but over time concrete breaks down and gets uglier. Studies have shown that as a sidewalk gets uglier, people are more likely to avoid using it, and treat the city with less care; they will be more prone to litter, for example. This can bring down property values. The opposite is also true: when neighbourhood elements are attractive, the neighbourhood is attractive for people to visit and live there, thereby increasing property values. With the understanding that creating a pleasurable walking experience requires that streets and sidewalks look good and be interesting, some neighbourhood developers and property owners work with cities to make the sidewalks look better by experimenting with different materials.

Brick is used in historic neighbourhoods to give a more noteworthy, prestigious feeling, but the bumpiness makes it hard to walk on, push a stroller or ride a bike. Brick is also less durable than concrete and gets slippery in the snow and rain.

Cobblestone, famously used on the streets in Paris, gives a neighbourhood a high-quality feel and is more durable than brick. Like brick, however, it's harder to use because it's bumpy and slippery when wet.

Some cities have been using granite and marble. These materials look great and are durable, but they can be slippery when wet and are prohibitively expensive to install on a large scale.

CASE STUDY

Toronto

Realizing the impacts that tall buildings have on a city's neighbourhoods, Toronto introduced tall-building guidelines for the design of condos. Planners in Toronto realized the huge potential condos had for revitalizing its major streets and creating anchors for vibrant neighbourhoods for others. In order to achieve vibrancy and revitalization, planners and developers spend much of their effort on how the base of the condo will look and perform. Developers are required to submit drawings to the planner that focus on the base and show as much detail as possible. Regulations pay particular attention to the base's design, height, facade, type of use and integration with the street, to ensure buildings not only achieve excellence in architecture, but also create a successful relationship with the neighbourhood. Regulations are strictly enforced and building permits are not granted unless the developer sticks to its approved plans.

The Middle/Shaft of the Building

The middle or shaft of a building falls between the base and the top of the building. The design of the shaft will be usually be uniform to ensure cost effectiveness and fast construction, so the design is very important. Visual impressions aside, the design of the shaft will govern how the floor plans will be laid out, what your view will be, how your building performs and how much wind, sunlight and shadows you will have.

To consider the design of the middle, we need to break down our understanding of the shaft into three parts: exterior and interior design, building performance and interaction with natural environment.

Exterior Design

Design is what most people critique when looking at a building. How a building looks doesn't just come down to what the builder decides is best; there is a complex set of constraints that impact how the building will look. These constraints include the land conditions where the building is to go up, engineering issues, city zoning rules, market forces, local weather, building time and material availability.

A multitude of small decisions is made that impact the final appearance of a building. Buyers need to understand that development is a fluid and constantly changing field in which no builder, no matter how skilled or experienced, can guarantee that what is shown in a rendering will be exactly what is built, while coming in on time and on budget. This is why condo developer contracts have clauses giving the developer the right to make substitutions. Naturally, good developers usually work hard to limit changes that take away from the appeal of the building and features promised in a rendering.

Generally speaking, architects like to design buildings that are aesthetically pleasing, but constraints force them to find the answer to the following question: How can I take the existing site, with the given city guidelines, to quickly build a structure with units that have an appealing floor plan, and do so profitably?

City building guidelines and the nature of the site will limit the different forms of the floor plate. The shape of the floor plate impacts the design of interior floor plans. Typically, in Canada, what the consumer wants drives the process. This is called the "inside-out process" of design. An example of an "outside-in" approach can be seen in projects in Dubai. In Dubai, astonishing and breathtaking buildings are in demand because labour costs are cheaper and, during Dubai's boom, revenues per unit were a lot higher.

Canadians are more conservative in what they will spend to meet their tastes. This has two outcomes. First, our unit mix is generally smaller, to keep prices lower, and this limits the number of angles and curves in the floor plate (thus ensuring more usable interior space). Second, Canadians value interior space and finishes much more than exterior aesthetics, so the limited revenue generated per unit needs to be balanced between the cost of designing a great interior space versus the cost of building a more complicated exterior.

CASE STUDY

Absolute World, Mississauga

The negotiation between city planners and developers is instrumental to the design of a tower. Realizing this, some cities have set up design review panels to ensure that a tower is aesthetically appealing by negotiating with the developer to place a higher standard on design, in return for allowances that would make a project more profitable. The best example of this in Canada currently is the Absolute World development in Mississauga. The idea for the design was born between the chief planner of Mississauga at the time, Ed Sajecki, and the president of Cityzen Developments, Sam Crignano. Mississauga wanted something special for an intersection that made up the gateway to the central business district, and Cityzen wanted to maximize the height and density of a large parcel of land. Crignano offered to set up an international design competition, if the city planners in Mississauga would give him the tools to increase his revenue over the entire community. If there was a major pushback from buyers and sales targets were not met, or if there were huge cost overruns because of the complicated design, Cityzen would be in a better position if it could make up those revenues from more traditionally designed buildings on the same site.

What happened was a little unexpected. The site sold extremely well and quickly, even though there was a premium price. Crignano has reported that buyers who bought early are selling their units at a higher price compared to other properties in the area.

 TIP

Landmark buildings increase in value faster than others

"Landmark buildings"—those with exceptional architecture—are worth a premium in the market, and in some cases can appreciate faster than the general market index.

18 Yorkville in Toronto is an example of a building that would be considered landmark for design and, on average, has almost doubled in value over the past five years, far outpacing the appreciation for the entire condo market. The rents in the building are also among the highest in the city in its market class. This building, designed by Architects Alliance, was built by an experienced team of architects who knew how to balance design with cost.

What does it mean to have an exceptionally designed building? In his TV show, *The Perfect Home*, host Alain de Botton explores the notion of idealism in architecture and explains that "architecture should reflect back to its audience a selective and flattering image of who it is." With so many different people with different tastes, is it really possible to build a consensus to the question of what good design is?

Styles and moods change often. Currently, in Toronto and Vancouver, glass panels are the material of choice; before that, concrete, marble and granite were popular. Each aesthetic decision—whether shapes, textures, colours or materials—creates an impression in the viewer that is unique, since each individual is governed by culture and personal preferences. For example, studies on the emotions created by the colour red show that reactions can range from the positive (love and romance) to the negative (anger and rage).

What this means is that you should focus on what's important to you rather than trying to decode what architecture critics are saying on Internet forums. For example, an architect can use scale, light and height to create that feeling of awe within you. If the design of a building draws your eyes up, and there is lot of light reflection, this can make people feel positive, even worshipful or spiritual (all of which are closely linked to awe). If critics call this building gaudy or an eyesore, but it makes you feel good to look at the building, don't stress: buy into that project.

The best way to determine what you like is to look at buildings in real life. See what you like and then carefully look at the renderings to see if that project will create that feeling within you.

Interior Design

After considering that the design of the exterior creates the shape of the floor plan, which is instrumental in how liveable a unit is, how can developers take this a step forward to make the interiors more liveable?

If office buildings have been designed to decrease absenteeism and increase productivity, and university libraries have been designed to increase educational achievement, why can't your home be built to make you more comfortable and happy? From an aesthetic point of view, you may have experienced mood changes from being in space designed a certain way. For example, large, ornate and decadently designed buildings can make a casual type of person feel uncomfortable.

Brightness and openness usually make most people feel more positive. As previously mentioned, the use of colours, shapes, light and textures can have dramatic effects on your mood, effects that are over and beyond individual tastes.

With the idea that buildings can create a particular mood in you, think back to a place you really found comfortable and think of the elements you would like to bring to your own home.

Building Performance

Energy efficiency is usually uppermost in people's minds when they assess building performance, but there are other aspects to building performance that are also critical to its liveability. All the elements of a building must come together for a building to become holistically liveable. An evaluation of performance should consider how effective the building is in terms of comfort, energy efficiency, indoor air quality, durability and maintainability.

Comfort

Comfort and enjoyment within a building can actually be created and measured. A huge number of complaints about buildings arise from problems with humidity, ventilation, heating and cooling, and noise.

Humidity

Moisture content of the air in condos is very important to comfort. Air needs to have some level of moisture content. Air that is too dry can lead to physical discomfort, static electricity, and even an increase in health problems such as allergies to dust and bacteria. When air is too damp (humid), condensation and mould can result, along with health problems such as allergic reactions and even breathing problems.

 TIP

Take control of humidity and ventilation—before you buy, and after
Before you buy, ask the salesperson how humidity can be controlled. Is there a centralized system? If not, can you add a system yourself? Does the unit have

heat recovery ventilators, which circulate fresh air into the unit? Does it have the necessary kitchen and bathroom exhausts?

If your unit doesn't have extra systems to prevent excess humidity from building up, ensure that you adequately ventilate your unit by opening windows or by opening blinds to allow air from heaters to blow on the glass. One of the first things warranty providers look for when investigating a claim for buckling floors or condensation is humidity levels. It is usually the occupant's responsibility to ensure the unit's humidity level, so be proactive.

Ventilation

Condos today are tightly sealed to decrease drafts from high winds and increase the efficiency of insulation. The downside of such tight sealing is the buildup of condensation on walls, window sills and window frames. Condensation occurs when warm, humid air contacts a cold surface; the air cools and the water in the air is deposited on the surface. Water buildup can result in windows being soaked, water stains on walls, and mould. Over time, water damage and mould can become serious issues. The key to limiting condensation is through proper ventilation, by opening windows and keeping the fan on in your vertical fan coil unit. In the winter, though, this could be uncomfortable.

Indoor Air Quality

Air that is fresh and free of pollutants and particles has been shown to directly impact student learning and worker productivity. Air quality can be increased by the choosing of finishes that are low in volatile compounds and by ventilation systems that bring in a constant source of fresh air. Recently, certain developers have taken a leadership role to increase air quality by redesigning the building's ventilation to include indoor air quality management systems. These systems ensure a constant source of fresh air is available in the units and common areas.

Air quality should also consider the management of odours, especially due to cooking. In modern buildings, air is forced into corridors, creating a high-pressure gradient outside a condo, which should ensure that no odours from your neighbour's grilled fish escape their unit.

Heating and Cooling

Condos can be uncomfortable if heating and cooling systems do not evenly or adequately condition the air in the suite. Here are some systems that you might find in a condo:

- Forced air heating consists of fan coil units that blow hot or cool air into your unit. This is usually controlled by a central thermostat in the unit. In this type of heating and cooling system, water is circulated into the fan coil units. In summer months, this water is cooled and in winter this water is heated. Since these water loops are used, it may take some time for a building to change from hot to cold and back again. Forced air systems are the most common and cost effective; the downside is that it doesn't allow for even distribution of heat.

- Radiant baseboard heaters use electricity to heat an element, which then radiates heat into a room. These systems allow for temperature to be controlled in each room. Not as prevalent because of the cost to operate.

- Water-based heat pump systems allow for different temperatures to be set in different areas (or zones) within your condo. These systems allow for a comfortable distribution of temperature and are typically found in more luxury projects.

- Hydronic heating systems use hot water flowing through tubes under the floor, in the ceiling and walls, or through units that resemble baseboard heaters. Like heat pump systems, they allow for a more comfortable distribution of temperature and are found in more luxury projects.

 TIP

Don't just take the heat—ask about it!
Ask the salesperson what type of heating and cooling system is at work in the building. What measures have been taken to control the temperature in your condo? Note where the thermostat is. For forced air systems, if the thermostat is placed near a window, an air vent or a gas fireplace, it can be difficult to achieve consistent temperature control throughout the unit.

Noise

Noise is a common complaint for people living in condos. Owners have lobbied for more stringent building codes around noise insulation materials. Noise regulations in building codes usually only consider the minimum standards for safety and don't really consider comfort. The courts have had to intervene in some cases where noise transmission between units was so severe that the owner of a unit was sued to rectify the situation, even though the noise insulation met the building code standard. These cases are rare, and usually only occur with belligerent owners who have no care for their neighbours.

Unwanted noise in a condo can come through walls, between floors, and from the street. Typically, walls between suites are supposed to prevent the spread of fire, heat and noise, but in some cases these walls have been poorly constructed or perhaps had large gaps due to plumbing, wiring and ductwork. The source of the noise can come from neighbours, elevators, garbage chutes or plumbing. In higher-end buildings, developers may install sound-dampening acoustic batt insulation into the condo's interior walls during construction; this is the best practice for reducing noise travelling from unit to unit.[2] Adding extra insulation around water pipes can reduce water noise. If the building you are buying into doesn't have the extra insulation to prevent sound transmission, it doesn't mean end-users will have an unbearable time living there. Minimum building code requirements set out that you should only hear muffled sounds, at most, coming from people in other units.

Even though floors can be separated by concrete slabs and under-padding, noise transmission can be substantial, especially if the unit has hardwood flooring. Noise can result from the impact of walking, from furniture, or from mechanical devices such as garage doors. Acoustic underlays can be installed under finish flooring to reduce sound transmission from between floors.

 TIP

Ask about noise
Ask the salesperson: What is the builder doing to lessen noise transmission beyond minimum building code or new-home warranty specifications?

There is some recourse when noise travels within a building, but what happens when noise comes in from outside? As cities become more densely built up, development projects could be located in areas with industrial uses, nightclubs, train stations, streetcars and busy roads. Developers often protect themselves by placing warnings in disclosure documents and have clauses protecting them from making verbal representations (which will be covered in depth in Chapter 5). It's really up to the purchaser to do due diligence on the neighbourhood to discover how bad outside noise can be.

CASE STUDY)————————————————————————————————

The Junction, Toronto[3]

In Toronto, a new condominium townhouse development was built next to an abattoir. The noise from the 18-wheeler delivery trucks and squealing animals keeps residents up all night, and the stench at times is unbearable, especially when the wind blows from the east. Although the pig slaughterhouse, Quality Meat Packers, had been in this neighbourhood for more than 100 years, many condo purchasers either overlooked or downplayed the impact this would have on their units. But because the slaughterhouse's operations pre-date Toronto's city plans, the residents have little recourse. A simple walk around the neighbourhood, or conversations with area residents, could have revealed this unpleasant aspect of the condo neighbourhood before prospective purchasers moved forward.[4]

Some residents have threatened lawsuits stating that the salespeople, hired by the developers, told them that the abattoir would shut down soon after they took possession. This claim is very difficult to prove in court. The city did require the developer to disclose that a slaughterhouse was nearby, which was skated over in the purchase agreements, and the city plan still allows for other industrial uses for the area. The only hope for residents is that a developer will buy the abattoir and turn the land to residential uses, although some people estimate it would cost approximately $100 million to do so—an unlikely scenario.

Energy Efficiency

Buildings designed to demand less energy are becoming more and more important as heating and air conditioning costs rise. For end-users paying for their own utilities, having a building that minimizes energy through design features and specialized products could be very attractive. Energy-efficient appliances and lighting are the obvious choices, but also consider a builder that incorporates green thinking into their construction. Rather than being an afterthought, truly green features will have a real impact on reducing operating costs. Here are some examples:

- motion-sensing lighting within the common areas
- maximizing shading and natural lighting through design features
- high-quality insulating materials, especially in buildings that use a lot of glass

- energy management systems that ensure buildings are operating efficiently and decrease energy waste.

These elements may increase costs initially and should be balanced with cost savings.

Durability and Maintainability

Another often overlooked element of the shaft design is how durable it is. We have all heard stories about "leaky condos" in Vancouver; buyers should be forewarned about buying condos that are made with lesser-quality materials, especially if built by a builder not known for quality. Durability and maintainability can be measured in terms of maintenance and replacement costs, and the lifespan can vary greatly depending on location, weather and the quality of installation.

CASE STUDY

Curtain Walls vs. Window Walls

For residential condo construction, condos built with glass are usually built using a window wall design; in contrast, office buildings and hotels normally use curtain wall design. Window wall systems are installed between the concrete slabs of a building and use caulking and taping to create a seal that prevents moisture from entering the building. The two advantages for window wall systems are, first, they can be installed quickly and easily and are relatively cheap, which keeps individual condo units affordable. Second, they compartmentalize issues between floors. If spot repairs are required, they can be carried out with minimal disturbance. The compartmentalization also decreases sound transmission between floors. One disadvantage of window walls is that, over time (and in the worst-case scenario, with poor installation, in as little as five years), the seals can dry out and crack, causing water to leak into the building, which will result in expensive repairs to reseal the entire building. A second disadvantage is that, due to the weaker structural integrity of the glazing in a window wall design, the system has to be built with more pieces (mullions) and joints. This construction makes the building look less smooth aesthetically and, due to the number of joints, increases the risk of failure.

Curtain walls, which have been used mainly in commercial buildings, hang off the front of the building and are anchored on the concrete slabs using metal plates. Curtain walls are much more resistant to moisture, wind, heat and earthquakes and require less maintenance (again, if installed correctly). Curtain walls also have stronger structural integrity, meaning fewer mullions and joints; as a result, the buildings can look more aesthetically pleasing. On the downside, curtain wall systems can be anywhere from double to triple the cost of window wall design, and are typically found only in more luxury projects. Another disadvantage to a curtain wall system is sound conduction. Noise can be easily transmitted throughout the entire building, as it's conducted through the wall system.

As technology changes and costs go down, and with new supply options from China, curtain wall systems may become more prevalent in residential construction. Similarly, technology changes have made window wall systems less prone to leaks, by allowing for better water drainage. Either way, be sure you are working with a developer with a solid track record for any window system.

Ask the builder when the warranty for specific components ends. Sometimes suppliers state that warranty starts from when a large portion of the work has been completed, rather than on move-in day. Quality finishes should have a warranty; otherwise, it may be from a dubious supplier.

 TIP

More elevators mean higher costs

As more and more in-fill projects start sprouting up in major cities, the availability of large sites dwindles. This forces builders to take sites that could be as small as 50 feet by 150 feet, and put 10- or 15-storey towers on them. Most people won't think anything of adding that much density to these sites, but it has its design challenges that can impact your comfort, especially when it comes to elevators. If a building has more elevators, it ensures a short wait (known in the industry as "call time") and fast travel times from wherever you are in the building to your suite. But elevators are costly to build (as seen in Chapter 3, they can take up to 3% of the construction budget of $100 million or more), the shafts and equipment room take up sellable space from a developer and they are expensive to maintain, which increases maintenance fees. Naturally, because those buying these residential buildings are more cost conscious, a developer must balance the cost of adding more elevators against the cost of inconvenience to owners who have to wait a long time to move up and down a building.

There is no hard and fast rule to how many elevators a building needs to ensure comfort of residents. Elevator consultants take in many variables, such as speed of the elevator, elevator cab size, number of floors and parking levels in the building, the number of units and people per floor, the expected number of people during high-demand times, and the budgetary and design constraints of a building. So there is no way a regular buyer without elevator expertise will know the answer to the question: how many elevators do we need in a building? It can't really be answered unless you ask the developer to see the computer models prepared by the elevator company. Even if the developer does build the minimum number, if your building is largely investor occupied (with many tenants moving in and out), elevators would be required to go on service during tenant move-in days, which can make the models completely useless, because they don't take this kind of usage into account.

What about maintainability? If you are buying into a building with a reputable company behind the elevator system, you will likely have a durable elevator system that breaks down infrequently. Reputable elevator companies install and enter into inclusive contracts for elevator maintenance. If the elevator breaks down, they have to send for an elevator mechanic to fix the problem at their cost, so there is an incentive to make sure the equipment is installed properly.

To find out who are the reputable companies in your area, look at who currently maintains the high-quality commercial or residential buildings in your city. As elevators get more complex, especially with new security systems being installed, some elevator companies can offer a developer a lower price to install, knowing that the building management will have to sign a maintenance contract with them afterwards. If the elevator technology is proprietary, your condo will be forced to work with the company that installed it, even if they provide poor service. The only recourse for the condo board is to replace the entire system, which can be cost prohibitive.

Interaction with the Environment

The orientation of a building takes into consideration how the shaft will be designed and positioned. The orientation of a building impacts the amount of light each side gets, the impact it has on the skyline, and the views available to units.

With regard to natural light, at street level, buildings placed at the east and south sides of a street will have shadows that fall back onto the street. To maximize sky views and minimize the impact of shadows, a developer can design and build with a smaller floor plate. If the site calls for a more elongated floor plate, there would be less shadow impact if the building is oriented north to south, because east-west buildings cast the tallest shadows. Because of shadow impact, some cities will discourage buildings that are wide and have large floor plates. Toronto, Calgary and Vancouver have strict restrictions on the size of the floor plates (Vancouver and Calgary demand the smallest floor plates and Toronto closely regulates floor plate sizes, but makes exceptions in certain cases for buildings taller than 50 storeys, commercial buildings and hotels); other cities, such as Chicago, do not have strict limits on floor plate sizes.

The orientation of the building is very easy to determine in master-planned communities, because the developer can choose where to place the tower. For stand-alone buildings, however, the developer must get creative to let sunlight in. Articulating, or breaking up, the floor plate (like in the drawing below) allows for density without creating an ominous building that blocks out all sunlight to the neighbourhood.

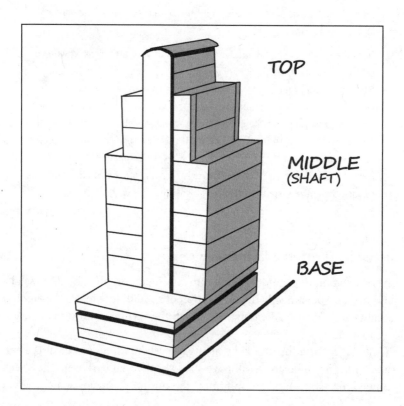

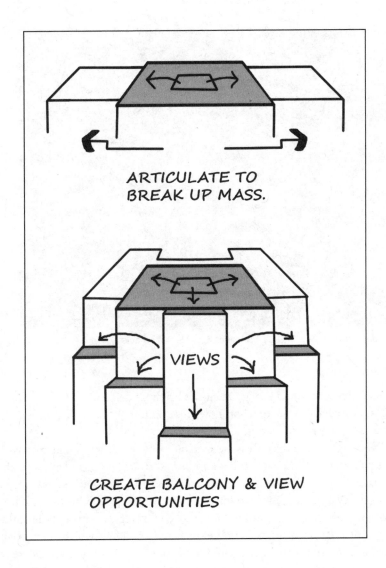

ARTICULATE TO
BREAK UP MASS.

VIEWS

CREATE BALCONY & VIEW
OPPORTUNITIES

Articulation can also maximize the number of units facing a certain direction, to take advantage of certain views. It can also allow the creation of very large terraces and balconies.

An example of a way developers manipulate views is with curved facades. Curved facades allow a bigger portion of a unit to face in a direction, while increasing privacy, since there is no direct overlook from one unit to another. For buildings placed close together, buying a building with

West Harbour City has large terraces because of setbacks.

a curved facade would be a good choice for those demanding more privacy. Most cities have regulations on how close buildings are to each other, but most are less than 30 metres.

Sunlight is not the only issue with buildings and their interaction with the natural environment; wind is another. At street level, wind gusts can be a real annoyance and will prevent uses such as lounging at a street cafe or walking. Winds come in two forms: vortex winds, which hit the building and are deflected downward to the street, could create a vortex at the building's entrance (creating a suction effect), and wind jets, which get accelerated around the corners of the building. In some cities, guidelines are in place to reduce the impact of wind at street level through the use of screens, roofs, canopies, colonnades and setbacks. In these cities, developers must provide a pedestrian wind tunnel model to demonstrate how these measures affect comfort. Despite the fact that cities have regulations to help limit wind problems, buildings will still have wind issues—the taller the building, the more impact it will have. A giant terrace on a high floor would be exposed to a lot of wind, making it less desirable to use, but condo rules surrounding the use of balconies may prevent you from building the wind breaks you would need to make it less uncomfortable.

Circular buildings can be designed closer together and maintain some level of privacy. (Photo by Chris Ho.)

Top of the Building

The top of the building is a developer's opportunity to give a building an identity. Normally the space is devoted to a building's mechanical systems, but the top or roof of a building can be a source of pride for residents, as they are able to easily pick their building out from a distance.

The height of a building is often a result of negotiation among the developer, city and community. Some cities have strict limits on building heights; for example, Vancouver has height limits to protect views of the mountains, and San Francisco uses height controls to protect its image of a city of rolling hills. Calgary, Toronto, New York and Chicago don't have specific height limitations in certain districts, but indirectly manage height through regulations. Calgary, New York and Chicago offer developers an opportunity to increase density and height through providing public benefits. Examples of public benefits include:

- rehabilitation and preservation of historic buildings
- building new public space (plazas, parks, streetscape improvements, public art pieces)
- creating pedestrian connections within a block and improving local transit facilities
- providing facilities for day cares, or arts and culture institutions
- developing sustainable energy projects
- providing affordable housing.

Toronto planners have taken a slightly different approach than other cities. In Toronto, planners have created similar provisions to other cities for granting height increases in certain districts in exchange for providing other community benefits; however, planners differentiated themselves by demanding a stricter focus on the form of the building, to ensure that it creates a strong, liveable community at the street where the building is located.[5] Toronto planners look at how the building, impacts the street through the design and use of the base, and the impact the building will have on wind and sunlight at street level. These regulations have huge consequences as to how buildings are designed.

It's clear how these design regulations forge the character of a city. New York and Chicago have big downtown metropolises, Vancouver combines the natural beauty of the mountains and ocean with the modern skyscraper to create a stunning skyline, and Toronto is a city of neighbourhoods.

The Contract

Overview of the most important aspect of the buying process: the paperwork, contract and disclosure documents.

So far the topics we have looked at cover the importance of determining location and amenities, studying the economics, and choosing the right suite in the right building. That was the fun stuff. As you get deeper into the process you must not fail to adequately consider one of the most important aspects of buying a pre-construction condo: the legal contract.

Buying real estate involves a contractual obligation where a lot of money is being paid out by one party and the other must fulfill its obligations. The emotional stress caused by entering into an agreement and not completely understanding the risks you take on can cripple the purchaser if things go wrong.

The contract protects the buyer's interests because it spells out the buyer's rights, terms, restrictions and obligations in the transaction. It also protects the builder's interests, as we will see.

The Standard Agreement

There is a real estate board in every province in Canada and each has a standard agreement for the purchase and sale of a property. These agreements are typically no more than five letter-size pages, and are usually designed to protect both the buyer and seller.

In comparison, builder contracts are usually non-standard, can be up to 50 legal-size pages, and are loaded with clauses to protect the builder. This means everything in writing provided by a builder should be carefully analyzed to completely understand the risks you are undertaking when purchasing a unit.

Builder contracts are full of technical language and small print, and are onerous to get through. They can be open to a lot of interpretation; you must have a competent lawyer to review them for you and a skilful agent to negotiate them on your behalf.

So, are builders being sneaky?

All builders, good and bad, must have contracts written in a way that offers them protection. They are working with many buyers, all with different personalities, and they are investing millions of dollars in order to build you a home. There would be absolutely no way anyone would invest that kind of money without the ability to protect themselves from savvy fraudsters.

In addition, the process of buying a newly built (or yet-to-be-built) property is a much more complex process than the buying process for an existing property, and the more specific the contract, the better it is for all parties involved.

From colour selections to location of ductwork to the types of amenities available, condominiums come in many combinations and permutations. These considerations force both you and your builder to cover every detail, every scenario, every practice and every requirement to reduce potential confusion and conflicts.[1]

COMPONENTS OF A CONTRACT[2]

SECTION	COMPONENTS	IMPORTANCE	TIPS
Description	• Model name • Unit number • Floor plan • Renderings • Elevations • Product and material specifications • Leased equipment in common areas • Construction plans • Condo Disclosure Statement	Ensures what you were "sold" on is what you get.	Don't rely on sales literature and marketing material as a guide to what you'll get. Specifics must be in your contract, or details are likely subject to change. Beware: wording in contracts can be intentionally ambiguous.
Price	• Unit price • Upgrades and options • Sales taxes (ask whether the price includes HST or GST) • Payment schedules	To get a clear idea of your financial obligations.	Ask the builder to list all additional charges to the purchase. Don't make assumptions on what is included in the purchase price.

SECTION	COMPONENTS	IMPORTANCE	TIPS
	• Handling of deposits • Deposit receipts • Additional costs and surcharges • Handling of payments for upgrades • Adjustments	The cost of buying a new home consists of not only the price but the extra fees and adjustments that the builder can charge.	You may be taking on loans or leasing back common elements.
Financing	• Builder mortgage • New mortgage	As a condition for the sale, the builder might require you to get a pre-approval in place prior to accepting the agreement.	Most lenders will require you pre-qualify before you close on your condo (even if you qualified at the time of your first builder deposit). Check with your lender well in advance of your registration date to ensure you can get the mortgage on closing.
Conditions	• Cooling-off periods • Right to have a lawyer review the contract • Builder receiving municipal approvals • Impact of rising construction costs and increasing prices • Developer's right to terminate an agreement • Time frames for builder to refund deposit	These clauses must be part of the agreement to protect yourself and your deposit during the pre-construction process.	Ensure your deposits are placed in trust with a law firm rather than given directly to the builder.
Restrictions on Title	• Easements • Obligations and restrictions (covenants)	Details any restrictions on title.	Check to see what spaces are public and private. Sometimes as a condition for

SECTION	COMPONENTS	IMPORTANCE	TIPS
	• Community guidelines • Site plan	All properties have limits on what you can do which are passed down from developer to you.	development, green space built by the developer may be open to the general public.
Construction Schedule	• Start and completion dates • Process and details if delays occur	Notes the approximate date for construction and indicates what will happen if construction gets delayed.	Check if your new-home-warranty province has a process to deal with delays.
Construction Standards	• Building code guidelines	Get an idea if your property will be built exceeding minimum code requirements for certain components.	Ask if your builder will exceed standards for building code to reduce your building's environmental footprint.
Site Visits During Construction	• Processes • Pre-delivery inspection restrictions • Liability waiver	Site visits give you an opportunity to visit your unit to spot deficiencies and defects before you get the keys to the building.	Carefully check the builder's inspection policies before you sign the contract. Sometimes you are prohibited from bringing along family members or professionals to inspect your unit.
Colour Selection	• Colour selections • Upgrades • Options	Builders offer a wide variety of options to finishes such as cabinets, counters and flooring.	Document everything, because proof is essential in any disputes. Get your finish options documented in writing. Create a log to document any phone calls with a time, date and

SECTION	COMPONENTS	IMPORTANCE	TIPS
		The contract will stipulate certain timeframes for you to select the different options available.	person you spoke to (noting that any agreements made by builder and not included in your original agreement are not enforceable).[3]
Deviations from Plans	• Builder's right to substitute products and materials • Rights to make changes (siting, plans, specifications, architectural details, exterior finishes)	There are a number of reasons why a builder may have to change details of your property; some of these changes can occur without notifying you.	Get a clear response from the builder to this question: If the builder deviates from the plans, and it's not to your liking, do you have the recourse to get a refund or select another unit?
Warranty	• Builder warranty • Third-party warranty • Manufacturer's warranty • List of items not covered • After-sales policy	Depending on the province in which you reside, you may be covered by third-party warranty programs. In addition, the builder will pass along the manufacturer's warranty on products used in the construction of your home.	Verify that your unit qualifies under the new-home warranty program.
Insurance	• Builder's insurance policy details used during the construction of your unit	You may be asked to take over the builder's insurance policy after closing the unit prior to closing your condo.	Verify what insurance you need to cover your contents. Condo insurance does not cover your personal items.

SECTION	COMPONENTS	IMPORTANCE	TIPS
Disputes	• Process for handling disputes • What is covered by your new-home warranty program	Once all conditions are met, it's very difficult to cancel or change a contract unless a builder agrees.	Try to get references on how a builder deals with disputes in the past by talking to your lawyer to see if there are any legal disputes by the builder.
Completion	• When will the occupancy period begin • What is meant when the unit is "substantially completed"	Buyers are required to pay the builder in full even after certain work needs to be completed.	Talk to your lawyer to ascertain if there is a history of how legal disputes are handled by the builder. Check to see how quickly your builder moves from interim occupancy to registrations by looking at past history.
Privacy and Consent to Disclosures	• Authorization for disclosure • Privacy policy	You provide a lot of confidential information to a builder, including copies of your ID, SIN and personal cheques.	If you wish to keep the purchase confidential, instruct the builder accordingly.

CASE STUDY

Condo Disputes[4]

After getting engaged and starting a new job that required regular junkets to Europe, an owner of a fairly new condo in New York unit decided it was time to sell. After the credit crisis, prices for new condos in the city plunged, and she was prepared to list the apartment at a price lower than what she had paid four years earlier, during the pre-construction phase. After dropping her asking price substantially, the owner finally accepted an offer at a loss of about $100,000. A condition was attached to the offer: the buyer had the right to review all the condo documents. Upon review, the buyer's lawyer discovered through the condo board minutes that the residents in the building complained frequently about structural problems and were in the process of suing the developer. A pending lawsuit severely limits the financing options available to a buyer, because no mortgage insurers will finance a purchase in a building with pending litigation (because of the risk associated with special assessments to pay for damages if the condo board loses). Since the owner was selling the condo for much less than what she had paid for it, she didn't have the option of offering seller financing or discounting the price further. Her only hope now is for a speedy and successful settlement of the lawsuit.

The Rescission or "Cooling-off" Period

It's the usual practice for a developer to release the contract, disclosure statement and proposed condo documents only after you have committed to purchasing one of its condos.

After you have signed the contract and written a cheque for your initial deposit, the clock is ticking. You now have a number of days to have your contract reviewed by your real estate agent and lawyer to understand what the clauses mean. This time is typically referred to as the cooling-off period and can range from three to ten days. During this time period, you have the right to back out of the contract with a full refund of your deposit, at no penalty.

HOW LONG YOU CAN COOL OFF ACROSS CANADA

British Columbia: 7 days
Alberta: 10 days
Saskatchewan: 10 days[5]
Manitoba: 48 hours (new legislation is in the works)[6]
Ontario: 10 days

 TIP

Buy more time if you need it
If you need extra time for the cooling-off period, have your lawyer request this in writing. Builders are usually amenable to it.

If you choose not to review the contract, you leave yourself open to considerable risk. Builder contracts have been known to contain clauses that give them the ability to:

- modify your floor plan

- alter what floor your unit is on

- move your parking spot

- change your finishes

- add substantial fees and levies.

It's vitally important that you know what you are getting into before you let the cooling-off period lapse. Always have your lawyer completely review the contract of sale and disclosure statement within the legislated cooling-off period.

What to Expect from a Developer's Contract[7]

Developer contracts are prepared for the sale of multiple units and include many clauses that may or may not have any impact on the sale of your condo. From our experience, this results in a huge amount of work (and legal costs) on the part of the purchaser, to review every detail with specific situations in mind. This is why it's absolutely imperative that you have a competent lawyer review your contract, and you must convey to your lawyer all the details as to why you are purchasing this particular condo.

Sample clause: Adjustments to Purchase Price

The cost of water, gas and/or electricity meters and/or check or consumption meter installations, if any, water, gas, electrical and sanitary and storm sewer service connection charges and hydro, gas, water and transformer installation, if any, and all utility and service connection or energization charges for the Condominium and/or the Unit, the Purchaser's proportionate share of such installation and/or connection or energization charges and costs by charging the Purchaser in the statement of adjustments with that portion of the charges and costs. A letter from the Vendor confirming the said charges and costs shall be final and binding on the Purchaser.

What this clause means: You have to pay for the installation of water, gas, and electricity meters, connection charges for sanitary and storm sewer service, hydro, heating and cooling, and transformer installation. These costs are typically not able to be financed by a mortgage and you must have the cash on closing.

Why it's there: This is an example of an additional cost that is usually referred to as "adjustments." Rather than increasing the purchase price for condominium units, developers will often include some of their development costs in the adjustment clause of the agreement.

What you can do: Often times the developer will allow you to cap or delete some of the charges. An experienced real estate agent can help you negotiate.

Sample clause: Consent to Sell or Rent

The Purchaser covenants not to list for sale or lease, advertise for sale or lease, sell or lease, nor in any way assign his or her interest under this Agreement, or the Purchaser's rights and interests hereunder or in the Unit, nor directly or indirectly permit any third party to list or advertise the Unit for sale or lease, at any time until after the Title Transfer Date. The Purchaser acknowledges and agrees that once a breach of the preceding covenant occurs, such breach is or shall be incapable of rectification, and accordingly the Purchaser acknowledges and agrees that in the event of such breach, the Vendor shall have the unilateral right and option of terminating this Agreement and the Occupancy License effective upon delivery of notice of termination to the Purchaser or the Purchaser's solicitor, whereupon the provisions of this Agreement dealing with the consequence of termination by reason of the Purchaser's default, shall apply. The Purchaser shall be entitled to direct that title to the Unit be taken in the name of his or her spouse, or a member of his or her immediate family only, and shall not be permitted to direct title to any other third parties.

What this clause means: This clause prevents a purchaser from leasing or selling his or her unit by way of an assignment of the agreement prior to taking title to the unit, unless he or she has the consent of the vendor. If you are planning to keep the property as an investment property, the unit will have to sit empty for months while the building goes through its occupancy phase (if your area has one). This doesn't mean the assignment will not be allowed; it just gives the developer the power to allow an assignment or lease and to charge any fee it determines for it. The clause does allow the unit to be transferred to an immediate family member without the payment of any fee.

Why it's there: This is to discourage people from buying units as an investment and flipping them (encouraging end-users rather than investors). Developers are of course aware that many people who buy pre-construction condos are investors who intend to sell their unit down the road at a profit. So how does a developer balance its needs against those of an investor? It is often the case that the last 10% to 15% of units sold to end-users is where the developer makes its profit. If there are unsold units during the occupancy phase, the developer may want to control the supply to ensure it can still hit its targets for price and still attract end-users, who typically don't like purchasing in a building that has a high proportion of renters. In some cases, the developer may want the flexibility to control rental rates if the developer decides to rent unsold units.

What you can do: Sometimes the developer will allow an amendment to the agreement to allow a fee to be stipulated, if the purchaser feels that it is important to have the ability to assign the agreement at a later date. Make sure you also get written permission to rent and advertise the unit.

CASE STUDY

Short-Term Rentals in Toronto get the Axe by Condo Board[8]
A Toronto-area developer allowed condo units of a luxury condo to be sold without any restriction on the number of units sold to investors or blocks to be sold by corporations. Since the building had a number of features that attracted people looking for short-term rentals, some investors began to market their condos as hotel-like units. Short-term rentals were actually encouraged by the developer, who marketed the units to foreign investors; however, to many of the actual owners, they became a nuisance. The increased traffic through the building by tenants made residents feel less safe, increased the condo's insurance costs and burdened the common elements and services for residents by tenants who expected hotel-like service from the building's staff. The condo board later passed a by-law that prevented tenancies of less than three months, and the condo board took the investors to court to in order to make them comply.

Sample clause: Builder's Right to Make Changes

The Purchaser acknowledges and agrees that the Vendor may, from time to time in its sole discretion, due to site conditions or constraints, or for marketing considerations, or for any other legitimate reason, including without limitation any request or requirement of any of the governmental authorities or any request or requirement of the Vendor's architect or other design consultants:

- change the Property's municipal address or numbering of the Unit (in terms of the unit number and/or level number ascribed to any one or more of the units comprising the Unit);

- change, vary or modify the plans and specifications pertaining to the Unit or the Condominium, or any portion thereof (including architectural, structural, engineering, landscaping, grading, mechanical, site servicing and/or other plans and specifications) from the plans and specifications existing at the inception of the project, or existing at the time that the Purchaser has entered into this Agreement, or as same may be illustrated in any sales brochure(s), model(s) in the sales office or otherwise, including without limitation, making any change to the total number of dwelling, parking and storage intended to be created within the Condominium, and/or any change to the total number of levels or floors within the Condominium, as well as any changes or alterations to the design, style, size and/or configuration of any dwelling within the Condominium;

- change, vary, or modify the number, size and location of any windows, column(s) and/or bulkhead(s) or change to ceiling height within or adjacent to (or comprising part of) the Unit, from the number, size and/or location of same as displayed or illustrated in any sales brochure(s), model(s) or floor plan(s) previously delivered or shown to the Purchaser, including the insertion or placement of any window(s), column(s) and/or bulkhead(s) or change to ceiling height in one or more locations within the Unit which have not been shown or illustrated in any sales brochure(s), model(s) or floor plan(s) previously delivered or shown to the Purchaser (regardless of the extent or impact thereof), as well as the removal of any window(s), column(s) or change to ceiling height and/or bulkhead(s) from any location(s) previously shown or illustrated in any sales brochure(s), model(s) in the sales office or otherwise; and/or

- change the layout of the Unit such that same is a mirror image of the layout shown to the Purchaser (or a mirror image of the layout illustrated in any sales brochure or other marketing material(s) delivered to the Purchaser);

- and that the Purchaser shall have absolutely no claim or cause of action whatsoever against the Vendor or its sales representatives (whether based or founded in contract, tort or in equity) for any such changes, deletions, alterations or modifications, nor shall the Purchaser be entitled to any abatement or reduction in the Purchase Price whatsoever as a consequence thereof nor any notice thereof (unless any such change, deletion, alteration or modification to the said plans and specifications is material in nature (as defined by the Act) and significantly affects the fundamental character, use or value of the Unit and/or the Condominium, in which case the Vendor shall be obliged to notify the Purchaser in writing of such change, deletion, alteration or modification as soon as reasonably possible after the Vendor proposes to implement same, or otherwise becomes aware of same), and where any such change, deletion, alteration or modification to the said plans and specifications is material in nature, then the Purchaser's only recourse and remedy shall be the termination of this Agreement prior to the Title Transfer Date (and specifically within 10 days after the Purchaser is notified or otherwise becomes aware of such material change), and the return of the Purchaser's deposit monies, together with interest accrued thereon at the rate prescribed by the Act.

What these clauses mean: Anything that has been sold to you, either from the marketing material, model suite, or even a verbal promise made by the salesperson, can change, and there is nothing you can do about it unless the change is considered "material in nature." Deciding what is material in nature may be up to the courts, which would be a costly battle to fight. If the courts determine that the builder has made a change that is "material in nature," or if the builder decides not to go to court, your only recourse is to get your deposit back. If the condo has gone up in value, you will lose that profit and only receive the interest paid while your deposit was held in trust.

Why they're there: Many developers will go to market with a proposed number of units, layout and levels, and once the sales start taking place, the details may change, based on the demands of the marketplace, or if the municipality demands changes to the design once permits are applied for, or to cover any mistakes that occur during construction. The changes cover a wide array of areas and may include changes to the number of storeys, the number of units, the layout of the unit, the finishes and the amenities. This clause allows developers the flexibility to complete a building in a timely matter and on budget without any costly delays.

What you can do: Buy only from a builder you trust. Significant legal action would be required to terminate an agreement, stating that the changes were significant enough to be considered material in nature. Your only recourse is to get your deposit back. If prices have risen, you will lose the gain. It's important to work with a knowledgeable lawyer and real estate agent to advise you on what to include and to manage your expectations.

CASE STUDY

Changes to Floor Plans and Unit Size[9]

In Vancouver, a couple purchased what was to be their dream condo. The layout showed a large den that would double as a second bedroom if they ever decided to have a family. The couple happily signed a purchase and sale agreement that had a clause that stated the dimensions and size of their condo as indicated in marketing materials was "approximate only" and might differ from the actual as-built size. Upon moving in, the couple discovered their den was the size of a small walk-in closet. The builder made these changes without providing notice after a redesign of the building's plumbing system, and the sellers were only informed during their pre-move-in inspection. The couple had little recourse in court and could not make a claim to their warranty program, since the coverage didn't include changes to size.

Sample clause: Completion and Move-in Dates

(a) The Unit shall be deemed to be substantially completed when the interior work has been finished to the minimum standards allowed by the Municipality so that the Unit may be lawfully occupied notwithstanding that there remains other work within the Unit and/or the common elements to be completed. The Purchaser shall not occupy the Unit until the Municipality has permitted same or consented thereto, if such consent is required and the Occupancy Date shall be postponed until such required consent is given. The Purchaser shall not require the Vendor to provide or produce an occupancy permit, certificate or authorization from the Municipality, and the Purchaser shall satisfy himself/herself in this regard. The Purchaser acknowledges that the failure to complete the common elements before the Occupancy Date shall not be deemed to be failure to complete the Unit, and the Purchaser agrees to complete this transaction notwithstanding any claim submitted to the Vendor and/or to the TWC in respect of apparent deficiencies or incomplete work, provided always, that such incomplete work does not prevent occupancy of the Unit as, otherwise, permitted by the Municipality.

(b) If the Unit is substantially complete and fit for occupancy on the Occupancy Date, as provided for in subparagraph (a) above, but the Creating Documents have not been registered, the Purchaser shall pay to the Vendor a further amount on account of the Purchase Price specified in paragraph 1(b) hereof without adjustment save for any pro-rated portion of the Occupancy Fee described and calculated in Schedule "C," and the Purchaser shall occupy the Unit on the Occupancy Date pursuant to the Occupancy Licence attached hereto as Schedule "C."

What these clauses mean: As soon as the interior work has been completed to a minimum standard allowed by the municipality, the unit may be lawfully occupied, and thus the purchaser is required to complete the occupancy and pay the occupancy charges. This means the common amenity spaces may not be finished when you get your keys, and it could be uncomfortable living in your unit while construction in other areas is occurring.

Why they're there: In order to lower the risk of a developer running out of cash while construction is ongoing, having an occupancy period can give the developer a revenue source to service its construction financing debt while the building is being completed. Occupancy fees are never enough to cover a developer's cost during the interim period, and developers are much better off having a short occupancy and getting all their funds on closing.

What you can do: Perform due diligence on your builder to see what kind of track record it has regarding time to registration. To lower the risk of long occupancies, ask the occupancy fee to be waived.

Sample clause: Opposition to Future Development

The Purchaser covenants and agrees that he shall not directly or indirectly object to nor oppose any official plan amendment(s) rezoning application(s), severance applications(s), minor variance application(s) and/or site plan application(s), nor any other applications ancillary thereto relating to the development of the Property, or any neighbouring or adjacent lands owned by the Vendor or any affiliated, associated or related entity within the area bounded on the west by 1st Avenue, on the east by 2nd Avenue, on the north by 2nd Street West, and on the south by 1st Street West. The Purchaser further acknowledges and agrees that this covenant may be pleaded as an estoppel or bar to any opposition or objection raised by the Purchaser thereto.

What this clause means: You have given up your right to have any opposition to any development in the area outlined in the contract. If any developer wishes to place a tower close to your building, even though you believe the proposed tower may adversely impact your enjoyment of the property (changing your view, bringing low-income housing to the area or increasing traffic), you have no right to object.

Why it's there: The amount of land that the city has deemed as appropriate for development in urban areas is limited. Land is priced based on the amount of buildable feet it allows; if there were restrictions on land use in future, the lost opportunity costs would have to be priced into a project.

What you can do: If you are buying a property because it has a particular view (for example, a park), even if there is a premium paid for the units fronting the park, by purchasing a unit with the above clause you are giving up your right to oppose any further development. In cases of parks or outdoor recreational areas, have your lawyer verify if the title to the land will be transferred to the condo corporation as part of its common areas. If you are in an urban area, look to see the city's plan for the adjacent land. If this clause is in the contract, you can't ever rely on the developer's word, the salesperson's word, or even the marketing material, that the surrounding land will not be developed.

CASE STUDY

Outdoor Space[10]

In the early 1990s, a multi-phase condo project was marketed as an urban woodland community with a recreational complex nestled among a grove of trees at its centre. The project was to have towers and townhouses that surrounded an outdoor recreational area consisting of a small forest, tennis courts, an outdoor pool and a putting green. Some of the purchasers relied on the marketing material and some in the high-rise even paid a premium to have a view of the wooded area. Over time, the developer decided to change the context of the development and decrease the number of towers and increase the townhome units. Since the townhome units were of a lower density, the builder scrapped plans to include the outdoor recreational area and instead planned to build townhomes on the land, essentially breaking its word to provide the space.

The residents went to court to stop the developer from building on the land, with the argument that they were the rightful owners of the land and the developer did not have permission to build upon it. The court eventually ruled that a clause buried in the documents "prohibited the purchasers from objecting to any construction" and that the developer did not require "the purchasers' consent to any rezoning or input as to how the outdoor recreational area is to be developed." The court also ruled that there was nothing in the contract that led purchasers to believe the land would be transferred to their condo corporations and they should have received professional advice.

As a result, the residents lost their outdoor space. According to the Ontario Real Estate Lawyers Association, this case sets the following precedents:

1. Any discretionary promises made by the developer should not be considered a real promise;

2. Purchasers have to read and understand all the extensive documentation provided by developers; and

3. Any agreement that gives a developer the option to redevelop nearby sites should be understood to mean that the sites will indeed be developed in the future.

Sample clause: Developer Obligations for Upgrades

The Vendor will undertake to incorporate the work covered by the sales extra in the construction of the Unit but will not be liable to the Purchaser in any way if for any reason the work covered by the extra is not carried out. In that event, any monies paid in connection with the same shall be returned to the Purchaser, without interest. Additionally, if for any reason the transaction of Purchase and Sale is not completed, the total cost of extras ordered is not refundable to the purchaser.[11]

What it means: If you were to request an upgrade or change to your condo and for whatever reason it is not included, the developer can simply return the money you paid and you have no recourse. Also, if you were to pay upfront for the extra and decide not to close on the condo, the costs would not be refundable.

Why it's there: The process of development of condos is complex. Since most of the heavy design work is done by the time construction starts, which could be almost a year after the agreed changes are made, a developer may find later on that it is no longer feasible, either from a time, design or economic standpoint, to proceed with the change. The fact that the costs are not refunded is due to the difficult nature of reselling a non-standard or unique layout, which may seem weird to later buyers.

What you can do: If upgrades are of vital importance to you, make sure the wording you have for upgrades is specific. If the extras are not included, it's very unlikely the builder will refund your money and may force you to close on the condo; however, it wouldn't hurt to ask for a provision that allows you to back out of the deal if the upgrades are not there.

Sample clause: Extension of Closing

Vendor can extend closing date up to 24 months.

Why it's there: Builders are at the mercy of weather, material and trades-people's availability. Work can be delayed for a number of different reasons, and it would be impossible for them to guarantee a closing date.

What you can do: Ask yourself if you are able to wait until the maximum term given (after adding extensions). Carefully consider if you would still be able to close on the condo, if two (or more) years from now you were in a substantially different stage of your life (unemployed, married, divorced, having children, etc.). Ignore what developer representatives say about completion dates. No one can accurately predict when exactly the building will be ready.

Sample clause: Excessive Noise from the Neighbourhood

a) Purchasers are advised that despite the inclusion of noise control features in the Condominium, the sound levels from increasing vehicular and road traffic from surrounding roads, including 1st Street, as may be extended and surrounding commercial establishments, as well as noise, vibration, electromagnetic interference ("EMI") and stray current from Transit operations, may be of concern, occasionally interfering with some activities of the dwelling occupants as the noise level exceeds the Municipality's and the Ministry of Environment and Energy's noise criteria. The dwelling unit will be supplied with a central air-conditioning system which will allow windows and exterior doors to remain closed, thereby ensuring that the indoor sound levels are within the City's and the Ministry of the Environment's noise criteria.

b) The Governmental Authorities, or their successors and assigns, has or have right of way rights-of-way or lines within 300 metres of the Property. There may be alterations to, or expansion of the rail facilities on such right-of-way lines in the future including the possibility that the Governmental Authorities, or their successors and assigns, may expand their operations, which expansion may affect the living environment of the residents in the vicinity, notwithstanding the inclusion of any noise and vibration attenuating measures in the design of the development and individual dwellings if necessary. Purchasers further acknowledge that the CNR owns or has interest in certain lands that are abutting or adjacent to the Property that are used for railway purposes, and Purchasers shall not object to the use of such lands for railway purposes or to noise, vibration or odour associated with such use.

What these clauses mean: If your condo is built near commercial and industrial properties that, from time to time, may create noises, vibration and odours that are uncomfortable, you cannot sue the surrounding businesses or the city to force it to stop, even if they exceed regulated norms.

Why they're there: As a city goes through re-urbanization, it is possible that the city will give approvals to a developer to build on a site in an industrial or commercial area. Since the area has already been established by the types of uses, planners cannot force the existing businesses out.

What you can do: Drive through the area during different times of the day, during the week, to get a feel for the area and what it would be like to live there. Ask the city planner about any proposals being implemented or encouraged in that area. There may be opportunities for the neighbourhood, if, sometime in the future, more former industrial sites will be redeveloped into residential.

Fees and Adjustments

Builders and developers must pay a number of costs that come up as they build your condominium. These fees are generally passed along to you and your unit holders and are not eligible for mortgage financing, which means that you have to come up with the cash out of pocket in order for the sale to be completed.

Determining the costs is difficult and they are not typically included in the purchase price for two reasons:

1. At the time when you enter into an agreement, some of these fee amounts are not verifiable or have not yet been charged (as is the case with city development charges).

2. It would make it difficult to compare prices with other projects if some developers included costs and others did not.

From experience, these clauses are non-standard, and some developers have favourite clauses they prefer to introduce in a contract.

It's clearly up to the buyer and the professional advice he or she receives to get a best guess as to the costs, or to request that the costs be capped at a certain amount, and if they exceed that amount, the balance would be deducted from the amount the purchaser will pay to the developer.

Common closing costs in Ontario include:

- Tarion New Home Warranty Program fee
- estimated property taxes for the first year
- initial reserve fund contributions
- paperwork fees for holding deposits in trust
- builder construction-financing discharge fee
- law society transaction levy
- interest charges on day of final closing to next banking day
- education levies
- municipal levies
- transit levies
- parks levies
- regional levies
- utility hook-ups (sewer, electric and gas)
- transit passes (Toronto)
- sales taxes (HST)
- land transfer taxes.

Common closing costs in Alberta include:

- estimated property taxes for the first year
- reserve Fund contribution
- condominium fees
- homeowners' association fees
- interest charges on late closing
- utility hook-up
- municipal levies

- lawyer's fees and disbursements
- GST.

Common closing costs in British Columbia include:

- HST on purchase price
- adjustments of property taxes
- maintenance adjustment
- notary or lawyer fees
- Land Title and Survey Authority of B.C.: Property Transfer Tax
- trust administration fee
- cost of form F: Certificate of Payment
- cost of insurance certificate.

The Disclosure Statement

In most provinces, all pre-construction condominium sales must include a "disclosure statement." It is called a disclosure statement because it contains all the information a vendor (in this case, the developer) is legally required to provide.[12]

Included in the disclosure statement are the following:

- notification as to whether the land the condo is built on is leased
- the full, legal address of the property
- whether the province's new-home warranty applies to the condo
- the number of condos the developer intends to lease
- what amenities will be available during the occupancy phase
- any risks associated with older buildings being part of your condo
- fees the corporation is required to pay.

The disclosure statement has many pieces of information that are vital to your ability to get financing, resell the property in the future, and your enjoyment of the property. It's critical that your lawyer review the document for you.

There are levels of disclosure, and they can be tricky

Developers have to clearly indicate what the common elements are in their disclosure documents. The definition of "clearly" was put to the test in Ontario. The town of Essex was home to a two-tower community that was to have a shared HVAC system. While performing an audit six years after the building was registered, the condo corporations discovered they didn't own the HVAC system they were sharing. It turned out that, prior to turnover, the developer had sold the HVAC system to a company that was re-leasing it to the two buildings.

The two condo corporations took legal action against the developer, stating that the lease wasn't adequately disclosed in the disclosure documents. In the disclosure documents, the only place a lease was mentioned was a line item in the project's first-year budget for the condo facilities. The line item indicated: "HVAC Lease $34,900 – Cost of the lease for air make-up and other air handling equipment in this area." Nowhere in the disclosure statement was there any mention of the specific items leased, or the terms, or who the owner of the equipment would be. The developer argued that the owners should have known about the lease and by making a line item in the budget they satisfied their disclosure requirements. The court ruled in favour of the developer, stating that a reasonable purchaser should have known a lease was in place and the annual cost from the budget provided.

This case illustrates that a competent lawyer must go through every single line item in a contract and should take nothing for granted.

UNDISCLOSED COSTS CAN REALLY ADD UP

by Bob Aaron, *The Toronto Star*

In reviewing the disclosure statement for a new downtown project with a client last week, I pointed out that after the condominium project is registered, all of the unit owners as a group will be required to purchase from the developer:

- Up to 6 guest suites at $200,000 plus HST each, or $1,356,000, plus 8% interest over 10 years;

- A superintendent unit for $565,000 including HST, plus 8% interest over 10 years; and

- A recreation centre for an astonishing $11.3 million, repayable without interest over 10 years.

Including $860,000 in interest on the guest suites and superintendent's unit, the unit owners as a group are on the hook to the developer for a total of slightly more than $14 million during the first 10 years of ownership. My client's share of the total cost works out to $69,560, or a hit of more than 7.4% in addition to his purchase price. None of these charges were disclosed in the sales office, so when I calculated it out for my client, he was in shock at the total amount of the costs.

The following table lists important information about your contract and disclosure statement. It should be given to your lawyer. The far-right column has questions that should be used to guide the lawyer on specific items that have been agreed to. The "comments" column briefly gives space to make notes on the issues in a manner that you can clearly understand. The "page(s)" column indicates where the clauses or information can be found within the contract or disclosure documents. Once this table is completed, keep it for future reference.

KEY INFORMATION CHART ON CONTRACTS

KEY INFORMATION	COMMENT	PAGE(S)	KEY QUESTIONS DURING THE OFFER AND DISCLOSURE DOCUMENT REVIEW
Rescission ("cooling-off") Period			• How long do you have?
Price and Closing Costs			• Do you understand your financial obligations? • Are sales taxes included in the price? • Who gets sales tax rebates? • If the condo is for resale and you have to close first, do you forfeit sales tax rebates? • If the unit is for rental, are you eligible to apply for the rental residential sales tax rebate? • Are you able to cap the closing costs?

KEY INFORMATION	COMMENT	PAGE(S)	KEY QUESTIONS DURING THE OFFER AND DISCLOSURE DOCUMENT REVIEW
Maintenance/ Condo/Strata fees			• What's included in the fees? (Utilities?) • What leases does the condo board have to take on? • What purchase agreements or loans is the condo obligated to take on? • What is being leased in the unit and common areas? • When do the agreements start? (One year after closing?) • What are the terms and financial obligations of the loans and leases? • Is the reserve fund study complete? • Has the reserve fund been funded? (applicable provinces) • What are the builder's obligations toward the reserve fund? • What is the likelihood that common expenses are too high or too low as compared to similar buildings in the area?
Size			• Does your contract include room-size measurements and total square footage? • Is a measured floor plan attached? • Does the builder have the right to change size or layout?
Feature Sheet			• What provisions are in place to ensure what you are sold is what you get? • What substitutions are possible (e.g., materials or colours)? • Are all important items included in the contract that were in the marketing material or model suite (including fixtures and appliances)?

KEY INFORMATION	COMMENT	PAGE(S)	KEY QUESTIONS DURING THE OFFER AND DISCLOSURE DOCUMENT REVIEW
			• Is anything missing from the feature sheet? (The sheet is a list of maximum features, not minimum.)
Conditions			• What are the ways the contract can be cancelled by the builder? • Is the contract conditional on your ability to get financing? • What conditions need to be satisfied before the condo registers? • Under what conditions can you cancel your contract?
Commencing construction/ Completion dates			• Were there any amendments to the condo disclosure statement after the building permits were granted (BC)? • When does the developer expect the condo to be completed? • How long can they extend the completion date? • What conditions does the developer have to satisfy before they can start to build? • How long is the interim occupancy period? • How much are the occupancy costs expected to be, and will the amenities be included? • Do you have the right to pay more money on occupancy to reduce the interim occupancy fees? (i.e., unpaid interest portion)

KEY INFORMATION	COMMENT	PAGE(S)	KEY QUESTIONS DURING THE OFFER AND DISCLOSURE DOCUMENT REVIEW
Deposit Money			• Is deposit held in trust? • Does the warranty program protect the deposit money? • If so, what is the maximum? • What is the interest rate to be paid? • Are deposits for upgrades protected?
Restriction on investment options			• Can you assign the contract? If so, are there any conditions (such as 90% builder sales)? • Is there an assignment fee? • On assignment do you remain responsible for performance for the original contract if the assignee defaults? • Is there a prohibition on advertising/listing/marketing or Internet promotion, even if you have permission to resell or lease? • Do you need permission to lease your unit? • What can you do if there is an absolute prohibition on assignment and renting before closing?
Warranty			• Is your unit covered by a new-home warranty program by the builder? • If not, is there one available? • What is the track record of the warranty program for handling deficiencies (basic structural)? • How long? (1–2–7 years?) • What is covered by the warranty program? • What is not covered? • Are there manufacturers' warranties for the different components?

KEY INFORMATION	COMMENT	PAGE(S)	KEY QUESTIONS DURING THE OFFER AND DISCLOSURE DOCUMENT REVIEW
Location issues			• Can anyone build an adjacent structure that would interfere with your enjoyment or view? • Are there any warnings about the location? • Can the developer make changes to the community plan? • What is the developer obligated to complete (e.g., shared amenities or recreational areas)? • Are there any zoning issues you cannot object to? • Can you object to any noise, dust, hydro lines, vibration and smell issues from nearby buildings now and in the future?
Condo Rules			• Are there restrictions to the use of the condo (e.g., running a business)? • Is there enough parking for residents and visitors? • Are pets allowed? • What kind of modifications are you allowed to make (hot tubs/satellite dishes, etc.)? • What type of commercial uses are allowed for units at the base?

The Importance of Proposed Condo Declarations

Condo declarations are the essential documents that are used to make up a condo corporation. Condo declarations outline:

- what the condo's common elements are
- what the private elements are (balcony, locker, parking)[13]
- what the particular unit holder's share of common expenses will be

- maintenance obligations of the condo board
- terms and conditions of use of the units and common elements.[14]

What to look for:

- extra charges for a superintendent suite, management office, guest suites, recreational facilities, amenity areas, green roofs (and other energy conservation equipment)
- amortization and interest for payback of extra charges and common elements developers "sell" to condo corporations[15]
- amenities that are actually included (versus those promised in marketing material and renderings)
- permitted uses of the unit and amenities (e.g., running a home business, bicycle storage, ability to rent suite out)
- whether pets are permitted.

Hiring a Lawyer

Hiring a lawyer who is competent, practical and understands your motivations for buying a condo is essential. As you go through the process of buying a condo, you will see the value of a powerful lawyer immediately.

An experienced and knowledgeable lawyer will ask you the right questions to determine what your needs are and will have plenty of experience working with particular developers to explain—and even mitigate—the risks you take before you complete your condo purchase. So the sooner you include a powerful lawyer in your pre-construction journey, the less likely you are to make a costly mistake.

Here's a quick guide on what to look for in a lawyer:

- **Find fighters:** Find lawyers who are advocates for buyers' rights or front and centre in buyer education. Non-profit advocacy groups, such as the Canadian Condominium Institute or Canadians for Properly Built Homes, would be a great place to start. Lawyers active in these organizations are always learning and upgrading their skills to keep pace with the law.
- **Find battle-tested lawyers:** Local news is a good source of intelligence to find builder horror stories. Lawyers who are involved in these cases will have a tremendous amount of experience protecting buyer rights.

- **Look for a lawyer in a law firm that is active in the development world:** Law firms with lawyers who represent builders are a great place to look for a lawyer who understands the reason for every clause in a condo agreement. Just be sure to find out if the law firm keeps the developer as a client, to avoid conflicts of interests.

- **Look for a lawyer in a law firm that is active in condo management**: Law firms that are active in representing condo boards will have a tremendous amount of experience dealing with particular developers as they provide after-sale service.

Here are some questions to ask a prospective lawyer:

- What are your qualifications? Do you belong to any professional organizations for condos? Do you belong to any committees pertaining to condo law?

- Have you ever been involved in condo law litigation? What was the outcome?

- Do you have experience preparing agreements for builders?

- Have you ever completed a condo assignment?

- Do you have experience representing condo boards?

Be a Cautious Client

In order for your lawyer to adequately protect you, you need to be completely open with him or her. Tell your lawyer why you are buying the condo (rental, for a family member, for yourself, as a flip, etc.), and explain to them how you will use your condo (for a business, for a place to stay part time, etc.). Also tell the lawyer about any verbal promises the condo sales staff may have made to you. This will ensure your lawyer knows what's important to you, so that he or she can help to craft an agreement that serves and protects your interests.

Negotiating with Builders

Imagine being in the builder's shoes when there are hundreds of buyers and agents lining up to purchase a unit from you in a sales centre at the prices you set. If one of those purchasers or agents asks to negotiate the price, you might send them away and deal with another person waving a cheque and a pen.

Does that mean you shouldn't negotiate with a builder? Well, you can certainly try. Buyers can gain leverage in a negotiation by first understanding what's in the contract; have your lawyer review the contract and find out what the builder has offered other clients by talking with your lawyer, realtor or past purchasers. Another way to increase leverage in a negotiation is to work with an agent who does a high volume of sales for a particular developer. A developer is more likely to negotiate with a real estate agent who is bringing in a few dozen sales over an individual purchaser responsible for one.

Builder Financing

In order for a builder to receive construction financing for a project, it is required to pre-sell a certain percentage of units to purchasers. In some areas, each purchaser can be scrutinized based on how many units they have bought in one project, how large their deposit is, and if they are pre-qualified for financing today.

Since some of the major banks may be involved with construction financing for a given development, they may also have mortgage representatives in the sales centre who can offer special capped rates. In an increasing interest-rate environment, offering a capped rate, when the mortgage will not be required for a few years in the future, is an excellent option, and you may not be bound to keep these rates if a lower one is available once you are ready.

In-house banks can offer interesting credit products to finance part of the deposit without charging interest until you are required to get the mortgage. Once the mortgage is ready, the interest payments are added to the costs or to the mortgage. (See more on financing alternatives in Chapter 7.)

After You Sign the Contract

Other concerns during the cooling-off period: proof of financing, strategic clauses and ownership options. The elements of a good financial plan. Tax strategies to maximize your investment profits. Joint ventures in condo investing. Staying on top of your condo investment.

In the previous chapter, we looked at the cooling-off period, and the importance of having your lawyer go over every line of the contract with you to be sure you understand the ramifications and the costs involved. The cooling-off period is also a time when your builder will need proof of your financing, and it's the moment when you should take the feedback from your lawyer to your realtor to have any necessary contract amendments created to address your concerns. If you are not satisfied with the builder's response, you are completely within your rights to cancel the deal. Your real estate agent will also help you to negotiate strategic clauses into your agreement.

Proof of Financing

During this period you will also be required by the builder to provide proof of a financial commitment to qualify for the purchase amount. Why is this relevant when you are closing three years in the future? Well, we suppose the builder reasons that if you qualify now, then you are likely to qualify three years in the future as well. The builder will have some conditions regarding your financial commitment. The builder will likely require that your mortgage pre-approval come from a major financial institution and *not* from a mortgage broker. They would ultimately prefer the mortgage pre-qualification to come from the lender the builder has chosen to be resident in the sales centre. This "mortgage pre-qualification" is exactly that, a pre-qualification: it does not include an extensive underwriting of your mortgage loan application or detailed verification of income. However, be prepared to sign off on an agreement to have the lender do a credit check and to provide proof of income. (We look at mortgage financing in more detail in Chapter 7.)

How Your Real Estate Agent Can Help You

If you have any thoughts at all about buying a condominium without a real estate agent—reconsider! There are numerous advantages that working with a realtor can provide.

Realtors get paid very well by the builders—at no cost to you, the buyer—to represent you. Commissions range from 2.5% to 6% of the purchase price, paid by the vendor. There is usually a small portion (up to 2%) paid 60 to 90 days after the deal goes firm, which is the date when all conditions are waived (at the end of the cooling-off period). The balance of the purchase price is paid at the registration date, which is three to six months after you (or a tenant) occupy the unit.

Realtors who understand the condominium market have competitive knowledge of the marketplace and can open the door to possibilities that will get you a better deal than you could have negotiated for yourself. They can assist in negotiating clauses that builders may not give to you if you are unrepresented. They also have access to pricing and incentives that the general public does not. This is generally through special relationships the builder may have with the real estate agent's brokerage firm. Some brokerages are able to negotiate bulk purchases at discounted pricing and then pass on the savings to you, the buyer.

Realtors want to get paid! So they are very focused on getting you the qualified resources you need to buy your condominium. These resources can run the gamut from a lender or lawyer to a home inspector.

Strategic Clauses to Add to an Agreement

1. Assignment clause: This clause allows you, the buyer, to assign the agreement to a subsequent buyer without you yourself taking deed to the property. Typically builder approval is required, but this approval cannot be unreasonably withheld. There is generally an assignment fee associated with this right.

2. Capping disclosed purchaser closing costs such as:

   a. The buyer's share for the cost of a performance audit done during turnover of the unit to the purchaser;

   b. The buyer's share for the cost of a reserve fund study done during turnover;

   c. The buyer's share for the cost of a site review;

    d. The buyer's share of development and school levies charged by the municipality;

    e. The cost of installing hydro meters.

3. Include upgrades or closing incentives such as cash back at close or free locker and/or free parking.

4. Delayed or reduced deposit required. Typically many builders will have pre-written contracts of sale with the deposit structure showing a 20% down payment, so an amendment to the original agreement would be added, showing that you purchased the building with only 10% total deposit required until occupancy.

5. Allowing the rental of the unit during interim occupancy.

6. Builder rebate of interim occupancy fee in full or in part.

Most of these strategic clauses will be requested by your realtor. Always have an experienced realtor represent you!

◎ **YOU SHOULD KNOW**

Every smart real estate investor is focused on annual ROI (return on investment), which is a ratio of profit over investment per year. This ROI declines every year your investment is tied up without generating income. The worst-case scenario is having your deposit tied up for a couple of years in a project only to find out it will not be built. In Ontario, Tarion has listened to the complaints of buyers concerned over developers using their purchases as a way of exploring a site's feasibility: builders can use pre-sales to test whether or not to go firm on the purchase of a site that they have optioned for development. Builders can also pre-sell while the development is still contingent on zoning changes being approved by local residents and the city; some projects never get that approval, and don't move ahead, meaning that all those buyers have their deposits returned—sometimes years after first making those deposits. For this reason, since June 30, 2008, Tarion now requires Ontario builders to disclose any contingent zoning approvals or sales numbers to be reached before going ahead with the project.

Ownership Structure and Other Considerations

During the cooling-off period, the developer will likely allow name changes and other material additions that stem from your consultation with your lawyer. These can include ownership structure, who needs to be on title to qualify for financing, and many other considerations. In this section, we will discuss legal and tax implications. It is important to get legal advice and qualified tax advice when considering these options.

When purchasing a condo, the buyer has several options for how they plan to structure the ownership. The most common options are as follows:

1. registered in one buyer's personal name

2. two owners registered as joint tenants versus tenancy in common

3. registered in the name of a child of legal age (usually 18)

4. registered in the name of a corporation.

Each of these options has some pros and cons that we will examine.

Registered in One Buyer's Personal Name

This is the simplest of all scenarios as it requires no additional legal work or costs. Many buyers choose to go for this option because they want to keep things simple and believe this is the best course of action. It is important, though, to distinguish between a principal or primary residence and an investment.

When a piece of real estate is purchased and is not the buyer's primary residence, there will be taxation implications down the road. The home in which you reside, known as your primary residence, is exempt from capital gains tax upon its sale. Any other properties you own are classified as investments and as such are subject to income taxes. For example, any appreciation in the value of your condo from the time of purchase to the time of sale will be classified as capital gains and must be declared in the year the property is sold. Half of this gain is subject to your marginal income tax rate in that year.

As an example, let's say that in 2005 you purchased an investment condo for $200,000. You kept this unit for a few years and in 2010 decided to sell it. You did so, receiving $250,000. Your capital gain is $50,000. If your personal income in 2010 is $60,000 and you live in Ontario, your marginal tax rate is approximately 30%. This means that for every dollar you earn over $60,000, the government will tax $.30. Only half of your $50,000 gain is subject to taxation so in this scenario the taxes owed on the capital gain would be $7,500 ($25,000 x .30). This leaves you with a "profit" of $42,500.

The above example does not include any real estate commissions or legal fees, but gives us a good idea of the tax implications of personal investing. Obviously, no one enjoys paying taxes, but there are some benefits to this scenario. If the unit was rented out during that five-year period, the condo would have generated rental income for the owner. Although this income is also subject to tax, the government allows investors to write off any expenses associated with the property against any income it generates. This means that if repairs are required, or you are paying interest on a mortgage for the unit, you can subtract this from any income you are earning. In this manner, many investors are able to effectively "write off" most of the income and thereby may avoid having to pay any income tax, or at least pay very little tax on the rental income. Depending on your marginal tax rate and the rental income you are receiving from a tenant, this can be a huge financial benefit to an investor.

Two Owners Registered as Joint Tenants versus Tenancy-in-Common

With this registration option, an investor is usually purchasing the condo along with another investor or partner. Tenancy-in-common is different from joint tenancy in a very important way. If a property is purchased jointly, often between two spouses, each individual does not own a specific percentage of the property—they simply own 100% of it together. This means that if one person were to pass away, the property would automatically belong in its entirety to the remaining individual. If that same property were to be held as tenancy-in-common, each individual would own a specific percentage of the property. This can be a 50/50 arrangement, but can also be any other combination of percentages. This would mean that if one person passed away, their percentage of the unit would not automatically go to the other owner, but would instead become part of their estate and be treated accordingly. In situations where investors are purchasing a condo as investment partners or joint-venture partners rather than romantic or familial partners, it is usually advisable to go tenancy-in-common, as this structure protects each party's estate and financial interests. It goes without saying that seeking legal advice before choosing a final option is always a wise decision.

As far as income tax implications in this scenario, it is very similar to sole ownership. The difference would be that the gains, expenses and income are all shared among the parties rather than simply falling on one person.

Registered in the Name of a Child of Legal Age (usually 18)

This option appeals to many potential investors because they view it as a way to manage their estate, minimize taxation and achieve better tax planning overall. This can be true, but one needs to be very wary of raising red flags with the government—especially when the child has little or no income of their own. Generally speaking, investment properties are purchased with a combination of down payment and mortgage. If a property is being purchased in the name of a child, the mortgage will also be in the name of the child. Unless the child is working and earning enough income to support this mortgage, this could prove to be a deal-breaker for the lender. Even if the parent will be making the mortgage payments, the lender will generally require the child to qualify on his or her own. This might be avoided or rectified by having the parent co-sign, but again this would have to be looked at on a case-by-case basis. If legal and financial obstacles can be overcome, a benefit to making a child the legal owner of the condo is that a Land Transfer Tax rebate is offered to first-time buyers. A child can qualify for such a rebate, and if he or she is a majority owner, this essentially eliminates the LTT as a closing cost, which can save you thousands of dollars.

Another advantage for first-time home buyers is the new non-refundable tax credit called the Homebuyers Tax Credit. For more details go to the Canadian Revenue Agency (CRA) website.

Something that many parents do not consider when considering purchasing an asset in the name of their child is what the future holds. If your child is married (or marries at a later date) and then goes through marital breakdown, any assets held in their name could become a part of the legal battle, thereby putting your condo investment at risk. A prenuptial agreement would protect the asset from the other spouse. Perhaps the child will have financial or legal problems in the future, including bankruptcy or lawsuits. This could also jeopardize the ownership of the condo. Although no one wants to think about bad things happening to their child, a savvy investor does not make decisions based on emotions, but rather on realities and rationalities.

Although there are some definite potential downsides to this registration option, the possible benefit is reduced taxes. This will occur if your child is in a lower tax bracket than you are, which is often the case. It can also be a great way to "save" for your child while potentially teaching them the value of smart real estate investing. Getting them involved in the real estate investing process from a young age can certainly be a beneficial thing, as it teaches financial literacy and the value of taking calculated investment risks.

Registered in the Name of a Corporation

This final option requires a little more work than the previous options we have examined. A corporation is a legal entity which exists independently of its shareholders. It can continue beyond its original owner's lifespan; it files its own tax return; and it can be bought and sold. Some condo buyers choose to use a corporation to purchase their properties. The primary reason for doing this is to shield the individual from any potential legal problems that might result from owning the property, and it also may potentially shield the shareholder from any legal proceedings that may occur with the individual. It is important to note that if mortgage financing is obtained, in order to have complete liability protection, the personal covenant or "guarantee" of the corporation's director should not be given to the lender. In other words, the bank must be satisfied to hold the equity in the property and just the property, in exchange for the mortgage outstanding.

As an example, Mr. X uses a corporation to purchase five condo units. The units are rented out for a number of years and eventually are shown to contain harmful mould. The tenants decide to sue their landlord, believing that this mould has potentially caused a negative health impact on their families. Because the units are held in the name of a corporation, Mr. X's personal assets and family assets are protected from this lawsuit. He has shielded his other assets, and only those assets belonging to the corporation are now at risk if the tenants are successful with their lawsuit.

Obviously any legal matter is more complex than the above example, but this gives us a good overview of why a corporation can be a useful tool in limiting liability. The downside of using a corporation for real estate investing is two-fold. There is a cost to setting up and keeping a corporation. This involves the initial legal set-up fees as well as the ongoing fees associated with filing separate annual income tax returns, bookkeeping and preparation of financial statements. Some investors see this additional cost and work as being too high to justify the benefits. Holding the condo in a corporation eliminates the Principal Residence Capital Gain Exemption. Furthermore, the income derived is likely income from business (100% taxable) versus income from property (50% taxable).

Another disadvantage is that the taxation rate for the passive business of rental property is the highest corporate tax rate, which far exceeds the highest personal marginal tax rate. This can be changed if the corporation becomes an Active Business Corporation, which is defined under the Canada Revenue Agency as having more than five full-time employees dedicated to running the real estate business, which has a tax rate of 21% for the first $200,000 of income and a $500,000 capital gains exemption for the shareholders. These benefits show that a sophisticated real estate investor could benefit from using corporations.

Corporations also cannot obtain high-ratio financing from insurers such as CMHC, Genworth or Canada Guaranty for condominiums.

We have looked at four different condo registration options. Each one has some benefits and some downsides. We strongly advise any investor to carefully consider all alternatives and seek out legal advice before making a final decision. The easiest and least expensive option is always appealing, but is not always the best option.

What to Expect from the HST

As of July 1, 2010, a harmonized sales tax (HST), combining the federal GST of 5% with the provincial tax rate (varying in each province), is now applied to new condominiums purchased directly from the builder.

HST rebate programs are in place as follows.

In Nova Scotia, the provincial portion of the HST qualifies for a rebate. Contact Service Nova Scotia and Municipal Relations.

In British Columbia and Ontario, there are programs in place for a provincial portion of the HST to be rebated. There is a provincial "transitional" rebate if at least 10% of the construction was completed by July 1, 2010.

The maximum Ontario new housing rebate amount that is available is $24,000.

The maximum British Columbia new housing rebate amount that is available is $26, 250.

In most instances the builder includes the HST in the price of the condo and requires that you sign over the rebates to the builder. In this case, the builder has you sign an affidavit that you as the owner are occupying the condo, to allow for the maximum rebate allowable. There are rebate programs in place for rental condos, but for lesser amounts, which would require the builder to collect additional HST from you at close.

Be warned that your intentional use of the condo will have tax implications and be sure to consult with a tax professional on how to handle your HST filings. For more information online go to the CRA website.

 TIP

Transition to HST in 2010 affects profitability

When the government implemented the new harmonized sales tax in Ontario, it had a very real impact on the cost of maintaining a condo. Whereas in the old system, with separate GST and PST, services were exempt from provincial sales tax, overnight this changed. Because condo maintenance fees are partially used to pay utility bills and service contracts, the additional cost of

8% is being passed along to condo owners. Although it may not immediately translate to a full 8% increase, it will certainly have an impact. This means that the average condo owner who owns a 700-square-foot unit with $0.45 per square foot maintenance fees will now be paying approximately $25 more per month. Although these numbers do not seem large, as an investor you should be concerned: when costs go up without a corresponding revenue increase, profitability decreases and rates of return go down. The HST is a strong reminder to real estate investors and owners that surprises can happen at any time, so a thorough understanding of carrying costs and the overall financial picture of your units is vital in order to avoid slipping into negative cash-flow territory.

The Big Picture: Real Estate and Financial Planning

Like any investment decision, it is important for real estate investors to look at the overall bigger picture in their investment plan. Unfortunately, most investment counselling occurs at the bank, where topics of RRSPs, mutual funds and GICs are the only topics of discussion. Rarely, if ever, is there a discussion about "non-traditional" elements of a financial plan, including real estate.

The Elements of a Good Financial Plan

1. Budgeting

A wise investor knows that even with a good tenant, surprises can occur and a plan for managing potential monthly shortfalls is imperative. A tenant can leave unexpectedly; condo maintenance fees can increase or one-time levies can be assessed; repairs to the unit may be required; mortgage rates can increase. All of these eventualities need to be considered and planned for in a budget.

2. Saving and investing

Most Canadians tend to think about mutual funds and savings accounts when they think about investing and saving. Owning an asset that appreciates and/or provides a regular stream of rental income is another way of investing. Rates of return on real estate have historically been equal to or greater than many other investment options that exist. Additionally, most real estate investors are only paying for a portion of their investment upfront (via the down payment) and finance the remainder (through a mortgage). Their return on their initial investment is greatly magnified due to leverage.

Let's look at an example of the power of leverage.

Bob is an avid stock investor who has $40,000 to invest. He invests it in a great stock that proves to be the right move, because in one year the stock has appreciated 50%.

Jill is a real estate investor with $40,000 to invest as a down payment. She finds a property, buys it for $160,000 and uses her cash as down payment. The property appreciates in one year by 50%.

Who received the highest return on his or her investment?

Bob sold his stock for $60,000. With an investment of $40,000 he received $20,000 profit, which is a 50% cash-on-cash return.

Jill leveraged her money, so after selling her investment property for $240,000, paying mortgage payments of $6,000 over the year, plus paying property taxes of $3,000 and paying off the mortgage, which has a balance of $115,000, she nets cash proceeds of $116,000, which is a 290% cash-on-cash return!

The banks are the best investors in the world, so why not follow? What asset will they lend you up to 95% of its value to buy? There is only one asset that falls into that category: real estate.

Having real estate within your portfolio can be a great way to save for retirement and plan for your estate. Because your property can continue to grow in value until you retire, it can become an integral part of your retirement savings. It is also an asset that will form a part of your estate and therefore can be willed to your desired beneficiaries.

Real estate is a great way to diversify existing investments, as it is very different from stocks, bonds and GICs, and will respond differently to market conditions than other investment vehicles. Real estate is a strong asset class and should always be considered within a financial planning context. This will ensure that you as an investor are giving the necessary thought to how it will fit into your overall plan and can then serve to strengthen your portfolio and help you work toward being financially better off.

3. Insurance

A good financial plan includes the use of many types of insurance.

- Default insurance for your mortgage. This is the realm of your mortgage broker, who will get your mortgage written with guidelines from

Canada's three mortgage default insurance providers: Genworth, CMHC and Canada Guaranty.

- Title insurance to protect any title defects. Your lawyer will give you advice as to why you would want to get title insurance. The most obvious reason is that there may be a "defect" in the legal title, at no fault of your own, and now that you are the owner, the fault has been found. Examples include properties incorrectly registered with name errors, or defined incorrectly and carried through for many years.

- Condominium common element insurance. Included in your maintenance fee is insurance against perils that affect your common elements.

- Content and liability insurance to protect your unit finishes in case of fire or flood and any injury to residents or guests. There is also vacancy insurance for lost rent during the repair time.

- Life insurance is a great estate planning tool to pay for deemed disposition costs of assets to be transferred to beneficiaries. It is also a solid tool to make your investment properties both mortgage-free and cash-flowing assets for your beneficiaries.

- Disability insurance protects you in case you lose your ability to earn income due to injury.

4. Managing your credit

Making credit work for you is a powerful tool, so understanding your Equifax and TransUnion credit bureaus and ensuring all errors are fixed and all information is reported accurately is important to your financial health.

Preparing to qualify for mortgage financing requires an understanding of your gross debt service ratio (GDS) and your total debt service ratio (TDSR). GDS is your total monthly payments of principal, interest, taxes and condo fees divided by your annual income. TDS is your total monthly payments to cover all of the items in GDS plus all other debts, divided by your annual income. Generally, only 50% of the condo fees have to be included in the equation.

Lenders will look at a very comprehensive grid of factors, including your ratios along with your Beacon Score, otherwise known as your Equifax FICO credit score, to determine the highest purchase price you could qualify for. It's important to keep your credit in good standing to avoid jeopardizing your condo closing due to an inability to obtain financing, since closing may occur years after the contract is signed.

5. Tax management

Canada Revenue Agency qualifies income upon the sale of a property to be business income (100% taxable) if the seller intended its use be for profitable gain, like a contractor purchasing a property to flip. The income becomes a capital gain (50% taxable advantageous) if the seller has owned a property that has been tenanted. The gain becomes tax exempt (most advantageous) if the property was owner-occupied (a principal residence) when sold.

These are some of the factors that CRA looks at to determine what income type applies:

1. the intention of the taxpayer at the time of purchase

2. feasibility of the intention

3. geographical location and zones use

4. extent to which the intention was carried out

5. evidence that the intention changed after purchase

6. the nature of the business of the taxpayer

7. how the property was financed

8. length of ownership

9. other owners and their occupation

10. factors which motivated the sale

11. evidence the taxpayer had dealt extensively in real estate.[1]

For example, let's say that you purchased a condo in Ottawa and intended to occupy the unit, but your company transferred you to Toronto. In this case you failed test 3 above and will likely pay at least 50% capital gain upon sale. If you obtained open financing, which is financing that has no penalty if prepaid substantially or paid off any time during its term (failed test 7), had flipped 10 other condos like this within one year of ownership (failed test 8), and/or are a registered real estate agent in Ontario (failed test 6), then CRA will conclude that you are likely in the business of condo flipping, and all the income will be 100% taxable as business income.

If you are trying to keep your investment proceeds from being treated as business income (100% taxable), there are strategies you can use. It is important to note, however, that there is much case law in this tax area and there is no one single factor that determines the taxation of the proceeds of sale. However, it is important to *document everything* to prove your case:

- Keep utility bills, cable bills and your driver's license to demonstrate that you, as the owner, occupied the condo.

- Obtain five-year financing, but go variable with the option to lock in, so the penalty is maximum three months' interest, rather than facing a potential huge interest rate differential penalty.

- Obtain a one-year lease or longer with a tenant, showing your intention to hold onto the property for a reasonably long time, and then document why you decided to sell in the middle of the lease.

- Properly document your reasons to sell the property after you bought it to keep as a rental. Personal reasons to sell an asset would be separation, divorce or sudden financial stress.

- Buy an investment condo within a one-hour drive of where you live.

- Hold the condo personally.

- Keep copies of your rental ads to prove your intention to tenant the property and the cost of doing business to keep it as a rental.

By comparison to other investment vehicles, pre-construction condos have some distinct tax advantages. Once the purchase agreement is signed, you now have what is essentially *an option* to purchase a condominium in the future at a pre-determined rate. Since this is an option, its gain is un-taxable until realized. In other words, every year, as your option grows in value (as the condominium grows in potential market value), this potential gain is not required to be reported to CRA, nor are taxes payable. So, with pre-construction investing, the gains are tax-deferred, which is in essence interest-free money that you are investing at compounded returns.

Compare that tax situation to others. With a REIT (Real Estate Investment Trust), as the REIT buys and sells real estate holdings within the trust, the capital gains are taxable every year, even if you have not sold your REIT units. With bonds, as you earn interest income, the income is fully taxable in that year. Mutual funds have MERs (management-expense ratios) that are about 3% of the fund; this amount is used to pay fund managers, and it is paid from the fund every year, thereby reducing the investable funds to compound.

6. Estate-planning strategies

According to a Royal Bank of Canada report from 2007, "Fifty-seven per cent of baby boomers in Canada have or expect an inheritance, in what is projected to be the largest ever inter-generational transfer of wealth." In addition, "Sixty-one per cent of those expect to give money—during their lifetime—to their own children," the report said, "adding that more than two-thirds of those who intend to pass it on early say they want to see their children enjoy their lives."[2]

How can parents transfer wealth to their children with a new condominium purchase? Here are some strategies.

The first strategy is: Own the condominium in joint tenancy with a child of legal age so that, upon your death, the condo becomes the asset of the child.

The advantages of such an arrangement are as follows:

- It simplifies the administration of an estate.

- It minimizes probate fees to the court to administer a will.

- It ensures the asset goes to the intended person without contestation or interference.

Some possible disadvantages are:

- Loss of control, as the parent cannot, on his or her own, change inheritance in the future.

- Exposing the asset to the child's creditors and/or ex-spouse in the case of a future marital breakdown (a pre-nuptial contract should be insisted upon).

The second strategy is: Freezing the estate to arrange for the appreciation of a property to accrue to the children while the parent is still alive, within a corporation, so that there will be less taxable growth to be taxed in the parent's estate. (You will need the services of a qualified lawyer to set this up.) Here's how it works.

The parent owns all the Class A common shares of a corporation that owns the condominium. The estate freeze occurs when the common shares are converted to preferred retractable (redeemable at the option of the holder) shares and new Class B common shares are issued to the children. The preferred shares will have the same market value of the Class A shares, but have dividends at a fixed amount for reasonable return preferred over the common shares. The "reasonableness" test is to qualify under CRA rules and will be created with your tax consultant.

Upon the death of the parent, the preferred shares would be entitled to the fixed redemption value plus any unpaid dividends. As a result, the children have the Class B shares for the corporation that owns the condominium with Class B share dividends that have not been distributed, thus no taxation or probate fees.

As an example, let's say Mr. Smith wanted to pass on $1 million today to his children, Mike and Sue, but wants to maintain control. Mr. Smith bought three pre-construction condominiums. He signed the contracts in 2008 in the name of ABC Corporation for a pre-construction price of $1 million, which took title to all three condos when they were completed in 2011. At the date of registration the condos were valued at $1.2 million and Mr. Smith converted his Class A shares, valued at $1.2 million, to retractable preferred shares with a nominal dividend. Mr. Smith also retained voting rights to maintain control. Class B shares were issued to Mike and Sue, valued at one dollar each.

When 20 years have passed, Mr. Smith dies and his estate has preferred shares valued at $1.2 million that are subject to disposition taxation; however, the condominiums are now worth a total of $4 million as of 2031. Thus Mike and Sue have Class B shares worth a total of $2.8 million with no probate fees and no taxes to pay.

So Mr. Smith has retained control of the condos until his death and passed on the future growth of the condos, tax free, to his children. This is a perfect example in a perfect world, so it is important to talk to your tax and legal professional before attempting this type of estate freeze.

7. Retirement planning

Deriving income from long-term property holdings versus an RRSP can be a preferred strategy: whereas mutual fund performance can be uncertain, there will always be tenants who need somewhere to rent. And while the tenants pay your rent, your mortgage will be paid down. Ideally, once the tenants have paid off your mortgage, you would be into retirement and the rent will be primarily cash-flow.

Understanding Joint Ventures in Real Estate

You may own an investment property or two and take care of all the repairs, marketing, tenant selection, legal structuring, financing and improvements. The problem with a "one-man show" is that the individual quickly suffers from restricted cash, mortgage financing, time and even profits, since he is working from a smaller portfolio.

The purpose of a joint venture is to allow individuals to specialize in their roles while allowing the business of real estate investing to grow. The business of joint venturing can be scalable to raising lots of capital, investing in different geographies and having profitable investments in different property types. All parties to a joint venture bring a portion of these ingredients to the deal:

1. time

2. expertise

3. money

4. mortgage qualification.

Finder

There are in essence three roles in joint ventures. The first role is the finder, who is the individual that has found the property, contracted for the property and carried out due diligence. The finder also has the expertise to assess the quality of the investment. The finder is usually the deal scout or real estate agent who understands the neighbourhood or type of investment. The finder has expertise in negotiating the contract, financing and terms of ownership. The finder usually produces an agreement of purchase and sale for the joint-venture partners to review, in addition to market data and financing options.

Manager

The second role is the joint-venture manager. The manager is the property manager, or someone who manages the property manager, and the financial manager. The property management deals with tenants by selecting them, collecting rent from them, procuring bids for any necessary repairs and advertising for new tenants. The financial management includes the creation and reporting of the income and expenses for the joint venture, including filing for income taxes and HST. The financial manager deposits rent cheques, reviews the utility bills, property taxes and repair bills, and makes sure payment is made.

Investor

The third role in a joint venture is the investor. The investor will come up with the deposit for the agreement of purchase of sale and the down payment for the purchase, and participate in the mortgage qualification.

The investor usually plays a more passive role and is dependent on the expertise of the other two parties of the joint venture.

Among joint-venture partners, the percentage of contribution, ownership, distribution and responsibility is negotiable. An example on one side of the spectrum is a parent assisting a grown child to buy his or her first house. Let's use the example of a mother and a son. The mother can fulfill the role of the investor by providing the down payment and co-signing on the mortgage. The son can fulfill the role of the manager, responsible for paying the mortgage, utility bills and repairs. Additionally, the son can also be the finder who works with his realtor to find the property that he wants to live in. The requirements for cash calls on major repairs may be the full responsibility of the son or the son may make a cash call to Mom to pay for special assessments or replace an appliance, because it would be in both of their interests to protect the value of the asset.

The parties may have an arrangement that, upon the sale of the condo, Mom would get her down payment back plus half the profit from the sale. If the son chooses to replace the carpet with hardwood and upgrade the kitchen cupboards to modern glass and the countertops to granite, the additional $20,000 that he invested in the condo would be paid back to him upon the sale before the profit is distributed. Mom may require that a separate bank account be kept and funded by both parties 50–50 every year in the amount of $2,000, which will be the repair fund for the property, and Mom may require a review of the repair quote if more than $2,000 is being paid out of the account for the repairs.

Legal Forms of Ownership in a Joint Venture

Just as with sole ownership, joint-venture ownership can be structured in a variety of ways, with various pros and cons for each.

Joint Tenancy and Tenancy-in-common

The parties of a joint venture could both be on title in the form of joint tenancy or tenancy-in-common. Joint tenancy is equal ownership where, upon the death of one party, that joint tenant's interest automatically goes to the other joint tenant. The liability of the mortgage is "joint and several," meaning that both parties are responsible for the mortgage qualification and the mortgage liability.

Tenants-in-common own a property in a percentage of interest, and upon the death of a tenant-in-common, the percentage of ownership goes to their estate. The liability is again joint and several. The percentage of ownership interest can be sold to any third party, unless the joint venture contract states that the other joint venture party has the first right of refusal.

Partnership

The above forms of ownership can be carried out by individuals, who are sole proprietors or legal corporate entities. These two entities can form a partnership, which is a legal entity that must be registered in each province in which the partnership is doing business, and is an entity that must file taxes for the partnership in addition to the individuals. Also, all cash distributions of gain or loss must be passed on to each individual. The danger of such a partnership is that one party can sign cheques or make commitments on behalf of the partnership and the liability of the partnership is joint and several, meaning that all partners are liable for the commitments or liabilities of an individual partner.

Limited Partnerships

Limited partnerships are a sophisticated form of ownership of a property. Limited partners are simply money partners that play a passive role and are only liable for their investment. There can be many limited partners, but there can only be one general partner. The general partner can be a person or a corporation that is the active manager and owner of the property and has liability beyond its capital investment. Limited partnerships that raise money through many unrelated parties are selling securities and thus must register an Offering Memorandum with the provincial securities-regulating body. Those that sell these securities in Ontario are called Exempt Market Dealers.

Bare Trustee

What happens if an investor does not want to be on title or on the mortgage for various reasons, including confidentiality and limited liability beyond their investment? In this case, the property and mortgage qualification would be carried out by the individual in the joint venture who will hold the property "in trust" for the joint venture. This individual is known as a Bare Trustee. The individual has full title ownership and is on the mortgage. An investor will hold ownership interest in the property by contract with the Bare Trustee, which can be registered on title in the form of a Caution. In the Ontario Land Registry, a Caution requires that all parties make themselves aware of the Caution registered before the mortgage is refinanced or the ownership interest is transferred. Another way for an investor to register their ownership interest is in the form of an equity-participating mortgage registered on title.

Corporations

A corporation is a very practical Bare Trustee. Although a person can also be a Bare Trustee, it is difficult to shape the person's rules, motivation or ethics. A corporation can be completely divisible and an agreement can be drawn up to guide its "behaviours" and rules. The corporation has share ownership in the form of joint-venture percentage interest. The joint-venture agreement can be in the form of a shareholders' agreement. Shares can be held by persons and corporations. The benefits of corporations holding property are limited liability of shareholders; the privacy of the shareholders; and the separate accounting, banking and tax filing that are required. The disadvantages of corporations are the additional paperwork and costs to maintain the records and file taxes. This form of joint-venture vehicle is for sophisticated parties and mainly commercial properties with sophisticated commercial tenancies. A potential issue for an investor is that shell corporations that are formed for the purpose of holding property have no credit history and require shareholders to give their personal "covenant" for the liability of the mortgage.

Certificate of Independent Legal Advice

All parties to a joint venture must, without exception, receive legal advice to completely understand the implications of the joint-venture relationship and agreement. In the courts of law, the unsophisticated investor can weasel out of an agreement by claiming ignorance, and a sophisticated party, such as a realtor or manager of a joint venture, would be liable for releasing the unsophisticated party, unless the investor received independent legal advice.

Cash Calls, Property Reserve Bank Account and Operating Account

The financial manager will deposit the rental income and pay the expenses of running the property. To prevent additional cash calls beyond the initial capital invested, the joint venture may require that a reserve be funded with a minimum of 12 months' gross rental income before there are distributions to joint-venture parties. Controls must be placed on the way funds are being spent by the financial manager; for example, all joint-venture parties must sign off on any expenditure over $1,000.

What if a cash call is made and an investor does not fund within a reasonable time? In that case, other investors may be able to acquire additional ownership interest by funding the required capital.

Reporting, Notifications, Distributions and Sale

Modes of communication should be properly defined either by mail, email, fax or phone. The frequency of accounting, investor relations and property management communication by the financial manager should be agreed upon, giving investors comfort that the property is being taken care of and all needs are being met to protect and grow their investment.

Distributions of rental income, proceeds from refinancing or proceeds from sale of the property are definitely something to celebrate and bring comfort to investors. Sale of ownership interest should give current investors the first right of refusal to retain ownership within the original ownership group.

Staying on Top of Your Investment

So you have just bought your condo and it has gone firm by virtue of the passing of the cooling-off period. Your agent says thank you and you go on with your everyday life. But this is just the beginning of your condo purchasing experience. Smart condo buyers know that their home is their biggest investment, so they treat it that way. There is no better way to keep on top of your investment than by building a network that supports your efforts, and this is how you do it:

1. Maintain communication with your agent on new projects and "word on the street" of projects being sold or completed by your builder or their competition.

2. Get prices from new projects as they get released and compare the price per square foot to your own unit.

3. Watch for the kind of amenities being offered in the new projects.

4. Note local improvements such as new public transit or expanded transit; new superstructures such as bridges, highways and airports; or community projects such as schools, libraries, recreation centres and parks.

5. Be aware of unionized trades going on strike or financial market downturns that could potentially freeze development.

Monitor your municipal development activity by checking your municipality's website on a frequent basis. Look for "development applications." It is important to monitor upcoming projects coming to market; this information may even tell you what is happening with your project behind the scenes.

6. Visit the condo development site and keep in mind the milestones. Not surprisingly, if the average person visits the site a month before the scheduled date for roof completion on a 50-floor building and sees that excavation has just begun, she can be fairly certain that the project is not on schedule. Milestones like this for "Tentative Occupancy" to become "Firm Occupancy" are observable by the average purchaser.

7. Get to know other agents who are familiar with the project. These agents are usually well represented online and have clients who have purchased in the project. These clients may have purchased before you at a VIP launch or even through friends and family introductions. You will likely learn more by calling the realtor, as their purchaser has strict restrictions preventing the marketing of their assignment; however, the realtor can market to his own database of clients or prospects on behalf of the original buyer (legally known as the assignor).

8. Get to know the insider agents that have assignments and enquire on what the assignment values are going for. This network will always be valuable for your own condo. For example, when you are ready to assign your unit, it is the other realtors who attended the VIP launch that may have waiting buyers, as well as your own agent. The market value you assign your condo may be done with the advice of other agents who have done a few assignments in the building. They can help you gauge how high or low assignment prices are for your condo project.

Getting the Keys

The risk of delayed occupancy: what rights do you have and what rights does the builder have? The pre-delivery inspection: what can possibly go wrong with a brand-new unit? Understanding new-home warranty programs. Should you consider "assigning" the unit rather than taking possession?

When buying a condo pre-construction, especially a high-rise, you must always plan for delays. Before you start planning to refinance your other investment properties to get the equity needed to close on the new purchase, you had better understand builder delays and your rights.

Delays can result from many factors, such as a builder experiencing lower-than-expected pre-sales; problems the builder may have with financing or finalizing condominium residence architecture, design and master plans; and delays in trades and materials. *A delayed condo project does not mean it is cancelled.* Delays can occur at any time during the life cycle of the project, including design, pre-construction, during construction/building and at completion. Examples of such delays include zoning change applications being delayed due to a local ratepayer association's objections. Final closings can be extended at the municipal level due to the backlog of applications that have occurred lately as more and more condominiums are being built. A definitive timeline will be re-set, although it will mean a later move-in date.

In most agreements of purchase and sale, as well as in disclosure statements, a developer can delay a project for a certain time period without the consent of the buyer for any reason. After that period, how you deal with a delayed move-in date depends on your province and the terms stipulated in your agreements. Ensure that your lawyer completes the key information chart in Chapter 5, so you can find the information easily within your contract and discuss it with your lawyer when a delay occurs.

CASE STUDY

Real Estate Development Act, British Columbia
According to the Real Estate Development Act (REDMA) of British Columbia,
a developer must amend its disclosure statement to advise purchasers of a

delay in the building's completion date, and this notice has to delivered to the client. Otherwise, the developers' agreements with purchasers could be in jeopardy.

In the case of *Chameleon Talent Inc. v. Sandcastle Holdings Ltd.* (2009 BCSC) the British Columbia Supreme Court held that an agreement of purchase and sale between the buyer (Chameleon) and the developer (Sandcastle Holdings) was no longer enforceable because the developer failed to amend its disclosure statement properly. The original disclosure statement contained estimated dates for issuance of building permits, commencement of construction and completion of construction, all of which were missed. The developer then sent the client an amended disclosure statement, once it received building permits (also required by REDMA), where the dates for commencement of construction and completion of construction were not updated. According to the courts, this disclosure statement failed to disclose a material fact and as a result is unenforceable. The courts ruled that the deposit must be returned to the buyer.

 TALES FROM THE TRENCHES

Leslieville, Toronto
by Marc, condo purchaser

I bought a condo in an up-and-coming neighbourhood in Toronto in 2008. I loved the layout; it had lots of windows and high ceilings. The original move-in date was supposed to be October 2009, and as of now (2011), the builder still hasn't submitted the required paperwork to get approvals. I purchased the unit for $364,000, and my realtor estimates it's worth about $420,000. The developer offered to take my deposit back, but now prices for other units have increased, and I would lose my potential $56,000 in profits.

The Pre-Delivery Inspection (PDI)

For most buyers, being called for your PDI is a time of great emotion. Speaking from experience, we know that these emotions can cloud your judgement if you are feeling low on disappointment or too high on excitement. This is why you must become informed and keep a level head.

Before you get the keys to your unit, a customer service representative (CSR) for the builder will contact you to book a walk-through of your unit for a PDI. The approach of the PDI is a little different than a home inspection, for two reasons:

1. One, you may still be entering a construction site. Trades may be working and could be coming in and out of the hallways.

2. Two, you have to be extremely detailed-oriented about noting any and all imperfections. If you have limited time, don't focus on items already covered by your warranty. It may seem counter-intuitive not to check that the lights work (for instance), but the reason is that if you miss a chip, scratch or dent during the PDI because you were too busy playing with the electrical box, you may be blamed by the builder for causing the damage during your move in because you didn't mention it during your PDI. (See more on warranties in the next section.)

The objective of this first walk-through is for the CSR to show you how the condominium unit actually is, compared to what was promised, and document any requirements needed to get it to the promised condition. The CSR will show you how the heating and cooling system works, show you how to enter your unit with the security system and electronic fob, and acquaint you with the building. The CSR should also begin noting any deficiencies.

During the PDI it is important not to have a false sense of security that the builder's CSR will make note of all deficiencies. Be prepared by bringing in your features list and go through every item. If pressed for time by the CSR, focus on items that are not covered by the performance guidelines.

⚫ TALES FROM THE TRENCHES

Unit Not Ready

by J. Wo, condo purchaser, Toronto[2]

I've waited three-and-a-half years to move into my condo and today I had my pre-delivery inspection. I was so happy and excited to see the unit that I almost overlooked some of the glaring omissions in the unit. Now that the rose-coloured glasses have come off, I am wondering if it is fair to show me a unit that really isn't move-in ready? Here are the major things that are missing or still to be installed: fridge, kitchen faucet, running water (cannot test dishwasher, toilet, shower, etc.), bathroom sink, bathroom mirror, and the walk-in closet railing/shelves. The ventilation system does not work either.

Of course all of these were noted by the inspector and written down on the PDI form. But my move-in date is in seven days and I sincerely hope all of these major items are fixed before then!

Before your PDI:

- Ask if you could bring an extra set of eyes (a family member, realtor or inspector).
- Go over your schedules in your agreement to determine what is supposed to be included in your unit.
- Bring a high-powered light to shine against all surfaces.
- Bring a list of upgrades paid for.
- Bring your colour chart.
- Bring an electrical outlet tester to test for outlets that are not grounded, have reverse polarity or other electrical defects. This can be bought at almost any hardware store.
- Bring a marble to test out uneven floor or counter-top surfaces. This is especially important for high-rise condominiums that have poured concrete floors, which may be uneven.
- Bring sticky circle dots from an office supply store to mark your deficiencies.
- Study your floor plan.
- Temper your expectations—expect to be disappointed.
- Read over your warranty provider's construction performance guidelines.
- Bring a Swiffer and a wet buffing cloth to clean dusty surfaces (dust can hide cracks, scratches and chips).
- Print out your checklist.

During the inspection:

- Remove any protective packaging on finishes (plastic on carpets, appliances and counter tops).
- Use the Swiffer to clean the non-carpeted surfaces of dust.
- Place stickers on all deficiencies and note them on your floor plans for your record.
- Note whether any items are incomplete, damaged or missing.

ENTRANCE	OK	NEEDS REPAIR	INCOMPLETE	MISSING	DESCRIPTION	KEY POINTS
Doors, closets						Look for rough surfaces, discolorations, flaking, chips, cracks, splits, dents, scratches or any other imperfections. Do the doors operate properly? Are the doors warping? Are there raw wood edges? Are the kick plates installed? Are there any paint or plaster flaws (e.g., hinges) painted over? Are the closets the size you expected?
Walls, trim						Look for rough surfaces, discolorations, flaking, chips, cracks, splits, dents, scratches or any other imperfections. Are the walls out of plumb? Are the surfaces uneven? Have the trim pieces been installed properly? Are they straight? Are they loose, buckling? Any paint or plaster flaws? Have they been painted the right colour? Evidence of water damage?
Floors and floor coverings						Look for rough surfaces, discolorations, flaking, chips, cracks, splits, dents, scratches or any other imperfections. Is it the right material? Right colour? Is it installed properly? Are they straight? Any evidence of water damage? Is it level? Is it sagging or bowing?
Ceiling						Look for rough surfaces, discolorations, flaking, chips, cracks, splits, dents, scratches or any other imperfections. Is it the right material? Evidence of water damage? Is it level? Is it sagging or bowing? Are the areas protected by your contract the right height?

(continued)

ENTRANCE	OK	NEEDS REPAIR	INCOMPLETE	MISSING	DESCRIPTION	KEY POINTS
Windows, screens						Look for rough surfaces, discolorations, flaking, chips, cracks, splits, dents, scratches, condensation or any other imperfections. Do windows open and close easily? Is the screen damaged? Any signs of leakage?
Electrical fixtures						Look for rough surfaces, discolorations, flaking, chips, cracks, splits, dents, scratches or any other imperfections. Are all electrical fixtures present? Are they the right style?
Other						
Other						

KITCHEN	OK	NEEDS REPAIR	INCOMPLETE	MISSING	DESCRIPTION	
Walls, trim						See walls, trim above
Floors and floor coverings						See floors and floor coverings above
Ceiling						See ceiling above

KITCHEN	OK	NEEDS REPAIR	INCOMPLETE	MISSING	DESCRIPTION
Counter tops, sinks					Look for rough surfaces, discolorations, flaking, chips, cracks, splits, dents, scratches or any other imperfections. Are counter tops and sinks the right style? Installed properly? Is the caulking done properly?
Cupboards, doors					Look for rough surfaces, discolorations, flaking, chips, cracks, splits, dents, scratches or any other imperfections. Do the doors operate properly? Are the doors warping? Are there raw wood edges? Are the kick plates installed? Is there any paint or plaster flaws (e.g., hinges) painted over?
Range, hood					Look for rough surfaces, discolorations, flaking, chips, cracks, splits, dents, scratches or any other imperfections. Are the range and hood both present and installed? Are they the right style?
Refrigerator					See above
Dishwasher					See above
Windows, screens					See windows above
Electrical fixtures					See electrical fixtures above
Other					
Other					

(continued)

LIVING/DINING ROOM	OK	NEEDS REPAIR	INCOMPLETE	MISSING	DESCRIPTION
Walls, trim					See walls, trim above
Floors and floor coverings					See floors and floor coverings above
Ceiling					See ceiling above
Closets, doors					See closets, doors above
Drapes, rods					
Windows, screens					See windows above
Electrical fixtures					
Other					
Other					
BEDROOM 1	OK	NEEDS REPAIR	INCOMPLETE	MISSING	DESCRIPTION
Walls, trim					See walls, trim above
Floors and floor coverings					See floors and floor coverings above
Ceiling					See ceiling above
Closets, doors					See closets, doors above

BEDROOM 1	OK	NEEDS REPAIR	INCOMPLETE	MISSING	DESCRIPTION
Drapes, rods					Look for rough surfaces, discolorations, flaking, chips, cracks, splits, dents, scratches or any other imperfections. Are drapes and rods all present? Are they the right style? Do they work?
Windows, screens					See windows above
Electrical fixtures					See electrical fixtures above
Other					
BEDROOM 2	OK	NEEDS REPAIR	INCOMPLETE	MISSING	DESCRIPTION
Walls, trim					See walls, trim above
Floors and floor coverings.					See floors and floor coverings above
Ceiling					See ceiling above
Closets, doors					See closets, doors above
Drapes, rods					See drapes, rods above
Windows, screens					See windows above

(continued)

BEDROOM 2	OK	NEEDS REPAIR	INCOMPLETE	MISSING	DESCRIPTION
Electrical fixtures					See electrical fixtures above
Other					
Other					
BEDROOM 3	OK	NEEDS REPAIR	INCOMPLETE	MISSING	DESCRIPTION
Walls, trim					See walls, trim above
Floors and floor coverings					See floors and floor coverings above
Ceiling					See ceiling above
Closets, doors					See closets, doors above
Drapes, rods					See drapes, rods above
Windows, screens					See windows above
Electrical fixtures					See electrical fixtures above
Other					
Other					

MAIN BATHROOM	OK	NEEDS REPAIR	INCOMPLETE	MISSING	DESCRIPTION
Walls, trim					See walls, trim above
Floors and floor coverings					See floors and floor coverings above
Ceiling/fan					See ceiling above
Electrical fixtures					See electrical fixtures above
Closets, doors					See closets, doors above
Windows, screens					See windows above
Toilet					Look for rough surfaces, discolorations, flaking, chips, cracks, splits, dents, scratches or any other imperfections. Is the toilet installed and functional? Is it the right style?
Bathtub, shower					See above
Sink, vanity, mirrors					Look for rough surfaces, discolorations, flaking, chips, cracks, splits, dents, scratches or any other imperfections. Are the sink, vanity and mirrors all there? Are they installed properly? Is the caulking done properly?
Other					
Other					

(continued)

2ND BATHROOM	OK	NEEDS REPAIR	INCOMPLETE	MISSING	DESCRIPTION	
Walls, trim						See walls, trim above
Floors and floor coverings						See floors and floor coverings above
Ceiling, fan						See ceiling above
Electrical fixtures						See electrical fixtures above
Closets, doors						See closets, doors above
Windows, screens						See windows above
Toilet						See toilets above
Bathtub, shower						See bathtub, shower above
Sink, vanity, mirrors						See sink, vanity, mirrors above
Other						
Other						

Location	Item	OK	NEEDS REPAIR	INCOMPLETE	MISSING	DESCRIPTION	OTHER

ADDITIONAL NOTES:

Examples of deficiencies

south wall not plumb, approx deviation 1 inch in 12 inches

incomplete gap

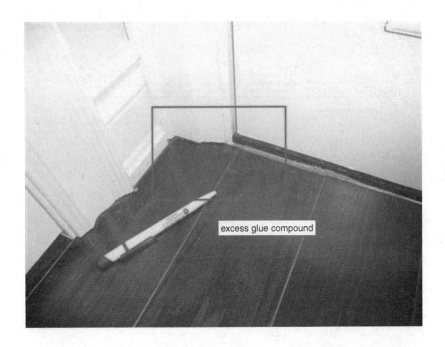

excess glue compound

threshold cut not finished

large gap in the flooring on the northeast corner of the master bedroom

chips and scratches in hardwood flooring

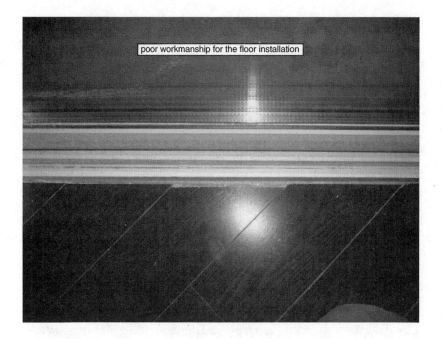

It is also possible to send a designate in your place for the PDI if you are unable to attend. This may be necessary for out-of-town or out-of-country investors, but in general it's advisable to be present at the pre-delivery inspection.

TALES FROM THE TRENCHES

by an anonymous home inspector, Toronto

Hiring a building inspector to do your condo PDI is tough because it really is the builder's show and the owner is on their clock. Many times, it makes the builder rep nervous, and as a result clients may not be served as well as we would like.

A PDI must always be completed, even if you cannot attend the inspection yourself. While you do not automatically lose warranty coverage if a problem is not listed on the PDI form, not making note of a problem makes it more difficult to prove that there was an issue before you moved in.

After the PDI

After you have completed the PDI and moved in, all warranty providers have opportunities for buyers to submit notices of further deficiencies during the time they are covering the issues. The date and timelines to submit lists of further deficiencies vary depending on your province and warranty provider (see chart on page 224).

At this time it may be valuable to hire a home inspector. An inspector can test for and point out some not-so-obvious defects. Examples include moisture from bad tile installation, unconnected dishwashers, reverse polarity electric outlets, leaks behind walls, an over-the-range hood that has not been vented properly, gas-fired hot water tanks not vented correctly, some building code deficiencies, such as electrical panel double-tapping, and other defects that are less obvious to the untrained eye.

Hiring a home inspector who has experience with condos should not be your only criteria, since buyers must also ensure that their inspector is able to deal with their warranty providers. A quality inspector is experienced and familiar with the warranty provider's processes and timelines for submitting paperwork, and has a full understanding of their construction performance guidelines.

If you decide to complete your own warranty deficiency lists, be sure you diligently complete all forms as objectively as possible and within the required timelines.

 TALES FROM THE TRENCHES

After Move-in Inspections
by Mark Benerowski, home inspector, Toronto

Most buyers don't understand their warranty provider's process for dealing with deficiencies. They think that once they give a long list during their PDI they are covered, but this is definitely not the case. Builders are so busy during the move-in process that they may not get to your deficiency list until after the move-in date or well after. The after move-in inspections and deficiency warranty forms are treated with a little more sense of importance than the PDI, as the results are also submitted to the warranty providers. From the time of the PDI to the subsequent inspection can be a really emotional time for a buyer, because they may be living with a set of issues on an ongoing basis, getting more frustrated as time moves on without having the builder fix the problem to their liking.

In one case, we identified major leakage in a unit that caused extensive moisture damage. We always provide an objective voice when filling out the warranty claim. In turn, the warranty provider was more open to looking at the client's issue objectively.

In this case I wrote the following:

> "Located throughout the home extensive moisture damage occurred from a plumbing leak several weeks prior to PDI. This plumbing leak occurred unnoticed for an approximate 24- to 48-hour period. The builder stopped the leak and began cleanup. Moisture cleanup consisted of water vacuuming, removal of cabinets, and wall cavity drying. Our concern is that limited remediation techniques were performed and not in accordance with industry standard IICRC S520 moisture cleanup protocol. Drying was performed probably 48 to 72 hours after initial plumbing leak. Moisture coverage was extensive. No apparent signs of drywall removal were observed throughout the home. The garage displayed high moisture levels on the day of inspection to surface building materials as a result of this plumbing leak. The garage area is insulated with spray foam insulation. This insulation is reducing the drying potential of the wood structure of the home. Recommend a qualified restoration professional remove all drywall and spray foam insulation within the garage area and perform industry standard."

When the warranty provider reads my take on it, they know the client understands what they are talking about; as a result, the conciliator or arbitrator will be more fair.

Had I not been there, the client's report may have looked like this:

"For weeks and weeks we have been living in misery, our condo had a leak that the builder refuses to fix and I think we may have mould."

Items that you will not be noting in either your PDI or after-move inspections are common elements, which are the responsibility of the condominium board. These items include:

- building foundation
- parking garage
- walls
- ventilation system
- windows
- doors

- elevators

- roof

- mechanical systems

- fire protection

- hallways

- balconies and terraces

- amenity space (party rooms, gyms, pools, etc.)

- landscaping

Your condo board will do a separate PDI for these items. Details of what your warranty provider covers and what is considered a common element will be outlined in your disclosure statement.

New-Home Warranty Programs

Buying a home with a warranty is a great way of protecting yourself from some of the costs associated with repairing deficiencies in your condo. Warranty programs provide a great advantage to buying a new condo over a resale condo.

Each province and territory has different ways of providing new-home warranties to buyers. The following table will guide you to find more information.

LUX–ATLANTIC CANADA CONDOMINIUM WARRANTY PROGRAM	http://www.luxrwp.com/
Mandatory	No
Deposit coverage	No
Defects covered[1]	• 1 year: Building code infractions
	• 1 year: Defects covered by the Lux Residential Home Warranty Performance Standards Booklet[2]
	• 5 years: Structural defects (option for 8 years)
	• Also available—extended warranty program for latent defects within the unit (renewable annually by owner)

Completion coverage	• No[3]
Common property coverage	Yes, with exceptions[4]
Mechanical Systems	No[5]
Maximal coverage's amount[6]	Different programs that the builder/ developer must purchase.
	Options
	• 1 year: Code infractions and performance standards defects maximum to $30,000
	• 5 years: Structural defects up to $35,000 per unit to a maximum of $500,000
	• 1 year and 5 years: Code infractions, performance standards defects, and structural defects
Appeal process[7]	• Negotiation
	• Mediation
	• Arbitration
Disclosure of claims to public	No
Customer satisfaction surveys	No
Special considerations	• Up to builder to purchase coverage
	• $3,500 additional living expenses covered as work is complete

QUEBEC NEW HOME GUARANTEE PLAN	Various administrators
	http://www.rbq.gouv.qc.ca/plan-de-garantie/le-plan-de-garantie-des-batiments-residentiels-neufs.html
Mandatory[8]	Yes for buildings 4 floors and under; not mandatory for buildings above 4 floors
Deposit[9]	• 4th floor or lower: $39,000
	• Above: $30,000
Defects covered	• 1 year: Poor workmanship
	• 1 year: Building code infractions
	• 3 years: Latent defects and major defects
	• 5 years: Major defects
Completion coverage	Yes[10]

Common property coverage	Yes, with exceptions[11]
Mechanical systems	No[12]
Maximal coverage's amount[13]	• Maximum $130,000 per unit to a maximum of $2,600,000 for the building
Appeal process	• Negotiation • Mediation • Arbitration
Disclosure of claims to public	Not online. Must request it over the phone after obtaining builder's *Régie du bâtiment du Québec (RBQ)* License #. Information limited.
Customer satisfaction surveys	No
Special considerations[14]	• Offers relocation benefits to a maximum of $5,500 • Not mandatory for buildings higher than 4 floors

ONTARIO NEW HOME WARRANTY PROGRAM (TARION)	http://www.tarion.com/
Mandatory	Yes
Deposit[15]	• $20,000 with any excess deposit amounts being protected by the trust provisions of Ontario's Condominium Act
Defects covered[16]	• 1 year: All items covered in their construction performance guidelines • 1 year: Building code infractions • 2 years: Water penetration through the basement or foundation walls; defects in materials, including windows, doors and caulking, or defects in work that result in water penetration into the building envelope; • 2 years: Defects in work or materials in the electrical, plumbing and heating delivery and distribution systems; • 2 years: Defects in work or materials which result in the detachment, displacement or deterioration of exterior cladding (such as brickwork, aluminum or vinyl siding);

	• 2 years: Violations of the Ontario Building Code affecting health and safety (including, but not limited to, violations relating to fire safety and the structural adequacy of the home)
	• 7 Years: Major structural defects
Completion coverage[17]	Yes
Common property coverage	Yes[18]
Mechanical systems	Yes[19]
Maximal coverage's amount[20]	• Common elements: $50,000 per unit to a maximum of $2.5 million
	• $300,000 per unit
Appeal process[21]	• Negotiation
	• Mediation
	• License appeal tribunal
Disclosure of claims to public	• Online
	• Limited information
Customer satisfaction surveys	Yes
Special considerations[22]	• Delayed occupancy coverage to provide compensation if your building construction is delayed[23]
	• Protection from unauthorized substitutions[24]
	• Builders are required to submit field review consultants to monitor progress of construction at different milestones

NEW HOME WARRANTY PROGRAM OF MANITOBA	http://www.mbnhwp.com/
Mandatory[25]	No
Deposit[26]	Maximum to $25,000
Defects covered	• 1 year: Building code infractions[27]
	• 1 year: Materials and workmanship covered in "Construction Performance Standards"[28]
	• 5 years: Structural defects[29]
Completion coverage[30]	No

Common property coverage	Yes, with exceptions[31]
Mechanical Systems	No[32]
Maximal coverage's amount[33]	• $50,000 per unit
Appeal process	• Negotiation
	• Mediation
	• Conciliation
Disclosure of claims to public	No
Customer satisfaction surveys	No
Special considerations	No coverage for buildings higher than 3 floors[34] and no complex without underground parking

NEW HOME WARRANTY PROGRAM OF SASKATCHEWAN	http://www.nhwp.org/
Mandatory[35]	No
Deposit[36]	15% of purchase price to a maximum of $25,000
Defects covered[37]	• 1 year: Building code infractions
	• 1 year: Workmanship and materials covered in "Construction Performance Standards"[38]
	• 2 years: Water leaks
	• 5 years: Major structural defects
Completion coverage[39]	No
Definition of structural defects	Defects in workmanship or materials that have or are likely to have an adverse effect on the performance of the load-bearing portion of the home
Maximal coverage's amount[40]	• Maximum $750,000 for entire building (excludes common elements)
	• Maximum per unit: $50,000
Appeal process[41]	• Negotiation
	• Arbitration
Disclosure of claims to public	No
Customer satisfaction surveys	Yes
Special considerations[42]	No coverage for buildings higher than 3 floors

ALBERTA NEW HOME WARRANTY PROGRAM	http://www.anhwp.com
Mandatory	Not mandatory, expected to change in 2012
Deposit[43]	15% of purchase price to a maximum of $30,000
Defects covered[44]	• 1 year: Workmanship and materials covered by the "Workmanship and Material Guide"[45] • 1 year: Building code infractions • 5 years: Structural integrity
Completion coverage	No
Common property coverage	Yes, with exceptions[46]
Mechanical systems	No[47]
Definition of structural integrity defects	Any defect affecting the load-bearing components of your unit
Maximal coverage's amount[48]	• Workmanship and materials: Maximum of $60,000 per unit and $1,500,000 per project • Structural integrity: $60,000 per unit and $1,500,000 per project
Appeal process[49]	• Negotiation • Mediation • Conciliation • Arbitration
Disclosure of claims to public	No
Customer satisfaction surveys	No
Special considerations[50]	• Maximum of $6,000 to cover living costs while work is being completed

SASKATCHEWAN, MANITOBA, ALBERTA: NATIONAL HOME WARRANTY	http://www.nationalhomewarranty.com/
Mandatory	No
Deposit	Maximum $25,000 [51, 52, 53]
Defects covered[54, 55, 56]	• 1 year: Workmanship and materials covered in "Performance Standards Guide"[57] • 1 year: Building code infractions • 5 years: Structural defects

Completion coverage[58, 59, 60]	Yes
Common property coverage	Yes, with exceptions[61]
Mechanical systems	Yes
Appeal process[62]	• Negotiation
	• Mediation
Disclosure of claims to public	No
Customer satisfaction surveys	No
Special considerations[63]	Details may change based on coverage the builder enrols in

BRITISH COLUMBIA, VARIOUS INSURERS	http://www.hpo.bc.ca/home-warranty-insurers
Mandatory	Yes
Deposit	• Depends on insurance program
Defects covered[64]	• All items covered in their construction performance guide (includes timelines broken down in 12-, 15- and 24-month intervals)[65]
	• 5 year: Building envelope
	• 10 years: Structural defects
Completion coverage	No
Common property coverage	Yes[66]
Mechanical systems	Yes
Appeal process	• Negotiation
	• Mediation
	• Arbitration
Disclosure of claims to public	No
Customer satisfaction surveys	Yes
Special considerations	Each warranty provider will have some unique considerations.

New-home warranty programs are mandatory in British Columbia, Ontario and Quebec, while in the other provinces and territories it is left up to the individual home builder to make a warranty available.

A new-home warranty usually covers the following:

- "Deposit insurance" provides protection to your deposit against builder fraud or bankruptcy.

- "Defects in work and materials" provides protection against shoddy work or defective materials. Most warranty providers have construction performance guidelines that clearly define the most common issues and what is covered by the warranty.

- "Building code violations" provides protection against work not completed in accordance with building codes. Coverage can range from all code violations to issues violating health and safety, depending on the policy.

- "Building envelope" provides protection against defects in workmanship and materials of the building envelope, which includes windows, doors, caulking, and other defects that could allow water to penetrate the building.

- "Major structural defects" provides protection against deficiencies in load-bearing components that can affect the structural integrity of the home. The exact definition will vary between warranty providers.

Less commonly, some warranty providers will also cover the following:

- "Completion insurance" provides protection if a builder is unable to substantially complete your unit.

- "Common elements" provides protection against defects of common property, such as hallways, mailrooms, amenity space and underground parking.

- "Building's mechanical system" provides protection of common mechanical elements such as elevators, garbage chutes, garage doors, and heating/air conditioning/ventilation systems (HVAC).

- "Unauthorized substitutions" provides protection against unauthorized substitutions. Items covered must be part of your agreement of purchase and sale.

TALES FROM THE TRENCHES

Dealing with Deficiencies
by an anonymous developer, Toronto

Clients are often frustrated at how long it takes for work to be completed. It's not that we are trying to ignore them; the process can be quite overwhelming from our side. We are trying to move in hundreds of people and working really hard to make other units fit for occupancy. This work involves waiting for municipal inspectors, finding tradespeople available to do the deficiency work, and managing any outstanding work that needs to be completed. Most developers do care about their reputations and want to avoid a blemish on their record, but some aspects are out of our control.

Most warranty providers do outline steps to take to get deficiency work completed before you can actually make a claim. The first step is usually a negotiation directly with the builder. At this time, you have submitted your PDI deficiency list to the builder and may have submitted your first after-move-in report. The negotiation process is informal and may involve the builder paying to fix the problem or offering a cash settlement.

If the builder is still unresponsive or the buyer is still not satisfied, the warranty provider will have to get involved. At this time, the warranty provider may order the builder to complete the problem or pay for it themselves.

If the buyer is unhappy with the warranty provider's or builder's response, mediation or arbitration and finally civil litigation can be used to settle disputes. These processes are more costly and some costs, including out-of-pocket costs to substantiate warranty claims, or fees to get legal advice, are usually not reimbursed, even if your claim is accepted.[72]

The most important warning we can give you is this: A warranty is not a complete guarantee to protect you from all defects or an excuse for not performing due diligence on your builder.

◎ YOU SHOULD KNOW

About walls that are not straight

New-home warranty providers do give builders some leeway in determining what a deficiency is. For example, in Ontario, if a wall is out of plumb less than 25 mm in a 2400 mm vertical measurement, it's not a warrantable defect. While you may not be happy with a wall that is not completely straight, your warranty provider will not require the developer to fix it.

OUT OF LEVEL   OUT OF PLUMB   BOWED WALL

Joe and Joanne West, new home buyers, Hamilton

Joe West and his wife, Joanne, purchased a new detached home in Hamilton, Ontario. While a house is not a condo, their story should be seen as a warning to those who don't do due diligence on their builder and warranty provider before purchasing. Joe and Joanne bought their home for under $300,000, but were amazed at the poor level of workmanship seen throughout the home. The deficiency list was so bad, the house didn't even pass the building code inspection and the city began to take steps against them to make their home code compliant. This flabbergasted the West family, since the city was responsible for ensuring the home was compliant by doing inspections while the home was under construction. It seems the homebuilder built the homes and the city provided them permits afterward, and the city inspectors may also have failed to do a thorough job of inspecting the property before the West family were granted occupancy.

The builders, who were a fly-by-night operation, refused to fix the problems and later declared bankruptcy. When the West family reported the claims to the warranty provider, the warranty provider refused to make a payout to them. The West family had to hire an independent engineering firm to detail all the issues of the home, and they discovered it would have cost $462,000 to repair all the problems. Even though the maximum payout by the warranty provider is $300,000, the West family says the warranty provider still refused to acknowledge all the claims and make the payout. The family was then forced to escalate the issue to the province of Ontario's License Appeal Tribunal. At the tribunal, the chairperson ordered the warranty provider to have its own third-party engineer detail the problems. The warranty provider complied and the engineer agreed with the engineer hired by the West family about the severity of the issues. Even after the verification from the engineer they hired, the warranty provider still refused to make the maximum payout and offered the West family $90,000. The Wests felt the warranty provider was using these tactics in hopes that they would drop the matter and not spend the extra money to take the matter further.

The warranty provider wanted the West family to sign a release absolving them of further liability, but the West family took the $90,000 and refused to sign the release, leaving them free to pursue the issue in the future. So far, because of delay tactics and the need for legal help, the West Family is out more than $100,000 in legal fees (outside of the license appeal tribunal) and have spent years fighting for justice. It has taken a substantial toll on their family.

When researching their problems with the warranty provider, the Wests have found others who have gone through similar situations, but when pressed to either fight for their rights or just stay quiet and quickly sell the property, most chose the latter. The West family finds it frustrating that the province of Ontario has only one provider to administer the warranty program, which gives buyers no choice on which company to enrol with.

CASE STUDY

Penhorwood Condominiums, Fort McMurray, Alberta

Many condo purchasers assume that if a project is approved and being built and sold, it will be a safe and solid structure in which to live. This is, sadly, not always the case. More than 300 residents of 168 units of a Fort McMurray condo building found this out the hard way in March 2011, when they received notice that they had 10 minutes to retrieve what belongings they could and evacuate their homes. After investigating the deteriorating conditions of this building, a remediation determined that it was no longer safe even for specially trained Health and Safety workers to re-enter the building to attempt repairs.

"It is with profound regret that we advise that it is highly unlikely that any person will ever enter any of the 7 Penhorwood structures again, for any reason," states the March 24, 2011, letter from Al Penner, the lawyer for the Penhorwood Condominium Association.

This condominium project, built during a building boom in the famous oil town, has severe issues with its roof and structural integrity. Could this have been due to lack of quality workers or materials at the time? Whatever the case, residents, who are still responsible for paying their mortgages on a condemned and uninhabitable home, are certainly wishing that they had known more about their builder and had fully understood their rights and responsibilities under the provincial warranty program. The owners' only recourse may be a costly and time-consuming class-action lawsuit against the builder.

Investors: Beware of Violating Occupancy Rules

In provinces that allow for interim occupancy periods, the building is still owned and managed by the developer, which means that, in essence, you are renting the condominium from the developer. Your mortgage has not taken effect. As such, there is an increased fire and insurance liability to the developer if tenants are occupying your unit.

Developers explicitly state in their purchase agreements that tenants are not allowed to occupy a unit during the interim occupancy phase. Many owners do not observe this clause and risk the chance of the developer taking legal action against them, which could result in fines in the thousands of dollars. Investor-friendly developers have been known to give schedules in their purchase agreements allowing for tenant occupancy, which requires further insurance costs for the developer. This is usually done as a sales and marketing incentive to encourage investors to purchase units. This is a specific section of the purchase agreement that should be negotiated with the builder upfront if you plan on renting your unit upon completion.

Assigning the Unit

You can't sell what you don't own, so although you purchased a condominium, you don't own its deed to sell it. So how can I sell my contract to ownership of a condominium? This is what an assignment is. In the past, a builder allowed buyers to assign their unit at any time, without any real control from the builder. This brought a lot of speculation into the marketplace, as the contracts for units were being sold to numerous buyers who had no intention of closing. As mentioned in Chapter 5, builders today must ensure that all buyers have the ability to close and they are concerned about the value of the standing inventory of units they have left; as a result, they want to control the assignment process.

Sometimes this can be detailed in a specific clause that you would negotiate with the builder upfront in your agreement of purchase and sale. Today, builders usually limit assignments as the building nears completion, meaning that the most opportune time for an investor to "cash out" is during the interim occupancy period. While some builders are proactive and have policies in place in order to deal with an assignment, these transactions can be still be complicated. The person who is selling their contract is known as an assignor, which is different from a vendor (in this case, the builder).

Why would an investor considering assigning the unit versus closing on it?

1. **To avoid costly closing costs:** As noted in Chapter 5, closing costs can be quite large. In Toronto, with the current additional municipal land transfer tax to the provincial land transfer tax, the cost is upwards of 2½% of the value of the property.

2. **The investor's ability to obtain financing is in doubt:** This could happen for any number of reasons. Job loss. Divorce. Or interest

rates have risen beyond the investor's comfort level (and that of the lender, too).

3. **Life situation of the buyer has changed:** Perhaps the investor wants a different lifestyle and the present address of the unit and its amenities cannot deliver it.

4. **The investor wants to avoid flipping competition:** Other investors may want to sell their unit by listing their property on the MLS® once it is registered, or even beforehand if the builder gives permission. Once a building registers and the deed is passed to the owner, investors who need to cash out will immediately list their property. The basic concept of supply and demand applies. More supply and same demand causes prices to drop.

5. **The market environment has significantly changed:** Smart sellers are constantly in touch with their real estate agent, who is monitoring sales and trends in the market. If values are declining and the sellers cannot wait out the decline, then selling the contract immediately is the smart thing to do.

6. **The investor needs cash elsewhere:** Good investment opportunities can come up, requiring the buyer to cash out the equity in the current deal and put the money into another.

7. **To reduce closing costs:** If the seller finds his own buyer, then paying a real estate commission is avoided. In such cases, it is highly recommended to work with a lawyer with condominium assignment experience.

Why would someone buy an assignment?

1. A smart buyer knows how much a seller would save by assigning rather than selling the unit. If the seller can realize savings of 3% (or more) of the value of the condominium, then why not negotiate a deal with the buyer in the middle?

2. A buyer may anticipate much demand for the units when they are registered and listed on the MLS®, so it is better to purchase without the competition.

3. Market values have increased. Builders price their remaining inventory units at market value, and a buyer who bought several years earlier may already have some equity and be willing to undercut the builder's price.

When dealing with a situation that requires the builder's consent, the process usually starts off with the assignor and assignee creating an agreement called the Assignment of Agreement of Purchase and Sale. The agreement is taken to the vendor (builder), who will decide if they accept the agreement, and they will usually want to ensure the buyer is pre-qualified to close the transaction. This could take some time, and if the seller doesn't close, you still may be on the hook to close the transaction. It's best to get the paperwork started on these transactions as soon as possible. A builder is less likely to grant the assignment if the building is close to registration, and the buyer (assignee) needs time to review the declarations, disclosures and agreements. Another roadblock to completing an assignment is lenders. If the agreement between the sellers (assignors) and buyer (assignee) isn't done properly, they may be too afraid of mortgage fraud and will not disburse funds on closing.

Having a lawyer or realtor who has a great relationship with the builder's staff is extremely valuable to a successful transaction, as they are more likely to know the inner workings of the individual builder's policies and may be able to get favours (such as extensions) from the builder's office staff.

Assignors beware: most builders require that there be no marketing of the assignment through public means such as MLS®, newspapers or websites. Builder penalties, which are stated on purchase agreements, are around $3,000 in fines upon the first incident, and the builder may declare the purchaser to be in default of their agreement and take the deposit. It is encouraged to seek legal advice on this matter when considering marketing your assignment and the repercussions it may have with your builder.

 TIP

Experienced lawyers and realtors are your ticket to a successful assignment. We cannot stress how important it is to have an experienced realtor and an experienced lawyer involved in this transaction, especially if you are dealing with a builder with no formal assignment policies or paperwork. We have seen some buyers' (assignees') lawyers convince their clients to kill an assignment deal because they don't understand what's going on. We have also dealt with sellers (assignors) with realtors who are so inexperienced they don't realize the risks to their clients' deposit funds with complicated agreements that will scare off buyers and lenders.

With an experienced lawyer and realtor on your side, they can structure the deal to protect your investment and make the paperwork clear, concise and easy for a buyer (assignee), their lawyer and lender to feel comfortable and confident that their interests are protected.

Checklist for Selling an Assignment

1. Confirm if you actually have the right to assign the unit.

2. Hire a competent lawyer and realtor, preferably one with experience working with the developer's head office, or one who has experience with assignments in the past.

3. Communicate your intentions to the developer. Confirm if you are still in good standing with your agreement. Find out all procedures and know who to talk to in the office. Confirm if you are able to market the unit on the MLS® or online.

4. Find out what your obligations are. Are there outstanding deposits? Money due on closing for extras and upgrades? Post-dated cheques for occupancy fees? Interest owing to you on your deposit? An assignment fee to be paid to the builder?

5. Prepare all agreements, amendments, condo declarations, disclosure documents, and colour and finish selections you received from the builder, to hand over to the buyer's (assignee's) lawyer.

6. Get written confirmation from the builder that you are up to date on your deposits.

7. Get written confirmation from the builder that there are no amendments changing the terms of the agreements you have signed.

8. Get any keys, remotes or security-access fobs ready for the assignee.

Checklist for Buying an Assignment

1. Use an experienced lawyer or realtor as part of the transaction.

2. Get pre-qualified by your lender.

3. Ensure you have received all paperwork from the assignor.

4. Have your lawyer go over all documents and understand the obligations you are taking on.

5. Find out how much cash you will need to close the deal. What can be financed by a mortgage? What are the occupancy fees? What are your closing costs? Do you have to pay the HST or GST? Do you have to pay any extra deposits? Are there any fees for extras or upgrades

that are due on closing? Are you liable for any income taxes on interest paid on deposits?

6. Ensure the warranty is valid and transferable (especially if the assignor has made modifications to the unit).

Essential Questions to Ask about an Assignment Agreement

1. Do you have the right to assign?

2. Who holds the deposit for the agreement, and how much is it?

3. How will the assignee protect themselves from the assignor flipping the unit to someone else?

4. How will the assignor's deposit with the builder be protected and paid back?

5. Who pays GST or HST? Who collects the rebate?

6. Who pays for the closing costs?

7. How will the balance of the purchase price and profits (if any) be paid?

MORTGAGE FINANCING

Preparation
by Calum Ross

Once you have bought your new condo, if you are like more than 90% of condo purchasers, you aren't going to be paying for the place with cash on the actual closing date (the date the deed of the title is registered to you). The challenging aspect of getting a mortgage for pre-construction units is that you don't know how much your mortgage will cost you on a monthly basis unless you get a pre-approval with a rate hold.

Most lenders and mortgage brokers can only provide a rate hold for 90 to 120 days. This is obviously not useful for buying a condo pre-construction unless the building is very close to completion.

Lenders do understand timelines involved with building condo towers, and this is why they work with builders to provide a range of products that offer more security and certainty for buyers. In return, the builder allows the lender to offer their products on site within the sales centre.

To ensure you will have the best mortgage ready for you at closing, it's important to do the following:

1. **Don't always bet on a pre-approval after you've signed the contract.** Far more than 50% of all the **mortgage** pre-approvals that are done are not worth the paper they are written on. Since most pre-approvals never fund and most clients are looking for the quickest answer, the system of pre-approvals is fundamentally set up to fail.

2. **If the builder has more than one on-site bank, get an approval from all of them.** Contrary to popular belief, having multiple lenders pre-approve you within a two-week period and subsequently checking your credit will not negatively impact your credit score, if all the requests are for the purpose of mortgage financing. Equifax (Canada's largest credit reporting agency) realizes that people will explore multiple options for mortgage financing and does not penalize people for visiting more than one financial institution.

3. **Don't look for the lender who will issue you the quickest pre-approval.** Look for the lender that will issue you the pre-approval you can rely on. There is a big difference between a simple pre-approval, which is nothing more than a rate hold, and a pre-approval that has been fully underwritten by a bank. Some banks/brokers will issue a pre-approval without even reviewing your details. These automated systems are nothing more than a rate hold with an asterisk that states the application will be underwritten at the time a "live" application is submitted.

4. **Understand your mortgage terms before you are ready to move forward with your lender.** While on paper it is pretty typical to see all the on-site lender options offering the same deal at the onset, the deals may vary considerably by the time you actually need the cash. This is because all too often the period that your rate and mortgage terms are guaranteed for comes to pass and the offer or options you then get can vary dramatically.

5. **Before closing, explore your options.** By having more than one option to explore at this time, and not being at the mercy of one lender's new offer, you have flexibility and typically a much different set of pro's and con's.

6. **Compare your interest rates.** If rates have gone down since you got your approval, feel free to call your own bank or a reputable mortgage broker that you know of. The commitment you signed with the on-site

lender typically has no fee to get out of, and it is by no means legally binding should you wish to explore other options.

7. **Get all of your documents in order.** No matter where you get your mortgage, the commitment letter should clearly state the outstanding conditions for the loan to be funded. While conditions such as final appraisal, building completion, and other things related to the project are out of your control, things such as satisfactory credit and income verification is within your control.

8. **Understand your personal situation fully.** Have a mortgage professional review copies of your tax return and credit rating.

9. **Work with the best.** Never forget that it always pays to work with the best people possible. Even if you have been pre-approved by the on-site lender, speak to an independent mortgage broker to see what other options are possible.

MORTGAGE FINANCING

A Cautionary Note

A lot can change between the time you sign a purchase agreement and the actual closing date. There could be some financing implications that could lead to your losing the condo if you are not prepared.

On January 17, 2011, the federal government announced that the Canada Mortgage and Housing Corporation (CMHC), a crown corporation that provides mortgage default loan insurance, which is then securitized and sold as mortgage-backed securities, will no longer provide the following loan products.

1. insurance for mortgages that are amortized beyond 30 years; or

2. insurance for refinances beyond 85% of the appraised value of a home (prior to the new legislation, insurance was available for refinances up to 90% of the appraised value).

3. CMHC will no longer insure Home Equity Lines of Credit (HELOC), which essentially discourages lenders from extending loans that represent more than 80% of the appraised value of a home.

Essentially, this changes the landscape for a first-time home buyer who had a commitment from a lender for a 5% or 10% deposit, which used to be sufficient to buy a unit. That amount also met the criteria for builder construction financing. Not anymore. And first-time home buyers can no longer take advantage of an amortization period that is longer than 30 years. What this means is that most buyers get "pre-approved" by a lender that can offer a fixed rate at the time of registration. This is very specific to a single lender that likely is involved in the construction financing. However, this "pre-approval" has many qualifiers, including the default insurance program at the time of qualification; default insurance includes CMHC and Genworth programs. So, with condo projects that are finally ready for occupancy, some of the CMHC and Genworth programs have changed, namely, the 10% down payment requirement for investment property no longer exists and the 40-year amortizations no longer exist. This changes qualifications completely. What smart builders did is they insisted on a 20% deposit, which has allowed for "conventional financing" that is not confined by high-ratio default insurance programs like CMHC or Genworth.

CASE STUDY

Taking Advantage of Time
Mike, condo buyer, Toronto

Mike purchased his condo in 2008 for $200,000 and put down a 15% deposit, or $30,000. Occupancy was slated for 2010 and his real estate agent said it could be worth around $260,000 by the time it registered. At registration, Mike wanted to avoid paying the CMHC insurance premium of 1.75% of the $170,000 mortgage amount, or $2,975, which is a one-time fee. Mike went to a lender who offered a bundled first and second mortgage with a 1% fee or $1,700 for one year, and then financed a conventional mortgage at 80% of the newly appraised value of $260,000, which is $208,000. There was no default insurance premium with his bank and the new raised loan amount allows him to pull out an additional $38,000 in tax-free dollars.

Frequently-asked Mortgage Questions

My unit has appreciated since I signed the purchase agreement so that I have more than 20% equity. Can't I just do conventional financing and avoid default insurance?

No, you cannot. The reason is that the bank will lend on the lower of contract price and appraised value.

A suggested strategy to take advantage of equity growth and avoid paying the non-refundable mortgage default insurance premium is to use short-term financing, such as a first and second mortgage, up to 85% of the appraised value. There are some major lenders that have these as "bundled" loans with their own "fee," which is almost equivalent to the CMHC mortgage default insurance premium. The short-term financing is typically for one year and it allows you to refinance with other programs after the one year is up. To take advantage of the increased equity, the refinancing after the one year can include conventional financing of the new appraised value, thus avoiding the CMHC premium.

My parents were going to refinance their home or get a HELOC to assist me with the down payment. Is that okay?

Under the new legislation, your parents can only refinance their home up to 85% of its appraised value, and a home equity line of credit cannot exceed 80% of the appraised value. If you don't have enough cash available you may have a problem.

How do I get extra cash for a down payment?

An alternative strategy is to have your parents go on title and declare the property as a second home, which may qualify the parents with 5% down. CMHC has a 5% down program to allow for a secondary home, which is typically used in the case of buying with a child or parent.

What can I do if I am having difficulty coming up with the final deposit at occupancy?

If you are challenged to raise the final deposit, you must clearly communicate this to the builder and request a delay in occupancy. It should be noted that delayed closing will cause the builder to tack on per diem (daily) loan charges for delays, which can be hefty over time. Use this time to work out an unsecured loan from your financial institution or get a secured line of credit on another piece of property you own. This is where finding a very good mortgage broker comes in handy for access to a "hard money lender" who will lend for short periods of time, unsecured, for an interest cost. This cost will be substantially higher than traditional secured financing, because there is no real estate asset to secure the loan against, since the condominium is not yet deeded and transferred in your name, and therefore cannot be deemed a security.

Alternative Sources of Financing for Deposits and Closing Costs

Deposit Loans

In order to encourage sales, some in-house lenders create aggressive deposit loan programs that provide a portion of the deposit in the form of an unsecured loan. The loans usually only require a minimum of interest-only payments, and at closing they are usually paid off. These loans may carry some extra obligations on the mortgage you take from the lender providing the loan. Consult with a seasoned mortgage broker if a builder has this option available; it is better to save your cash in hand for surprise closing costs than tie it up in the deposit.

Deposit Bonds

Some warranty providers offer a product in which a buyer can put a portion of cash toward their deposit and the unpaid portion is guaranteed by a bond. This is popular in British Columbia and Alberta and requires the buyer to be pre-qualified, showing that not only do they qualify for a mortgage, but they also will be paying the unpaid deposit at closing to avoid the warranty provider from making a payout. This program is meant for people who have the cash available from an investment or from equity from their existing real estate, but don't want to liquidate in order to make the deposit that will be held by the builder for a long time.

Private Financing

Private financing is another source for much-needed cash to close. Private financing can be in the form of loans from people you know or through mortgage brokers that raise cash from investors to be available to loan. These loans are generally non-insured loans and can be very costly in terms of upfront fees and interest rates. It's best to discuss this with a mortgage professional you trust.

FINAL CLOSING

The Deed Transfer

This phase of the closing occurs once the municipality has inspected the entire building for safe occupancy. Your deed can now be registered. You will need to sign the final documents in your lawyer's presence, including your deed and mortgage charge. At this closing you will be required to pay the remaining down payment, plus all disclosed closing costs. Be ready for some surprise adjustments, such as pro-rata property taxes, which is your portion of property taxes refunded to the seller if they prepaid a certain amount. Additional closing costs will include the land transfer tax, utility hook-ups and school levies. Be prepared for surprises!

Closing Costs: Are You Being Overcharged?

With all the taxes, closing costs and rebates available, some buyers may feel they have paid too much on closing. Since these closing costs are discovered right before you are supposed to close on a property, you may not have enough time to fully understanding if you are being overcharged.

Lawyers who are experienced in closings have looked at thousands of statements of adjustment and have a pool of data that they can compare it with if they see anything out of the ordinary. However, those same lawyers may have many closings to deal with, and may not have or take the time to go through your agreement again to ensure you were treated fairly. As well, because the rules change so often, your lawyer may not even be aware if you overpaid. In Toronto, there has been an expected $150 million in rebates available since 2005, and only 30% have been collected. The rule of thumb is: if your instincts tell you have overpaid, you may have actually overpaid.

Examples of rebates or overcharges:

- Development charges or city levies that the municipality did not charge the developer
- HST or GST rebate (if you qualify)
- Land transfer tax rebate (if you qualify)
- First-time home buyer rebates
- Abatements (deductions due to mistakes by the developer or government)

Collecting rebates or overcharges is an arduous task, however, and may involve months and months of filling out forms and follow-up. It's best just to pay the charges upfront and get a second opinion afterward.

Get a Second Opinion!

After you have closed your document, have your lawyer go through the charges to see if there is anything you are uncomfortable with. Give your lawyer all information about your unit and its measurements. If your unit is smaller than promised, for instance, or if pillars that weren't in the original floor plan are now taking up valuable floor space, you may be eligible to collect an abatement.

If you are not comfortable with your lawyer, some companies have been formed just to collect these rebates in return for a percentage that they collect.

 TALES FROM THE TRENCHES

Collecting What Is Owed
by Wes Weber, condo rebate collector, Toronto

The process of collecting the Toronto Land Transfer Rebate is a difficult one. You will apply for it and provide every single piece of supporting documentation that is requested on the form; 120 to 150 days later, you may get a letter in the mail asking for something called a "Docket Summary." When this happened to me, I called the City of Toronto and the clerk that sent the letter did not know what a Docket Summary was, but they still wanted one before the rebate could be approved. Turns out that a Docket Summary is a printout from the lawyer's trust account indicating that indeed the Land Transfer Tax was remitted from his bank account to the city. I almost fell over laughing when I figured this out. I will tell you why: the City of Toronto Land Tax Office has, right on their computer screens, the day that you paid your Land Transfer Tax! It is there on the Land Registry Office Form #80. If you read the legislation behind Toronto's Land Transfer Tax, you will see that a provision was put forth that grants the city the absolute right to enter your home and confiscate your property if you do not pay the tax. They know full well whether you have paid the tax. It is on their balance sheet as well. If you did not pay they would be sending a letter very shortly after the provisional time expired.

The First Year of Ownership

The importance of keeping your new-home warranty intact.
Determining what you need to insure. Understanding and working
with your board of directors and property management team.
The importance of the "turn-over meeting." The status certificate.
Finding tenants for your unit. Deciding when to sell, and how.

Congratulations! You have now taken deeded title to your condominium and all the legalities have been completed for final closing. You are now part of a community of owners. Now the work begins in wealth creation and asset value preservation. As a community owner, you need to understand the rules you need to play by to maximize your return on your investment. How does your condo investment make the most money in today's real estate market? What are some strategies used by condo investors to get the most out of their investment?

Keeping Your New-Home Warranty Intact

Each warranty provider expects that condo buyers will take reasonable care to maintain their property properly. Damage due to neglect, abnormal use or improper maintenance will not be covered. Some builders provide a homeowner manual that will detail what needs to be maintained, how to do it and when the work needs to be done.

Some common issues for condos include:

Neglect:

- not disclosing problems within an adequate time period
- failure to minimize damage in a timely manner
- failure to adequately ventilate the property, resulting in moisture damage from condensation.

Abnormal use:

- operating a business within the unit
- renting or leasing your unit

- installing new or modifying existing mechanical and HVAC systems (e.g., adding humidifiers)

- installing new or modifying existing electrical components (e.g., adding recessed lighting)

- installing new or modifying existing plumbing systems (e.g., adding a hot tub)

- adding heavy appliances or furniture (e.g., waterbeds, pianos).

Improper maintenance:

- damage as a result of not following manufacturer's requirements for appliances

- not adequately cleaning the fan coil units or heat recovery ventilator.

Buyers should consult their warranty provider to understand if the way they plan on using their condo, or if any modifications or additions (especially for work done by someone who is not hired by the builder) may have the unintended effect of voiding their warranty.

 TIP

Taking matters into your own hands can be fatal to your warranty
Wanting to make his small condo brighter, a buyer of a condo tore open parts of his ceilings and, with a friend who was an electrician, installed pot lights. The friend was able to install the lighting by splicing into the existing electrical wires for the ceiling lights, and ensured that the circuit had enough capacity to handle the lighting. After it was finished, the ceiling was repaired and the work looked amazing. However, because this work was done without an electrical inspection or the permission of the builder, it will almost certainly void the warranty.

Understanding What You Should Insure

So far, you know that you are insured against builder defects by your new-home warranty, but what about other insurable risks? It is important to consult with a licensed insurance representative for your specific insurance needs.

Your maintenance fee allocates a portion to the condominium corporation's Master Insurance Policy, which insures damage to common elements plus the "standard unit," as defined in the condominium by-laws and Master Insurance Policy.

Standard Unit Definition

It is important to have your insurance agent review your condominium by-laws to confirm what the "standard unit definition" is in the condominium. If there is a fire or flood in your unit, what liability is covered by the condominium corporation? In other words, how is your liability defined, and how is the condominium's liability defined? The answers lie in the by-laws of the corporation, where a Standard Unit Definition is articulated.

The Standard Unit is defined in most buildings as being from the concrete floors to the concrete ceilings. The walls are usually drywalled and the standard unit is typically halfway between the neighbouring unit and the common areas. The balconies are considered common area.

Homeowner Insurance for Condominiums

As an owner, you need insurance for:

1. Structural improvements such as wall studs, ceiling drywall, carpet, counter tops (everything above and beyond the Standard Unit Definition).

2. Personal property such as appliances, furniture, ceiling and wall fixtures (everything unrelated to the structure).

3. Liability for harm you may cause in any part of the building or you may cause to anyone that lives in or visits the condominium building.

4. Loss assessment, which is your portion of the deductible charged to the condominium unit owners as a "special assessment" in the event of major flood or wind damage due to a peril. This is a very rare risk.

All of these four components combine to provide an "all-perils" or comprehensive insurance policy.

Cash Value versus Replacement Cost

Once you determine the appropriate amount of coverage, you'll need to decide what kind of coverage to buy. The basic distinction in insurance policies you should be aware of is the cash value versus the replacement cost.

Cash-value coverage replaces the value of the insured item minus depreciation. Replacement cost coverage replaces the actual cost to replace in today's dollars. This is a premium feature to your policy, but well worth the extra monthly expense.

If you rent your unit, make sure you tell your insurer that the policy is for business use, and consider additional insurance to cover such things as lost rent (for example, if your condominium needs repair following a major wind storm or other peril). This type of insurance does not cover you if the unit is rentable and you cannot rent the unit based on finding a suitable tenant.

Tenant Insurance

Never sign a lease with a tenant who does not provide you with a copy of their insurance policy, which must be a comprehensive policy. In case of tenant damage, not only will their contents not be insured, but their negligence will affect your existing policy with the condominium.

Turn-over Meetings

The first year of operation from registration date is called the "turn-over" year, which is the year that the developer turns over the operation of the condominium corporation to the owners and its elected board members. During this turn-over year, the Condominium Act requires the developer to hand over to the new board of directors (who were voted in at the "turn-over meeting") all documents pertaining to the running of the condominium.

Each province will have different procedures on when and how to transfer control from the developer. Transfer of the corporation usually occurs when a certain percentage of units have been transferred to the owners.

At the turn-over meetings, the new condo board usually receives documents from the developer. Examples include:

- current declaration and by-law rules
- architectural drawings, specifications and site plans
- copies of all agreements entered into by the corporation (property management, deeds, leases, etc.)
- copies of all insurance policies
- bills of sale or transfers for all assets of the corporation.

There are many documents that are detailed for the new board to receive by law, and sometimes the developer may not have them all. Some documents require the board to sign releases, waivers and acknowledgements. This is why it's best to have an experienced lawyer or experienced impartial property manager at the meeting.

A common complaint by condo board members is the lack of interest among owners in participating in the election of board members at turn-over meetings. Only when owners organize themselves will they have some control over how their condo is run.

 TALES FROM THE TRENCHES

Turn-over Meetings Gone Wrong
by Armand Conant, lawyer, Toronto

Usually developers want turn-over meetings to take place as soon as possible; however, I have seen situations in which the developer wishes to retain control as long as possible.

An example of this is the corporation for which I was appointed administrator by the courts. In this case the developer retained ownership of all the commercial units and just enough residential units to maintain control and ensure he did not have to hold a turn-over meeting.

The limited records turned over showed that the developer-controlled board had not collected common expenses from the developer for the 28 commercial units, nor had any liens been registered. At the same time that he controlled the board, he acted as property manager of the building.

What to Expect from the Board in Your First Year of Ownership

Smart investors will keep themselves well informed of the annual operational budget shortfall or surplus for the first year, plus any deficiencies or excesses in the reserve fund. This will help you be aware of any impending increases in maintenance fees. Being in constant communication with property management or a board member would be well advised. As a unit owner, you also have the right to request a copy of board meeting minutes to keep yourself abreast of current news occurring in the building.

For the first year, the condo board will be required to complete:

- **Performance audits:** Performance audits are reviews of all common elements in a building. These audits are done to determine if there are any deficiencies of common elements. Sometimes this may include surveys of all unit owners for deficiencies lists. Performance audits are mainly looking for building code issues. Problems related to design are usually not covered by new-home warranty providers and will have to be dealt with directly with the developer or through legal action, if the board decides to go that route. If your warranty provider covers common elements, audits should be done before each warranty milestone to ensure that if damage has occurred, it will be covered by the new-home warranty.

- **Reserve fund study:** A reserve fund is a fund that is set aside to deal with repair and maintenance of major parts of the building's common parts (foundation, garage, ventilation, roof, mechanical system, etc.). These items are outside the regular maintenance that occurs throughout a building. The reserve fund study should be updated regularly; some of the better buildings update them at least every three years.

It's important for the condo board to hire the best engineering firm to complete a performance audit and reserve fund study. All too often boards fall into the trap of looking strictly at price when choosing a firm to complete the work. This is a mistake. These reports are extremely important and will have a lasting impact on the value of your building.

Among the characteristics of a quality firm to perform technical audits and reserve fund studies are the following:

- has experience with the warranty provider and their processes

- is able to explain to the board all the steps required to complete the audits

- has in-house experience (rather than subcontractors) to deal expertly with all components of a building.

A property manager should be able to advise the condo board on the merits of choosing one firm over another. They will be able to educate the board on the scope of work being provided and the depth of the firm's experience.

◎ YOU SHOULD KNOW

Cities are not infallible

In doing research we have found many examples in which a municipality failed to properly inspect a property during construction (for example, see Joe and Joanne West's case in Chapter 7). Many condo boards realize only after their technical audits are complete that buildings don't meet minimum standards for safety, even though their municipal inspector has approved it. Experienced engineering firms take nothing for granted, not even past inspection reports. This is why it's important to have the best firm available to complete the audits. Repairing build-ing issues can be costly, and if the board is going to take steps against the city, developer or warranty provider, it's always the responsibility of owners to prove a deficiency exists. Having a reputable firm will provide solid evidence for the board in any legal action.

Understanding Your Condominium Corporation, and Its Rules and Politics

As a new owner in a condominium corporation, you need to understand how this type of corporation works, and what will be expected and required of you.

Let's return to some of the basics about condos that we touched on in the first chapter of this book. A condominium is a form of ownership cre-ated in Alberta in 1966; Ontario followed suit in 1967. British Columbia uses a different method of recording title to condominiums, called strata corporations; in Quebec they are called *"syndicats de co-propriété."*

The board of directors is the part of a condominium that is run by a group of volunteer owners. They steer the direction of property manage-ment and how funds are budgeted in the condominium. A smart owner is always aware of condominium activity, in order to make good investment decisions. Any owner or tenant can volunteer to be elected to the board.

The board's decisions to run the corporation, with the help of property management, are generally not subject to owner approval, unless specified in the Act, such as where the board must borrow money on behalf of the condo-minium corporation or if they make "substantial alteration or improvements" to the common elements. In such cases, at least 66 ⅔% of all the unit owners, either present or by proxy, must approve the board's action in a vote.

The experience, financial knowledge and business acumen of the board members is of paramount importance for a well-run building.

The board uses the operational advice of property management and, for the first year, the budget created by the developer to "steer" the condo-minium corporation in the right direction, financially and operationally.

Creating a Good Condo Board

We have all heard of stories of people who let their election to the condo board go to their heads and make the lives of other residents a nightmare. It's important to have a condo board that is not divided by petty differences, a board that works in unison. But we know that's easy to say and difficult to accomplish, especially if and when parties are in disagreement Here are some steps to ensure your condo board is run well:

1. Eliminate gossip. All important discussions should take place at board meetings where the condo board can take the minutes. Board members should not be commenting on issues to other owners or tenants outside of meetings or pointing fingers at other board members if they do not agree with a decision. This only creates mistrust and positions can be misinterpreted.

2. Include your property manager in your decision-making process. Property managers will be implementing the decisions made by the boards. To ensure a seamless implementation, getting the manager's input and advice is important.

3. Develop agendas and action plans. The board should work with the property manager and other owners to anticipate the needs that must be addressed in the building.

4. Communicate regularly. Newsletters and notices should be published regularly (either monthly or quarterly) and be easily found by owners and tenants. They should be placed on bulletin boards or at the concierge's desk. The newsletter should not be prepared by the manager; instead, the board should elect someone to write them. The report should cover upcoming events and explain to other owners and tenants why decisions were made. Many residents and tenants are starting Facebook groups, email distribution lists and websites dedicated to communicating.

5. Be organized. The chairperson should ensure the agenda is followed and control the meeting to give each board member a chance to speak. Meeting minutes and agendas should be distributed well in advance of upcoming meetings. Board meetings should be quick and efficient: if the above tips are followed, no meeting should extend past two hours.

 · TIP

Let the magnitude of the issue determine the time spent on it
Property managers and board members can become frustrated when it takes hours to discuss trivial issues (such as whether free weights can be added to the gym to supplement the machines) when larger issues that may cost the board hundreds of thousands of dollars are approved with a quick motion. Focus your time on what matters.

Property Management and You

Property management directly and indirectly affects the market value of your condominium. How satisfied residents are with the responsiveness of property management, how easily the owners or tenants can book and use common element facilities, and the overall safety of residents will become part of the building's reputation. Residents and real estate agents will either become "raving fans" or "raving naysayers."

Here's an example of how property management can affect you as an owner. As mentioned earlier, by the time your building is operational, the builder will have contracted with service providers such as property management, security and cleaning services. These are expensive services. In Ontario, under the Condo Act, the board can elect to cancel any contract the declarant (builder) entered into on behalf of the condo corporation. How well—and how efficiently—a building is run will impact your investment in a number of ways: it will affect the quality of tenant you can attract; it will affect the financial stability of your maintenance fees (and thus overall the competitiveness of the building's maintenance fees); and it will affect the marketability and resale value of your unit when you come to sell.

The board can only act on feedback from its owners, so *be active* in communicating with the board and requesting basic things, like a feedback survey form that can be handed in anonymously, and an open-door policy with property management that is attentive to owner and tenant concerns.

The Importance of the Status Certificate

The "status certificate," as it's called in Ontario (it's called the "information certificate" in B.C. and the "estoppel certificate" in Alberta), is a legal document issued by property management on behalf of the board, outlining details that are a snapshot of the condominium corporation. All buyers of your condo will review this document before purchasing and all lenders should review this before extending a mortgage. Information found in the certificate includes:

- common expenses for the unit, and default, if any
- a statement of increase/decrease of common expenses with explanations
- a statement of special assessments for increased financial obligations of the unit owner toward the condominium budget shortfall

- a copy of current declarations, by-laws and rules

- any outstanding judgements against the corporation and status of all legal actions the corporation is a party to

- a copy of the budget of the corporation for the current fiscal year and the last annual audited financial statements with auditor's report

- the amount in the reserve fund, a statement regarding the most recent reserve fund study, and current plans, if any, to increase the reserve fund

- a statement of board-proposed improvements to the common elements.

All lenders and buyers assess the risk of purchasing and lending in a condominium corporation based on the status certificate, so be aware of any negative red flags, such as:

- pending common expense increases

- special assessments imposing an increased contribution by own-ers over an extended period of time. This is to correct a current or projected insufficiency of maintenance fee revenue for common expenses. When this increases, the cost of ownership increases, which usually translates to decreased market value

- judgements or court action that may be costly for the condominium corporation

- an insufficient reserve fund balance, which would likely mean an increase in maintenance fees.

Keeping the Condo as a Long-Term Investment versus Selling

Many condo investors get into the pre-construction game for the quick flip. Many question how a condo can work as a long-term investment, with a high maintenance fee that eats up most of the cash-flow. We get asked this all the time from both experienced and newbie investors. Some typi-cal comments are: "You can't cash-flow with the maintenance fees!" or "The prices just don't make sense!" We usually respond by saying cash-flow with freehold can be just an illusion, if the owner is planning the numbers right.

Most investors who rent, say, a single-family home or townhouse, pocket their net cash inflow after expenses every month, until there is a major repair such as a roof repair, roof replacement or furnace replacement. Then the investor usually has to borrow to get the $5,000 to perform the repair. Now that was a huge negative month!

Condominiums are mandated under the provincial Condominium Act to have a mandatory Reserve Fund Study performed by an engineer and a plan in place to save toward the required capital over the life of the building systems. In other words, an investor will not have to pay for large capital repairs if the building is managed well. On top of that, all the condominium owners have an elected board of directors that manages the daily affairs with a qualified property manager who manages the whole building. How is that for a power team behind your investment? Obviously these qualified professionals are not cheap and the costs of repair are extensive for a larger building, but it is a cost shared among all the condominium owners in the building.

Comparing a Freehold Property to a Condo

A triplex is priced at $400,000, with three kitchens, three washrooms, washer, dryer and three sets of tenants, with property management costing 10% of gross rents.

The three one-bedroom apartments rent for $800 each plus utilities.

$100 per unit should be set aside every month for repairs and maintenance on the freehold, while for condos this repairs-and-maintenance cost is already being set aside in the maintenance fee. For a 1,000-square-foot condo, we will estimate a maintenance fee of $500.

We use an investment ratio called the "rent-to-price ratio," which is gross rent, less property management fees, less maintenance reserve, divided by price. In this case it is $2,400 − $240 − 300 = $1,860/$400,000, which equals .46%.

Now, let's look at a $400,000 condo that has two bedrooms plus a den in the GTA, with parking, where the tenant pays $2,200 per month plus utilities. The property management is about 6% because of the ease of management. The rent-to-price ratio is $2,200 − $132 − $500 = $1,568/$400,000, which equals .39%.

Right now this makes freehold look like the winner, but we are going to introduce the "hassle factor." This is a measure of energy used to manage a rental property. The hassle factor includes turn-over repairs to the property, advertising upon turn-over, showing to individual tenants, selecting tenants, dealing with tenant utilities, paying for plumbing and electrical repairs, snow removal, garbage, landscaping, and all the other fun things that come along with managing properties. The hassle factor is low for condos and higher for freehold, and incrementally more for multi-tenanted properties. In this example, the condo has none and the triplex has a hassle factor of $100 per door or $300. Let's take a look at the investment ratios now:

Triplex: $2,400 − $240 − $300 − $300 = $1,560/$400,000, which equals .39%.

Condo: $2,200 − $132 − $500 = $1,568/$400,000, which equals .39%.

Factors such as liquidity and ease of selling, legal retrofit status of the property, age of the property, quality of the tenant and demand for rental play important contributory factors as well. So this should illustrate that condominiums are at least equivalent in investment quality to freehold. We prefer condominiums because of the escalation of rents in the city core, the ease of renting, and the upside in property value appreciation in a relatively short period of time. So why rush to cash out? Have a tenant pay down your mortgage if you can handle the buy-and-hold process.

HOW MUCH CAN I RENT MY CONDO FOR?

by Chris Davies, realtor, Edmonton

Before buying any piece of investment real estate, you need to extend your due diligence to examine the potential income and expenses for every property. You can get reasonably accurate estimates for the expenses before purchase by talking with developers, sellers, other owners and professionals. The rent you can command for your property isn't much harder to estimate if you approach it the same way.

First, ask the owners or managers of other similar units in your building how much they've recently rented their properties for. It's important you look for the rents paid by people who have actually moved in! It's the same as using the prices of recently sold properties to estimate the value of a property for sale—offers don't count!

Second, ask professionals what recently rented properties went for, what currently vacant properties are being advertised for, and what impact the particular amenities within your unit will have on the price and rentability. Good people to build relationships with for this purpose include realtors, property managers, other investors and owners within the same building, complex or neighbourhood.

Third, look at ads for nearby rentals. You can do this by looking at popular rental sites, using search engines to search for the building's name, neighbourhood or address and the words "for rent," or by using a website such as Rentometer (www.rentometer.com).

Finally, take a moment to consider the prevailing vacancy rate. While you're talking to owners, realtors or property managers, ask them how long it's taking to fill a vacancy, and how many units they know of that are currently vacant. The vacancy rates published by CHMC are a useful barometer for an area, however, they only measure a sample of units, and then only for buildings with three or more units. This means that large condominiums, even if they have a huge number of units available for rent, typically aren't counted in the official CMHC numbers.

Doing some solid research before you buy will help you make the most financially sound investment possible.

Googling for Renters

Prospective renters use search engines for every stage of the research process. Every month more than 100,000 Canadians search Google with the word "apartments." When you consider all the possible keywords prospective tenants are using, there are easily a million people asking Google to help them find a place to live.

Realizing that search engines (particularly Google) are the starting point for your renters, try to follow the same path. Here's a quick way to figure out which rental sites your future tenants are seeing and where you should advertise.

1. Go to Google.com. Start typing "apartments for rent" and watch the phrases that Google suggests for you. These are typically the most popular ways of phrasing a query. Be sure to try different versions of a phrase: condo, apartment, flat or studio are all ways of describing the same property.

2. Search with three to four of the popular keywords and make a note of the sites that are consistently on the top five to six spots. They'll get the majority of traffic from your potential tenants.

3. Start by advertising on sites that consistently rank near the top of Google. Try to measure which sites are getting you the best renters by asking callers, using different phone numbers for different sites (cheap pay-as-you-go cell phones with voice mail are perfect for this), or setting up different email accounts for different sites, using Google's free gmail service.

There are a few sites that are hugely popular, but don't always rank well in search engines. Two of these are Facebook and MLS®. Facebook offers a free marketplace where you can list properties for rent. You can also promote your listings by sharing them on your wall or by purchasing ads within Facebook. Be sure to check you own security settings: it's never a good idea for your tenants to know your home address! MLS® has the ability to list properties for rent, but it's not used in every area. If you're investing in a place like Toronto, where rentals are posted on MLS®, ask your realtor to help you advertise your rental.

Using a combination of strong existing sites such as the MLS® system, and sites that rank well on search engines such as Google, will help ensure you fill your vacancies faster and get higher rents.

Quality websites to post your condominium for rent include:

- http://www.hometrader.ca

- http://www.viewit.ca

- http://www.gottarent.ca

- http://www.rentbc.com (B.C.)

- http://www.calgary.rentspot.com

- http://www.rentfaster.ca (Calgary/ Edmonton)

TENANTING YOUR INVESTMENT
by Chris Davies, realtor, Edmonton

Evaluating the rental value of your condominium is fairly easy, as there may be some activity on the MLS® or current owners advertising in your building, either on public boards in the mailroom or online on Kijiji or Craigslist. A local newspaper may also be a good place to investigate pricing for similar rents. You want to price your rental competitively to get a good tenant in a timely manner, because most quality tenants who use these resources to do a comprehensive search.

Online advertising for tenants is the best chance to get the best fit for tenants, because you can have lengthy descriptions and vibrant pictures of the unit inside, common amenities and even the view. Many technology-savvy investors feel more comfortable working with tenants that communicate online via email and show a strong online profile by having a website, Facebook profile, LinkedIn profile and strong online credentials. This is a quick way for a landlord to evaluate the prospective tenant.

The Rental Process

1. A rental application must be completed in its entirety:

   a. Make sure you get all the information you need, including the prospective tenant's SIN, to pull a credit bureau report and to populate a lease agreement, including legal names, as verified by a driver's license.

   b. Get income and employment information along with references. Usually if this cannot be obtained, or is incomplete, there is a bad story behind the tenant. Save yourself the time and expense of a tenant check.

   c. Have the prospective tenant provide a copy of their Equifax credit bureau, or use a service like www.rentcheckcorp.ca, which can also search landlord and tenant board past judgements on "professional tenants" that may have skipped out on previous landlords.

2. Sign the lease and collect a deposit:

   a. After you perform a tenant check and are satisfied, it is time to collect the first and last month's rent as deposit and sign the lease agreement.

   b. Verify that your tenant understands the condo building restrictions regarding pets.

   c. The lease agreement should be comprehensive and have specific requirements for proof of tenant liability and contents insurance before they move in.

   d. There should be a detailed account of what utilities are included in the rent and what the tenant must pay extra for.

   e. Most condominiums will require you submit this executed lease to the property management office to verify the tenant as an allowed occupant who will get access to the building through security and parking.

3. Perform a move-in day inspection report signed off by both landlord and tenant and forming a part of the lease:

   a. This allows you to walk through the condo and note any repairs needed, list blemishes and test all appliances, sinks, toilets and showers so that you may make the tenant responsible for any damage or unusual repair.

  b. This creates a working relationship between landlord and tenant as the tenancy will ideally be a long-term working relationship.

  c. Note the number of keys and electronic door fobs handed over to the tenant and have a clause making them aware of the cost to replace these if lost.

  d. Arrange for the tenant to be able to book the moving elevator to move in.

4. Check in with tenant in the first week to help with any set-up or moving issues.

5. Deal with repairs or problems promptly and treat the tenant as your customer or client who is helping you pay off your investment.

6. Perform an annual inspection of the condo to ensure its cleanliness, its safe use and its state of repair.

7. On move-out day, go through the move-out checklist, note areas that are damaged and collect the costs to repair or replace before the tenant leaves. Try to get a mail forwarding address to follow up if any surprises are found later.

Should You Rent Furnished or Unfurnished?

Most owners when renting their unit will go the easy route and rent it unfurnished and ask for a minimum one-year lease. But there can be many advantages to renting the unit furnished.

Furnishing your unit requires a large capital outlay that can be $10,000 or more, depending on the furnishings and size of the condo. Not only would you be bringing in furniture, but also the accessories, art, lighting, kitchenware, etc.—essentially everything required for someone to just move in and enjoy.

The benefits of doing so can translate into higher rents. Corporate clients, travellers and individuals in between homes are willing to pay the premium for a furnished condo. Why? It's a home away from home. And while you may be able to achieve rents equivalent to a nightly hotel rate, for the tenant, it generally means more space, a kitchen and a nice homely feel. And if you are lucky, you'll get a long-term tenant who wants a furnished unit simply because they have no desire to buy furnishing themselves.

The downside of a furnished condo can be the shorter lease terms. If you agree to rent to a traveller, it can be as short as a couple of nights. Many individuals that look for the furnished condo only need the unit for a few months. So while the rent may be higher during months of occupancy, you may also have many months of vacancy where you have to carry your mortgage costs. It may also take longer to see the payback on your furnishing costs.

It's important to evaluate your market and the demand for furnished condos to determine if this would be the right route for you.

Your Investment: What Is Your Exit Strategy?

Evaluating the value of the condo during occupancy requires a complex analysis of the value. Ideally, the analysis would be a comparison of sale price of similar condo units in previous phases of the same development. Otherwise, your real estate agent will help you compare the sales of condominiums in neighbouring towers. There is no "record" of resale activity during the occupancy period, which makes it extremely difficult to determine the current market price. However, as soon as the building registers and the deed is passed onto the owner, investors looking to flip their unit will list their condominiums for sale on the MLS® immediately. The listed price of similar units in the building will also affect the value.

How do you know where you are in the real estate cycle?

In his book *Real Estate Investing in Canada*, author Don R. Campbell notes that you should base your analysis on research specific to your market, rather than relying on general comments on the state of all real estate investing. You must also make sure your research comes from trusted sources of information. In today's climate, dubious research outfits publish research only to shock the media into getting a comment from them, and some bloggers have been used to misrepresent information.

When looking at research, look past headlines and analysis and look at the data yourself. Sources of information we use include the following:

- provincial websites
- city websites
- boards of trade
- universities

- CMHC: http://www.cmhc-schl.gc.ca
- Statistics Canada: http://www.statcan.gc.ca
- Canadian Real Estate Association and its local boards
- Real Estate Board of Greater Vancouver: http://www.rebgv.org/
- Calgary Real Estate Board: http://www.creb.com/
- Edmonton Real Estate Board: http://www.ereb.com/
- Toronto Real Estate Board: http://www.torontorealestateboard.com/
- Ottawa Real Estate Board: http://www1.ottawarealestate.org
- Greater Montreal Real Estate Board: http://www.cigm.qc.ca/
- Teranet: http://www.housepriceindex.ca/
- Major real estate brokerages
- Royal LePage: http://www.royallepage.ca/en/media/index.aspx
- RE/MAX Ontario and Atlantic: http://www.remax-oa.com/media-newsroom/
- Colliers: http://www.collierscanada.com/en/Research
- CB Richard Ellis Canada: http://www.cbre.ca/EN/Research/
- Mercer Human Resource Consulting
- Altus: http://www.altusgroup.com/
- Bank of Canada: http://www.bankofcanada.ca/
- Federal Reserve Bank and its state representatives: http://www.federal-reserve.gov/
- IMF (International Monetary Fund): http://www.imf.org
- World Bank: http://www.worldbank.org/
- Canadian Bankers Association: http://www.cba.ca/
- Canadian Association of Accredited Mortgage Professionals (CAAMP): http://www.caamp.org/
- Urbanation: www.urbanation.ca/
- N. Barry Lyon and Associates: www.nblc.com/
- RealNet: http://www.realnet.ca/

- Genworth Canada: http://www.genworth.ca/content/genworth/ca/en/about_us/Press_Centre/housing_reports.html

- Conference Board of Canada: http://www.conferenceboard.ca/

- RBC Economics: http://www.rbc.com/economics/index.html

- Scotia Economics: http://scotiabank.com/cda/content/0,1608,CID8338_LIDen,00.html

- BMO Capital Markets: http://www.bmonesbittburns.com/Economics/

- TD Economics: http://www.td.com/economics

- CIBC World Markets: http://www.cibcwm.com/wm/

When is a good time of the year to sell?

Condos have definitely changed the market landscape in terms of seasonal sales cycles. Traditionally, the best time to sell real estate was April to September. Before April, the weather would keep people away and after September, the kids would be in school and folks would be gearing up for Christmas and the winter. Condos have extended this period to almost year round (except December, due to Christmas): because condos are the choice of many first-time home buyers, worrying about changing the kids' school is not an issue, and because condos have little outdoor space, weather is not as much of an issue.

To determine when is the best time to buy or sell, speaking with a realtor who has a pulse on the market and can back it up with statistics would be extremely valuable. A good realtor can advise you that selling in February may be advantageous, because there are proportionately more buyers than available listings, and waiting until April, when everyone else lists their unit, may harm your profit potential because of competition.

Here are some suggestions a good real estate agent should be using in developing a sales and marketing strategy:

1. Timeline

If a sale must occur within 30 days, then the "asking price" should be close to what you think the condo is worth. If a sale can take 60 to 90 days, then price the unit higher and work your way down. The unpredictability of demand in a new development coupled with a premium of "new" can push a buyer to pay more for a "brand-new" condo versus old.

2. Amenities

Consider the competitive advantage or disadvantage your condominium has as an overall place to live compared to condominium towers within the vicinity. Things to consider include innovative common element features like commercial tenants, grocery anchors, brand-name bars or eateries, and adjoining high-end hotels.

CASE STUDY

Maple Leaf Square, Toronto

This project by Lanterra has transformed the condominium rental market in downtown Toronto forever, as it combines the best of built-in amenities such a 24-hour Longos grocery store; the Real Sports Bar (with the largest Sports Bar HD screen in North America with more than two floors and 900 seats); a connection to the underground PATH to the subway; office space; and a hotel, all of which are adjacent to the Air Canada Centre, which is home to the Toronto Maple Leafs and Toronto Raptors.

Record-breaking rental rates are showing that tenants want these amenities and are willing to pay for them. Bachelors rent for approximately $1,400; one-bedroom units for $2,000; and two-bedroom units for $2,800, all on one-year leases.

A lucrative investment area is short-term rental, which can be for as much as $200 per night or $1,000 a week, though it is important to note that some condominiums have by-laws prohibiting short-term rentals in the building. This is an example where the mixed-use amenities have caused tremendous tenant demand, making this building a fantastic investment in downtown Toronto.

---

3. Staging your unit

If you have the budget for staging or basically furnishing the unit for your enjoyment or the enjoyment of friends and family, this can significantly beat out the competition of vacant units for sale in the same building by showing how the space will be used and highlighting innovative storage solutions or special features like terraces and high ceilings. (See more on how to stage your unit below.)

4. Multi-phase projects

If your condo is in a tower that is the second phase, use the first phase resale values as a strong indicator of value.

5. Builder sales

Use the sales prices the builder is offering on its inventory as a strong indicator of what to beat. Usually builders have quality marketing, signage and access to real estate brokers to get their inventory sold.

6. Data mining prices per square foot

This is a statistic that changes on a quarterly basis for each building, and even a block of buildings. You can calculate this by looking at sale prices for similar units and dividing them by their square footage. This data is extremely valuable but costly to obtain. Consult with Realexperts.com or condoinvest.ca to get current data.

Staging

Why would you, as an investor, even consider staging? Well, remember that home buying is very much like shopping, and the retail industry spends massive amounts of energy and time in preparing its merchandise for sale. The reason is that first impressions are everything!

As an investor, your target buyer is not another investor, because these investors are looking for a deal with a discount. These investors are paid for having a vision, which in turn they use to sell the unit to an end-user like buyer or tenant. Your target buyer is an end-user who can pay "retail" for their condominium. How does a retail buyer buy something?

Buyers like to see merchandise organized, clear and easy to purchase. The same is true with a home. With the small sizes of condominiums and the strange configurations, buyers are sometimes confused with how an empty space will look or take the shape of a bedroom, living room or dining room. It is the stager's job to show the buyer how the space can be optimally used, being both functional and tasteful.

It is also important to ensure that the buyer's experience is laid out as clearly as possible, from entering the building to going through the condo unit. This requires working closely with your property management, security staff and realtor in communicating how access to the building is managed. Here are some suggestions:

1. Ask property management what the policy is for allowing realtors and guests. Is there a sign-in or registration at the front desk? Must the guest have your dial-in code at security? Are lockboxes permitted in the condominium and where?

2. In regard to security, what information does a guest or realtor need to access the building? Is there a special fob needed to access your floor in the elevator?

3. Make sure your realtor communicates these requirements to the agents showing the property clearly, as every showing counts. You don't want a frustrated agent not to show your property because they couldn't find the lockbox, couldn't park their car, or couldn't get to your floor.

Here are some common mistakes that investors make when they stage their own condo:

1. They don't paint. The builder's colour is usually basic white or beige and adds no value to the decor. Paint is a very cost-effective way to create an ambiance for the home.

2. They use furniture that is house sized. Condo furniture is different proportionally—it is smaller and more functional for the typical size of condo rooms. Oversized furniture will make the condo appear too small.

3. They don't have enough accessories. Accessories make the space and the condo feel like home.

4. They forget the lighting. Lighting is the secret to making a space feel larger and welcoming. Having sufficient lighting is critical in a condo.

5. They forget the window coverings. Along with lighting issues, window coverings address the subconscious need for privacy and provide an opportunity to add colour and style to a condo.

6. They forget the temperature. Although a condo is vacant, it is still true that first impression counts for everything, so keep the condo heated or cooled to a normal temperature.

Notifying Your Tenants

If your condo is tenanted, you must of course notify your tenant that you are listing the condo for sale and that there will be showings. Ensure there is clear communication.

Here are some suggestions:

- Give your tenant pointers on what they can do to make the condo show its best, because they may not even realize they are not being neat enough to meet your standards!

- Explain to your tenant what a lockbox is and how only registered, licensed real estate agents can access this key to show.

- Come to an agreement with your tenant on the best time to show the unit. Don't show outside of those times unless it is absolutely necessary. Suggest showings while the tenant is at work. This makes the prospective buyer more comfortable to peruse the space at his own pace.

- Ask your tenant to cage their dog or cat while they are not there, since animals can be a deterrent for a buyer who has a fear of or allergy to pets.

- Ask your tenant to leave on the lights, rather than have the real estate agent fumble around looking for light switches.

A Final Word

In 1851, the percentage of Canadians living in rural areas was 87%. Today, the percentage of Canadians living in rural areas is only 20%—that means a full 80% of us are urban dwellers. Canada is growing up and becoming more urban; as a result, sales of new condos are outpacing resale condos in major urban markets.

This book had to be written for the sole reason that buying pre-construction condos will become an option for home buyers in every major city in Canada in the near future, no matter where the city is in the real-estate market cycle. Guidance is needed, because this type of buying is so new and unfamiliar to so many.

But who knew buying a pre-construction condo would be so complicated? When you consider all the experts who were interviewed and the years of education and experience they have gained, it's really amazing that so much knowledge could fit into these pages. Congratulations: you are now more informed about pre-construction condo buying than 99.9% of Canada's population, and you are probably even more knowledgeable than some so-called experts in the field.

When buying a condo pre-construction and using this book, take the information you need as you need it. The best way to fully understand the pre-construction condo buying process is to use this book as a guide while you are in the process of moving forward. As you go through the process a few times, what took weeks to do due diligence will take minutes. Don't frustrate yourself with the amount of work needed to follow the steps outlined: delegate the work to a solid team that includes a realtor, lawyer, mortgage broker, accountant, home inspector, property manager and engineer. This book is here for you to understand what these players do, and we have provided you with the information to better hold them accountable. The responsibility of your success in reaching your goals ultimately lies with you.

Credits

Chapter 1

1. Aaron, Bob. 2008. "Court is an expensive way to deal with a noise complaint issue." Toronto Star. December 20. http://www.aaron.ca/columns/2008-12-20.htm
2. "Best source for vacancy rates: CMHC Rental Market Report." Accessed September 1, 2011. http://www.cmhc-schl.gc.ca/en/hoficlincl/homain/stda/index.cfm

Chapter 2

1. Carras, George. 2011. "GTA Residential Development Market Briefing." Speech presented at BILDgta. Toronto, Ontario. February 8.
2. Finnegan, Niall. 2010. "2010 High-Rise Market Outlook." Speech presented at BILDgta, Toronto, Ontario. September 24.
3. Altus Group. "Construction Cost Guide," Accessed April 1, 2011. http://www.altusgroup.com/Services/Construction_Cost_Guide
4. BILDgta. 2008. "Over the Top: The Impact of Development Charges on New Homebuyers." http://www.bildgta.ca/BILD/uploadedFiles/Media/Releases_2008/DC_REPORT_08_FINAL.pdf
5. CMHC. "Government-Imposed Charges On New Housing in Canada." Accessed April 1, 2011. ftp://ftp.cmhc-schl.gc.ca/chic-ccdh/Research_Reports-Rapports_de_recherche/eng_unilingual/CHIC_Government_Imposed%28w%29.pdf
6. GlobalTV. 2005. "Do your homework when buying a new condo." Canada.com. December 5. http://www.canada.com/

globaltv/calgary/consumerbeat/story.html?id= 4cc82591-532b-4ba9-b5d6-e6b28301a8a8

7. Barbaro, Michael. 2011. "Buying a Trump Property, or So They Thought." The New York Times. May 12. http://www.nytimes.com/2011/05/13/nyregion/feeling-deceived-over-homes-that-were-trump-in-name-only.html?_r=1&amp=&%2359;pagewanted=all&pagewanted=all

8. Tomkinson, Theresa. 1999. "Condominium Developers' Holdbacks - Cash Flow Crunch." Feldlaw.com.

9. Belford, Terrance. 2009. "How the plan to build Canada's tallest condo fell apart." The Globe and Mail. September 25. http://www.theglobeandmail.com/life/home-and-garden/real-estate/how-the-plan-to-build-canadas-tallest-condo-fell-apart/article1291333/singlepage/#articlecontent

10. CBC News. 2007. "Vancouver developer pulls out of condo projects due to financing difficulty." CBC News Canada. November 27. http://www.cbc.ca/news/canada/british-columbia/story/2007/11/26/bc-condo.html

11. CBC News. 2008. "Work stops on another Calgary condo project" CBC News Canada. September 17. http://www.cbc.ca/news/canada/calgary/story/2008/09/17/condos-calgary-halt.html

12. Sources: RBC Economics, Scotia Economics, BMO Capital Markets, TD Economics, CIBC World Markets.

13. Source: Employment diversity index, Conference Board of Canada.

14. Ibid.

15. BizMAP Market Area Profiles. "Yaletown Neighborhood Profile." Accessed September 9, 2011. http://www.bizmapbc.com/neighbourhood-profiles/yaletown-neighbourhood.pdf

16. Sources: RBC affordability index, KPMG Survey on Cost of Doing Business (results are usually found within a city's economic development office), Toronto Board of Trade Scorecard on Prosperity.

17. Sources: Toronto Board of Trade Scorecard on Prosperity, Mercer Human Resource Consulting Quality of Living Survey

18. Wolfe, David A. 2009. "Geography of Innovation." Speech presented at CIBC Scholar in Residence Lecture. Toronto, Ontario. May. http://www.conferenceboard.ca/Libraries/PUBLIC_PDFS/The_Geography_of_Innovation_SIRP_Lecture_May09.sflb

19. Pivo, Gary and Jeffrey D. Fisher. 2011. The Walkability Premium in Commercial Real Estate Investments. Real Estate Economics 39.2. 185-219.

20. MVA Consultancy. "Seeing Issues Clearly: Valuing the Urban Realm." Last modified September 2008. http://urbandesign.tfl.gov.uk/Guidance/Valuing-Urban-Realm-2.aspx

21. Macleod, Meredith. 2011. "Walkability and the new urbanism." TheSpec.com. May 11. http://www.thespec.com/feature/article/530147--walkability-and-the-new-urbanism

22. Copeland, Larry 2011. "City's design, transit system can ease gas costs." USA Today. March 22. http://www.usatoday.com/news/nation/2011-03-22-citygas22_ST_N.htm

23. Dirksen, Kirsten. 2011. "Happiness Research Ranks Commuting Low: One-Hour Commute Cuts Your Social Life By 10 Percent." Huffington Post. March 8. http://www.huffingtonpost.com/kirsten-dirksen/happiness-research-ranks-_b_829591.html

24. Michigan Public Health Institute: National Center for Child Death Review Policy and Practice. 2006. "United States Child Death Mortality." http://www.childdeathreview.org/national-childmortalitydata.htm

25. US Department of Agriculture Economic Research Service. "Food Desert Locator." Accessed September 9, 2011. http://www.ers.usda.gov/data/fooddesert/fooddesert.html

26. Lakhani, Nina. 2011. "UK gets its walking boots on and heads for the hills." The Independent. May 1. http://www.independent.co.uk/life-style/health-and-families/health-news/uk-gets-its-walking-boots-on-and-heads-for-the-hills-2277351.html

27. Stenger, Brad. 2011. "Designing Streets for Emergencies." Medill National Security Journalism Initiative. May 2. http://nationalsecurityzone.org/site/designing-streets-for-emergencies/

28. Florida, Richard. 2010. "America's Most Walkable Cities." The Atlantic. December 15. http://www.theatlantic.com/business/archive/2010/12/americas-most-walkable-cities/67988/

Chapter 3

1. Allison, David. 2011. Telephone Interview. Braun Allison. January.

2. Tarion. 2010. "Builder Bulletins Revised 19." June. http://www.tarion.com/New-Home-Builders/Policies-and-Guidelines/Pages/Builder-Bulletins.aspx

3. Backstage Toronto. "Views." Accessed September 9, 2011. http://www.backstagetoronto.com/views

Chapter 4

1. City of Toronto. 2007. "Regent Park Social Development Plan." http://www.toronto.ca/revitalization/regent_park/pdf/regent-park_sdp-part2_sept_16.pdf
2. HGTV. "Acoustic Insulation: Soundproof the Space Between the Walls." Accessed September 9, 2011. http://www.hgtvpro.com/hpro/bp_insulation/article/0,2617,HPRO_20150_3647563,00.html
3. Aaron, Bob. 2001. "What recourse do St. Clair W. homebuyers have?" Toronto Star. November 17. http://www.aaron.ca/columns/2001-11-17.htm
4. Alcoba, Natalie. 2008. "Condo residents face foul smell from slaughterhouse." National Post. July 2. http://network.nationalpost.com/np/blogs/toronto/archive/2008/07/02/condo-residents-face-foul-smell-from-slaughterhouse.aspx
5. City of Toronto. 2010. "Tall Buildings Inviting Change in the Downtown Core." April 30. http://www.toronto.ca/planning/pdf/Tall-buildings-Final.pdf

Chapter 5

1. CMHC. "Understanding Your New Home Sales Contract." Accessed September 9, 2011. http://www.cmhc-schl.gc.ca/en/co/buho/buho_004.cfm
2. CMHC. "Understanding Your New Home Sales Contract." Accessed September 9, 2011. http://www.cmhc-schl.gc.ca/en/co/buho/buho_004.cfm
3. Canadians for Properly Built Homes "Top 10 Things To Do - When you are buying a newly constructed home." Accessed September 9, 2011. http://www.canadiansforproperlybuilthomes.com/html/top_10_things_to_do.html
4. Haughney, Christine. 2011. "How a Building Dispute Can Sink a Sale." The New York Times March 21 http://www.nytimes.com/2011/03/22/nyregion/22appraisal.html?_r=1&hp
5. The Law Society of Saskatchewan. 2006. "Saskatchewan Practice Checklists: Condominiums." September. http://www.lawsociety.sk.ca/newlook/Publications/PracticeChklst2006/RE1_Condominiums_2006.pdf
6. Province of Manitoba. 2010. "Condominium Act Under Review." September 15. http://news.gov.mb.ca/news/index.html?archive=2010-9-01&item=9721

7. For the sample clauses and their interpretation in this section, we are indebted to lawyers Bob Aaron and Denish Lash, and are grateful to them for their kind permission to use this material.

Chapter 6

1. Michael Cadesky. 2002. Taxation of Real Estate in Canada. Thomson Canada Limited. Toronto. 1-10.
2. Canwest News Service. 2007. "Not all baby boomers passing on their inheritance: report." Canada.com. November 7. http://www.canada.com/topics/news/national/story.html?id=2742b4d5-5bf9-4206-ba6e-1e36ccda1c62&k=15849

Chapter 7

1. Lux Residential Warranty Program. "Condominium Warranty Program." Accessed September 9, 2011. http://www.luxrwp.com/Condominium%20Warranty%20Program.html
2. Ibid.
3. Hamilton, Kevin. 2011. Telephone Interview. Lux Residential Warranty. July 25.
4. Ibid.
5. Ibid.
6. Lux Residential Warranty Program. "Condominium Warranty Program."
7. Ibid.
8. Garantie Maisons Neuves APCHQ. 2006. "Guarantee Contract - Building Held in Dividing Co-Ownership." May 26. http://www.gomaison.com/gomaison/garantie/maison_neuve/pdf/En/GB-060AD%20%2806-2006%29.pdf
9. Ibid.
10. Ibid.
11. Ibid.
12. Ibid.
13. Ibid.
14. Ibid.
15. Tarion. "Deposit Protection." Accessed September 9, 2011. http://www.tarion.com/Warranty-Protection/Pages/Deposit-Protection.aspx
16. Tarion. "Warranty Coverage." Accessed September 9, 2011. http://www.tarion.com/Warranty-Protection/Warranty-Coverage/Pages/default.aspx

17. Tarion. "Understanding Delayed Closings and Occupancies for Freehold Homes and Condominiums." Accessed September 9, 2011. http://www.tarion.com/Warranty-Protection/Understanding-Delayed-Closings-and-Occupancies/Pages/default.aspx

18. Tarion. "Warranty Protection: Common Elements." Accessed September 13, 2011. http://tarion.com/Warranty-Protection/Warranty-Coverage/Pages/Common-Elements.aspx

19. Tarion Customer Service. 2011. Telephone Interview. March.

20. Tarion. "Warranty Protection: The Statutory Warranty - What's Included." Accessed September 13, 2011. http://www.tarion.com/Warranty-Protection/Pages/default.aspx

21. Tarion. "Warranty Protection: Appealing a Decision." Accessed September 13, 2011. http://www.tarion.com/Warranty-Protection/Statutory-Warranty/Pages/Appealing-a-Decision.aspx

22. Tarion. "Warranty Protection: Understanding Delayed Closings and Occupancies."

23. Tarion. "Warranty Protection: Unauthorized Substitutions." Accessed September 13, 2011. http://www.tarion.com/Warranty-Protection/Pages/Unauthorized-Substitutions.aspx

24. Tarion. 2010. "Builder Bulletin: CONDOMINIUM PROJECTS: DESIGN AND FIELD REVIEW REPORTING." May. http://www.tarion.com/New-Home-Builders/Policies-and-Guidelines/Builder%20Bulletins/BB19R%20-%20Final.pdf

25. Kosheluk, Lori. 2011. Telephone Interview. Manitoba New Home Warranty Program. March.

26. Ibid.

27. Manitoba New Home Warranty Program. "Warranty What's Covered." Accessed September 13, 2011. http://www.mbnhwp.com/warranty.htm

28. Manitoba New Home Warranty Program. "Construction Performance Standards." Accessed September 13, 2011. http://www.mbnhwp.com/standards.htm

29. Manitoba New Home Warranty Program. "Warranty What's Covered" Accessed September 13, 2011. http://www.mbnhwp.com/warranty.htm

30. Kosheluk, Lori. 2011. Telephone Interview.

31. Ibid.

32. Manitoba New Home Warranty Program. "Construction Performance Standards." Accessed September 13, 2011. http://www.mbnhwp.com/standards.htm

33. Manitoba New Home Warranty Program "Warranty What's Covered." Accessed September 13, 2011. http://www.mbnhwp. com/warranty.htm

34. Kosheluk, Lori. 2011. Telephone Interview.

35. Silliphant, Glenn. 2011. Telephone Interview. New Home Warranty Program of Saskatchewan Inc. March.

36. New Home Warranty Program of Saskatchewan Inc. "NWHP Coverage." Accessed September 13, 2011. http://www.nhwp.org/ about/about-coverage.htm

37. Ibid.

38. New Home Warranty Program of Saskatchewan Inc. "Construction Performance Standards." Revised January 1, 2011. http://www.beagleproductions.com/nhwp/main.php?pid=360

39. Silliphant, Glenn. 2011. Telephone Interview.

40. New Home Warranty Program of Saskatchewan Inc. "NWHP Coverage."

41. New Home Warranty Program of Saskatchewan Inc. "What if I have a problem?" Accessed September 13, 2011. http://www. nhwp.org/about/about-problems.htm

42. Silliphant, Glenn. 2011. Telephone Interview.

43. Alberta New Home Warranty Program. "The Alberta New Home Warranty Program's Warranty Protections for Multi Family Homes." Accessed September 13, 2011. http://www. anhwp.com/documents/MultiFamilyProtections.pdf

44. Ibid.

45. Alberta New Home Warranty Program. "Workmanship & Material Guide Home." Accessed September 13, 2011. http://www.anhwp. com/hbTemplates/WorkmanshipMaterialsGuideTemplate.aspx

46. Alberta New Home Warranty Program. "Condominium Common Property: Warranty Certificate Terms and Conditions." Accessed September 13, 2011. http://www.anhwp. com/documents/CondominiumCPTerms.pdf

47. Ibid.

48. Alberta New Home Warranty Program. "The Alberta New Home Warranty Program's Warranty Protections for Multi Family Homes."

49. Alberta New Home Warranty Program. "Dispute Resolution." Accessed September 13, 2011. http://www.anhwp.com/hbTem plates/ContentTemplate.aspx?Page=DisputeResolution#

50. Alberta New Home Warranty Program. "The Alberta New Home Warranty Program's Warranty Protections for Multi Family Homes."

51. National Home Warranty. "Warranty Benefits for Manitoba." Accessed September 13, 2011. http://www.nationalhomewar ranty.com/main_3.asp?content_id=4&prov=mn

52. National Home Warranty. "Warranty Benefits for Saskatchewan." Accessed September 13, 2011. http://www.nationalhomewar ranty.com/main_3.asp?content_id=3&prov=sk

53. National Home Warranty. "Warranty Benefits for Alberta." Accessed September 13, 2011. http://www.nationalhomewar ranty.com/main.asp?content_id=1&prov=ab

54. National Home Warranty. "Warranty Benefits for Manitoba." Accessed September 13, 2011. http://www.nationalhomewar ranty.com/main_3.asp?content_id=4&prov=mn

55. National Home Warranty. "Warranty Benefits for Saskatchewan."

56. National Home Warranty. "Warranty Benefits for Alberta."

57. National Home Warranty. "Performance Standards." Accessed September 13, 2011. http://www.nationalhomewarranty. com/PDF_doc/Guides/Defect_Guildelines_Performance_ Standards-07.pdf

58. National Home Warranty. "Warranty Benefits for Manitoba."

59. National Home Warranty. "Warranty Benefits for Saskatchewan."

60. National Home Warranty. "Warranty Benefits for Alberta."

61. Martin, John. 2011. Telephone Interview. National Home Warranty Program. March.

62. Ibid.

63. Ibid.

64. Home Owner Protection Office. 2011. "2-5-10 Year Warranty Insurance." July. http://www.hpo.bc.ca/files/download/ Bulletins/2-5-10.pdf

65. Home Owner Protection Office. 2011. "Residential Construction Performance Guide." February. http://www.hpo.bc.ca/ files/download/Res_Guide/Residential_Construction_ Performance_Guide.pdf

66. Home Owner Protection Office. 2011. "Options For Resolving Residential Construction Disputes." February. http://www.hpo. bc.ca/files/download/Res_Guide/Residential_Construction_ Performance_Guide.pdf

Acknowledgments

From Randy Ramadhin

- Brad & Lisa Lounsbury
- Concord Adex
- Denise Lash
- Loretta Ramadhin
- Aliya Ramadhin
- Mya Ramadhin
- Raymond Aaron
- Don Campbell & REIN
- George Carras
- Urbanation
- BILD
- TREB
- The Dhillons
- Robert Kiyosaki
- Harv Eker
- Tony Robbins
- Justin Cook

- Susan Toughlouian
- Virendra Srivastava

From Brian Persaud

My friends and family—Your support and love over the past nine months inspired me through this journey.

- Sabrina Rahaman
- Hazara Persaud
- Ranjan & Shantie Persaud
- Ronald & Priya Persaud
- Don Campbell, @DonRCampbell
- Philip McKernan, @PhilipMcKernan
- Kelly Langteigne, @KellyLanteigne
- Paul Oberman, @PaulDOberman

The rock: writing team—For a first-time author, I don't know where I would be without your expertise. Thank you for always pushing the extra mile for me.

- Don Loney
- Nicole Langlois
- Jeremy Hanson-Finger, @HansonFinger
- Pam Vokey

Idea makers, nitpickers and fact checkers—Thank you for spotting all my typos and giving great feedback.

- Mara Samardzic, @MaraSamardzic
- Alyssa Richard, @AlyssaJRichard
- Kerri-Lynn McAllister, @RateHub_Canada
- Corinne Korytkowski, @AllThingsC
- Kyle Pulis, @Pulis_IG

- Joey Ragona, @JoeyRagona
- Matt Goulart, @BankGuru

Artists, paparazzi and photographers—Thank you for making this book look so pretty.

- Chris Ho, Photographer
- Ben Frisch, @benfrisch
- Kent James, Photographer

On the shoulders of giants—This book is the culmination of hundreds of years of experience in home-building industry. To all the people in this list, I can't thank you enough for the thousands of hours you have invested into helping me make this book a great book.

Legal superstar team:

- Bob Aaron, Aaron and Aaron, Barristers and Solicitors—Toronto
- Denise Lash, Heenan Blaikie—Toronto
- Armand Conant, Heenan Blaikie—Toronto
- Mark Weisleder, www.markweisleder.com/—Toronto
- Donald Kramer, Biamonte Cairo & Shortreed LLP—Edmonton
- Ron Clarke, Canadian Condominium Institute—South Alberta
- James Polley, McLeod & Company LLP—Calgary
- Heather Bonnycastle, McLeod & Company LLP—Calgary
- Christopher J. Jaglowitz, @chrisjaglowitz—Toronto
- David Nakelsky, Green and Spiegel—Toronto
- Ivan De Grandpré, De Grandpré Joli-Coeur—Montreal
- Douglas Gray, www.homebuyer.ca/—Vancouver

Honoured development team:

- Harry Stinson, Stinson Properties
- Sayf Hassan, @symmetrydevelop
- Michael A. Smith, @canplanlaw

- Riz Dhanji, @rizdhanji
- Sam Crignano, @Crignano
- Jim Ritchie, Tridel
- Don Ho, Trans City Group of Companies
- Marisa DeBrincat, Lanterra
- Stephen Diamond, Diamond Corp
- Arni Thorsteinson, Shelter Canadian Properties Limited
- Gordon Harris, Simon Fraser University
- Scott McLellan, Pure Plaza
- Jeanhy Shim, Streetcar Developments
- Aidan Ball, Camrost Felcorp
- Andre Mihelic, Minto

Best design professionals in the business:

- Prishram Jain, Tact Design
- Elaine Cecconi & Anna Simone, Cecconi î Simone
- Carmen Dragomir, esQape Design
- Ken Greenberg, Greenberg Consultants
- Les Klein, Quadrangle Architects

Best financiers in the business:

- Calum Ross, Calum Ross Mortgage Team
- Frank Margiani, @FrankMargani
- Gary Berman, Tricon Capital

Super VVIP PLATINUM agents:

- Roy Bhandari, @TalkCondo
- Manny Riebeling, @yaletownliving
- Chris Davies, @wcdavies

- Mark Savel, @SavelSells
- Andrew Lafleur, @AndrewLaFleur
- Giovanni Marsico, @GiovanniMarsico
- Jamie Johnston, @RemaxCondosPlus
- Graham Connaughton,@GConnaughton
- Irma Eibich, RE/Max Condos Plus
- Lakhvir Randhawa (Rupinder Meelu & Amin Kainth), Century 21 Green
- Sunil Deonaraine, @Sunilhomes

Experts in sales and marketing:

- David Allison, @BAdavid
- Dan Floman, @DanFlomen
- Linda Mitchell Young, Baker Real Estate
- Eve Lewis, Marketvision Realty
- James Kilpatrick, @J_Kilpatrick
- Jane Renwick, Milborne Real Estate
- Vicki Griffiths, Vicbar Marketing
- Tim Ng, @tim_ng
- Rob Galetta, @BlackJetInc
- Parmjit Parmar, Montana Ridge

Canada's source for market intelligence:

- Matt Slutsky and Cliff Peskin, @BuzzBuzzHome
- Ed Skira, @Urban_Toronto
- Dave Reiss, New Home Buyers

Trusted economists and experts:

- Ben Myers, @benmyers29
- Pauline Lierman, @Daphne7411

- Steve Ladurantaye, @syladurantaye
- Jasmine Cracknell, @Jassy247
- Barry Lyon & Paul Dydula, N. Barry Lyon and Associates
- Niall Finnegan, Altus Group
- George Carras, Realnet
- Tsur Somerville, Sauder School of Business (University of British Columbia)

The fine details and warranty providers:

- Kevin Hamilton, Lux Residential Warranty Program
- Jim Smith, National Home Warranty
- Glenn Silliphant, New Home Warranty Program of Saskatchewan
- Lori Kosheluk, Manitoba New Home Warranty Provider
- Michelle Bilodeau, British Columbia Homeowner Protection Office
- Wes Weber, Residential Rebates

Construction experts and engineers:

- Michael Steele, Construction Control
- Mark Benerowski, Inspection Consultants Toronto
- Gerry Quackenbush, GTA Inspections
- Rory McNabb, Otis Elevators

Property management supreme:

- Tasso Eracles, Simerra Property Management
- Allan Rosenberg, Del Property Management
- Tim Bourdignon, Andrejs Management

Savvy investors:

- Joe West
- Nicholas Luca

- Astrum Nanji, @astrumnanji
- Wade Graham, @wgraham76
- Hwi Young Kim & Myungjin Lee
- Neil Uttamsingh, @Neil_Uttamsingh
- Marc Lalonde
- Jenna Lang
- Gurm Sehmbi

Index

Page numbers in **bold** denote definitions.
Page numbers in *italics* denote checklists, charts or graphs.

Other Wiley Real Estate Titles

AUTHORS OF THE BESTSELLERS REAL ESTATE INVESTING IN CANADA AND 97 TIPS FOR CANADIAN REAL ESTATE INVESTORS

REAL ESTATE JOINT VENTURES

THE CANADIAN INVESTOR'S GUIDE TO RAISING MONEY AND GETTING DEALS DONE

DON R. CAMPBELL & RUSSELL WESTCOTT

DON R. CAMPBELL | KIERAN TRASS | GREG HEAD

SECRETS OF THE CANADIAN REAL ESTATE CYCLE

AN INVESTOR'S GUIDE

with CHRISTINE RUPTASH

NATIONAL BESTSELLER • OVER 35,000 COPIES SOLD!

REAL ESTATE INVESTING IN CANADA 2.0

CREATING WEALTH WITH THE ACRE SYSTEM

Revised & Updated with FREE Property Analyzer Software that will help investors reduce risks and increase returns in any market conditions

DON R. CAMPBELL
CANADA'S #1 BEST-SELLING REAL ESTATE AUTHOR

SECOND EDITION FULLY REVISED & UPDATED

NATIONAL BESTSELLER

97 TIPS FOR CANADIAN REAL ESTATE INVESTORS 2.0

DON R. CAMPBELL

PETER KINCH | BARRY MCGUIRE | RUSSELL WESTCOTT

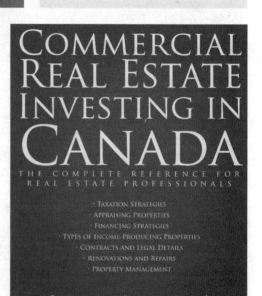